A Second Helping of Manna

Written by

Dr. Jay Korsen

This book is also dedicated, as was the first volume, to my wife Lori, the mother of my two wonderful children Lindsay and Ryan. Together, Lori and I have made a commitment to love the Lord Jesus Christ and to prioritize our relationship with God, through Him in the unity of the Holy Spirit, above all else in our lives.

I want to also express my gratitude to my Bible study partners Paul Buterbaugh and Wheeler Van Brocklin who have helped me build my faith every Thursday morning for more than 16 years. I also want to thank my new Bible study partners Gary, Mike and Steve for insight into the Truth contained in His Word that I have received in the last few months we have been studying together on Thursday nights.

I want to thank my parents and grandparents for having planted the seed of faith in me at an early age and I am grateful that the seed landed on fertile ground.

Thank you to all the prayer warriors I have surrounded myself with including my patients, friends and family (many of which fall into all three categories). All of you are truly Bright Lights in my life. Thank you for shining so brightly.

Thank you to my friend Doris who has shown me what real courage and faith is in the face of a real challenge and for teaching me to "Trust in God and let it go."

Thank you to my friend Donna who was the first one to purchase my book at a brick and mortar store (Wakefield Books in RI).

Thank you to Jan and Evelyn. Two sisters that always have a good word from the Good Book, a smile evident of their joy in the Lord and hearts filled with faith each week I see them in the office.

Introduction

I begin this book as I did my first, at the beginning…

I began writing a daily reflection on Facebook several years ago after being inspired by the daily messages I used to receive on my cell phone from what is now known as Gotandem.com. The messages seemed to speak directly to me and answered many of my biblical questions. I shared the messages with friends online and soon began receiving biblical questions from those friends who mistakenly thought I wrote the daily reflections. In an attempt to answer their questions, I used a similar format as Gotandem.com, did my research and posted the answers.

Over time, I began studying the Bible each morning or night for an hour or two to answer my own difficult questions with biblically sound answers. At the end of my daily study, I would try to summarize the answers I found in what my friends began calling my "Bible minute". I try to pick tough, modern day, real life questions to answer biblically but this is truly just an average guy's approach to try to get to the truth.

You should know that I am a chiropractor in Narragansett, RI. I have been practicing chiropractic for 28 years so you'll see several references to my profession although it is not my intention to teach you anything about chiropractic in this devotional. I wrote this devotional during two years that were filled with health challenges of my own. In January of 2017 I broke 3 ribs and instead of taking 10 weeks to fully heal, they were healed in 10 days. On October 10th 2017, I tore a disc in my lumbar spine. Instead of spinal surgery and 5 months recovery, two weeks later I was in the office working and fully healed BY GOD THROUGH JESUS CHRIST! Two true miracles! It is my hope that this book will heal any hurts in your soul and strengthen your faith.

I did go to Trinity College of the Bible for a year but I did my studies online and that was 17 years ago. You should know I didn't continue past my first year because I didn't think I was the guy to explain death or dying, especially if a child was involved, to a family. I didn't get it back then. Truthfully I still don't completely understand God's plan but I've found answers to the toughest of questions in the Bible. Just like you, I don't like all the answers I've found, but I believe that God has a plan and I trust that plan. I now believe with all my heart that ALL THINGS work together for good as described in Romans 8:28.

On most of the pages that follow, I've left some space at the bottom for you to jot a few notes of your own about the reflection and verses each day. Don't feel you have to write only about what you read on the page. Dig deep and come up with your own tough questions and find the biblical answers on your own and then share them on this book's Facebook group called, "Manna For The Spirit". I would love to hear from you in that group and get your feedback on this new devotional.

If you picked up this book and become inspired to learn more about biblical questions and answers, I'm going to advise you to join a Bible study. I'm a guy so the Men's Bible Study I formed at my old church turned out to be "just what the doctor ordered". At the time, I had a very enthusiastic, biblically grounded pastor that helped me form the group. (Thank you Dr. Bill Trench) If you're a gal or a couple or a teen, form a group that you can relate to and pick a book or a study that's appropriate for your group. Ask at your church and get one started if there's not one available now.

Along the way, while reading this devotional, if you have a great Bible question that's tougher than you anticipated, don't despair. That happens to me all the time. Email me at drjaykorsen@aol.com and maybe I'll be able to help you out.

I will make a suggestion before you begin reading this devotional. Assume my interpretation and summary of the scripture is incomplete and perhaps, just flat out wrong! Do your own research. Dig into YOUR Bible and decide if you agree with what I said based upon what you learned in your own study of the scriptures. God may speak to you differently than He did to me in His living Word, His gift to you and to me, the Bible.

Enjoy the read. It's my prayer that the words that follow, and the verses that accompany them, will inspire you, will increase your faith, will call you to action, and will warm your heart.

In Health and Faith,

Jay Korsen, DC

- Day 1 -

Father Jared made a great point in church last night. Joseph, as in Mary's husband and Jesus' stepfather, rarely get's the spotlight. The role he chose to fulfill is not one that takes the lead, garners the attention or steals the show but what he taught us through his deeds and actions is so very important. Just this one account in Matthew, when he is visited by an angel, speaks to the person he is and who we could aspire to become.

Matthew 1:18-25 Now the birth of Jesus Christ was like this; for after his mother, Mary, was engaged to Joseph, before they came together, she was found pregnant by the Holy Spirit. Joseph, her husband, being a righteous man, and not willing to make her a public example, intended to put her away secretly. But when he thought about these things, behold, an angel of the Lord appeared to him in a dream, saying, "Joseph, son of David, don't be afraid to take to yourself Mary, your wife, for that which is conceived in her is of the Holy Spirit. She shall give birth to a son. You shall call his name Jesus, for it is he who shall save his people from their sins." Now all this has happened, that it might be fulfilled which was spoken by the Lord through the prophet, saying, "Behold, the virgin shall be with child, and shall give birth to a son. They shall call his name Immanuel"; which is, being interpreted, "God with us." Joseph arose from his sleep, and did as the angel of the Lord commanded him, and took his wife to himself; and didn't know her sexually until she had given birth to her firstborn son. He named him Jesus.

A "Righteous" man. I like the sound of that. Here's a guy that was engaged to be married and finds out the love of his life is pregnant and it wasn't his. Instead of being vengeful, he decides to divorce her "quietly". He is visited by an angel in his dream and decides to Trust Completely in God. Despite the evidence in the natural, he took Mary as his wife, became the stepfather to God's son, and remained faithful. Righteous indeed.

- Day 2 -

Funny, we get all bent out of shape when unexpected events happen in our lives. We make mountains out of mole hills. What if we compare the occasional unexpected events to standing around one day and in an instant half the people we are looking at disappear? What if it was US that disappeared in that moment? Can't happen, you say? Can too...

James 4:14
Whereas you don't know what your life will be like tomorrow. For what is your life? For you are a vapor, that appears for a little time, and then vanishes away.
1 Thessalonians 4:16-17
For the Lord himself will descend from heaven with a shout, with the voice of the archangel, and with God's trumpet. The dead in Christ will rise first, then we who are alive, who are left, will be caught up together with them in the clouds, to meet the Lord in the air. So we will be with the Lord forever.
1 Corinthians 15:51-52
Behold, I tell you a mystery. We will not all sleep, but we will all be changed, in a moment, in the twinkling of an eye, at the last trumpet. For the trumpet will sound, and the dead will be raised incorruptible, and we will be changed.

Things in life can change in a moment, in a twinkling of an eye. One minute your life is going great and then... not so good AND vice versa. One minute you're going south, the next minute you're heading north. As the commercial says, "Life Comes At You Fast!" But, don't worry...ALL THINGS work together for good for those that love the Lord. Are you ready for the unexpected?

- Day 3 -

So here is a very tough one...honesty. It should be an easy one. Just tell the truth all the time. After all, honesty is the best policy, right? But what happens when you are talking with a friend and they ask you a question and if you answer honestly, it will hurt their feelings? That is really a conundrum. Tell the truth and it might jeopardize your friendship. Lie and you are technically sinning. What to do? What to do?

Psalm 12:2
Everyone lies to his neighbor. They speak with flattering lips, and with a double heart.
Proverbs 27:6
Faithful are the wounds of a friend; although the kisses of an enemy are profuse.
Proverbs 19:22
That which makes a man to be desired is his kindness. A poor man is better than a liar.
Ephesians 4:29
Let no corrupt speech proceed out of your mouth, but only what is good for building others up as the need may be, that it may give grace to those who hear.

Listen, there is no doubt that dishonesty has worldly rewards. Lying can bring about financial gain, power or temporary satisfaction but there is always a price to be paid. I have asked my wife on more than one occasion to just lie to me if the truth is going to hurt my feelings. What really have I asked her to do? I have asked her to sin and that's not cool. And yet, if push comes to shove, I myself will choose a "white" lie over the truth if it means sparing someone's feelings. I have chosen sin for myself in order to spare their feelings in the name of "love". Thank God for grace! What will you choose when confronted with this dilemma?

- Day 4 -

Have you ever disagreed with someone about something you are both very passionate about? Every comment from the other person stings and hurts to the core. On the other hand, every one of your comments (respectfully expressed or not) stings them and hurts to their core. It's a dilemma. What do you do when two people are 100% confident they are absolutely right about the same subject but their opinions are diametrically opposed?

Ephesians 4:31-32 Let all bitterness, wrath, anger, outcry, and slander, be put away from you, with all malice. And be kind to one another, tender hearted, forgiving each other, just as God also in Christ forgave you.
Proverbs 15:1 A gentle answer turns away wrath, but a harsh word stirs up anger.
Matthew 5:9 Blessed are the peacemakers, for they shall be called children of God.
James 1:19-21 So, then, my beloved brothers, let every man be swift to hear, slow to speak, and slow to anger; for the anger of man doesn't produce the righteousness of God. Therefore, putting away all filthiness and overflowing of wickedness, receive with humility the implanted word, which is able to save your souls
Romans 12:17-19 Repay no one evil for evil. Respect what is honorable in the sight of all men. If it is possible, as much as it is up to you, be at peace with all men. Don't seek revenge yourselves, beloved, but give place to God's wrath. For it is written, "Vengeance belongs to me; I will repay, says the Lord."

So, here is the take home message from the Bible: Don't always try to convince the other person what is right or wrong at the expense of being tenderhearted and forgiving. If you feel or even know that you know the TRUTH, share it in a non-threatening and civil way. If the other person tries to engage you in an evil, threatening or hurtful way, don't repay their evil with evil. Hold your tongue, be respectful and let God do the talking for you. A little bit of light shining in the dark is more powerful than all the darkness in the world. What will you do next time you are confronted with a person passionate about a view different than yours?

- Day 5 -

Today I had a unique experience. I was invited by a friend to go to the shooting range and do target practice with a wide variety of firearms and a wide variety of ammunition. Until today, I was a strong supporter of the second amendment of the Constitution of the United States but I had never fired a gun. I have to say it was pretty fun. To buy a handgun you need to take a test. One of the questions you are asked is to name the reasons to own a handgun. One of the reasons is self defense...

Luke 11:21   "When the strong man, fully armed, guards his own dwelling, his goods are safe.

Exodus 22:2-3 If the thief is found breaking in, and is struck so that he dies, there shall be no guilt of bloodshed for him. If the sun has risen on him, guilt of bloodshed shall be for him; he shall make restitution. If he has nothing, then he shall be sold for his theft.

Matthew 26:52 Then Jesus said to him, "Put your sword back into its place, for all those who take the sword will die by the sword.

Mark 10:19 You know the commandments: 'Do not murder,' 'Do not commit adultery,' 'Do not steal,' 'Do not give false testimony,' 'Do not defraud,' 'Honor your father and mother.'"

Firing the gun at a target 13 or 25 feet away is one thing. Using it against another human being, even if they are invading your home or threatening your life is quite another story. The Bible is clear about guarding your own dwelling and being held harmless if you shoot someone else, even kill them, defending yourself. But, there is also the whole "do not murder" thing and a warning that those that live by the sword, die by the sword. In the end, we never know what we will do if the situation presents itself. Even if we are prepared to defend ourselves and evil overcomes us, it is comforting to know who we are, whose we are and where we are going in the end. Do you know who you are, whose you are and where you are going in the end?

- Day 6 -

Have you ever spent time trying to share a message with someone and no matter what you said and no matter how much proof you shared, you never got anywhere. It was merely an exercise in knocking your head against the wall. The frustration level goes right through the roof and you wonder what's wrong with the way you are explaining your point of view or the inability of the other person to comprehend it.

Galatians 6:9 Let us not be weary in doing good, for we will reap in due season, if we don't give up.
Exodus 14:14 Yahweh will fight for you, and you shall be still."
Joshua 1:9 Haven't I commanded you? Be strong and courageous. Don't be afraid. Don't be dismayed, for Yahweh your God is with you wherever you go."
Proverbs 3:5-6 Trust in Yahweh with all your heart, and don't lean on your own understanding. In all your ways acknowledge him, and he will make your paths straight.

Listen, not everyone is going to "get it". Not everyone is going to think that what you think is important is important to them. It's called free will. As much as you may not like it, God Himself gave them that Free Will. But, do not be disheartened. Keep spreading your message and eventually it will pay off. What message have you had a hard time getting across lately? Have you prayed for God to help you? If not, what are you waiting for?

- Day 7 -

The Bible has a lot to say about knocking at the door. Remember when you were a kid and you rode your bike down the block to a friend's house, parked the bike in the driveway and went to knock on the door to see if they could come out to play? There was an excitement bubbling up inside you. You knew that there are occasions that your friend would not be able to come out and play but each time you knocked with expectancy.

Luke 11:9-10 "I tell you, keep asking, and it will be given you. Keep seeking, and you will find. Keep knocking, and it will be opened to you. For everyone who asks receives. He who seeks finds. To him who knocks it will be opened.

Acts 12:13-16 When Peter knocked at the door of the gate, a maid named Rhoda came to answer. When she recognized Peter's voice, she didn't open the gate for joy, but ran in, and reported that Peter was standing in front of the gate. They said to her, "You are crazy!" But she insisted that it was so. They said, "It is his angel." But Peter continued knocking. When they had opened, they saw him, and were amazed.

Matthew 7:7 "Ask, and it will be given you. Seek, and you will find. Knock, and it will be opened for you.

Revelation 3:20 Behold, I stand at the door and knock. If anyone hears my voice and opens the door, then I will come in to him, and will dine with him, and he with me.

Often doors we knock on are not opened. Usually that is because what is behind the door just wasn't for us. But, we are encouraged by the Word of God to knock persistently, knock with vigor, knock with anticipation and expectancy and if what is behind the door is truly for us and not against us, the door will be opened for us. What doors have we knocked on that in retrospect we are glad were not opened? What doors should we have knocked on that we talked ourselves out of knocking on?

- Day 8 -

So many people are stressed out these days trying to be "perfect". The media says we need the perfect clothes, the perfect car, the perfect food, the perfect kids, the perfect body, the perfect relationship, etc... In essence, we are led to believe that we should have perfect lives. That's not reality...

Hebrews 10:14 For by one offering he has perfected forever those who are being sanctified.

Colossians 1:22 yet now he has reconciled in the body of his flesh through death, to present you holy and without defect and blameless before him,

Matthew 19:21 Jesus said to him, "If you want to be perfect, go, sell what you have, and give to the poor, and you will have treasure in heaven; and come, follow me."

John 8:7 But when they continued asking him, he looked up and said to them, "He who is without sin among you, let him throw the first stone at her."

Only one person that walked the Earth was perfect, that was Jesus Christ. The rest of us never were, are not and never will be perfect while we are wearing this meat suit we call the human body. So, lighten up and stop trying to be what the media says you should be. Instead, put your time and energy into following Jesus and accepting Him in full faith for it is in Him, in His perfect love that we become perfect through His sacrifice. It can be done no other way.

- Day 9 -

I heard a good sermon about "secret frustrations". Nearly everything in our lives may be right. We can have our health, a wonderful family, a great job, everything looks great from the outside but there is one thing in our lives that we just can't seem to overcome. We are not alone. Many people in the Bible had secret frustrations too.

2 Corinthians 12:7 By reason of the exceeding greatness of the revelations, that I should not be exalted excessively, there was given to me a thorn in the flesh, a messenger of Satan to torment me, that I should not be exalted excessively.

2 Corinthians 12:9 He has said to me, "My grace is sufficient for you, for my power is made perfect in weakness." Most gladly therefore I will rather glory in my weaknesses, that the power of Christ may rest on me.

Exodus 4:10 Moses said to Yahweh, "O Lord, I am not eloquent, neither before now, nor since you have spoken to your servant; for I am slow of speech, and of a slow tongue."

Genesis 30:1 When Rachel saw that she bore Jacob no children, Rachel envied her sister. She said to Jacob, "Give me children, or else I will die."

The Apostle Paul had a "thorn in his flesh", Moses was a stutterer, Rachel could not bear a child for her husband and those are just a few examples. The hard times, the secret frustrations in our lives, are the proof of our faith. If we can stay in faith through the trials, His power is made perfect in us. We all have to deal with "stuff" in our lives. Just when we think our "stuff" is terrible and unbearable, we hear about other people's stuff that is way more difficult to bear than our "stuff". The trick is to trust God, praise Him and give thanks in the good times AND in the bad times. Easier said than done but it is the way to reach our highest potential in life.

- Day 10 -

I recently saw an interesting interview which was, in part, about addictions. It explained that there is a chemical produced in the brain of people that are addicted to smoking, gambling, drinking alcohol, eating and almost all addictions. This chemical is called dopamine. Turns out the brain craves it. Interestingly, guess what else produces dopamine in the brain and can be physically, chemically and psychologically addicting... The very thing you are doing right now... Social Media!

1 Corinthians 10:13   No temptation has taken you except what is common to man. God is faithful, who will not allow you to be tempted above what you are able, but will with the temptation also make the way of escape, that you may be able to endure it.

1 Peter 5:8 Be sober and self-controlled. Be watchful. Your adversary, the devil, walks around like a roaring lion, seeking whom he may devour.

James 1:12 Blessed is the man who endures temptation, for when he has been approved, he will receive the crown of life, which the Lord promised to those who love him.

1 Corinthians 6:12 "All things are lawful for me," but not all things are good for me. "All things are lawful for me," but I will not be enslaved by the power of anything.

Hey, we all have free will, we can do whatever we want to but addictions destroy lives. Be aware that posting on social media waiting for the next comment or "like" is really just an addiction waiting for the next "hit" of dopamine. Admitting you have a problem is the first step. Asking God for help is the second step. It is in our weakness that we are made strong through Christ who strengthens us.

- Day 11 -

Seems as though I'm putting more and more people on my prayer list for cancer, heart disease and Lyme disease these days. Toxins in our environment are becoming harder and harder to avoid. Mental stress seems to be becoming the norm and technology has caused us to become more and more sedentary. The only time we get any exercise is if we schedule a workout at the gym. It is indeed becoming harder to stay healthy but when we, or someone we know is stricken with dis-ease in the body, the Bible has a few things to encourage us and it even gives advice on what we can do to help our bodies heal.

2 Corinthians 4:16-18 ESV   So we do not lose heart. Though our outer self is wasting away, our inner self is being renewed day by day. For this light momentary affliction is preparing for us an eternal weight of glory beyond all comparison, as we look not to the things that are seen but to the things that are unseen. For the things that are seen are transient, but the things that are unseen are eternal.
Psalm 107:20   He sends his word, and heals them, and delivers them from their graves.
Matthew 9:35   Jesus went about all the cities and the villages, teaching in their synagogues, and preaching the Good News of the Kingdom, and healing every disease and every sickness among the people.
Joshua 1:9   Haven't I commanded you? Be strong and courageous. Don't be afraid. Don't be dismayed, for Yahweh your God is with you wherever you go."

We've all heard about people that were told by the doctors that they have only days or weeks to live who, in the end, outlive the doctors that told them that. Healing is talked about often in the Bible and we know that miracles are possible so we pray with passion, fervor and zeal knowing that not all prayers are answered the way we would like them to be. Still, we pray with intensity knowing that God's plan is always perfect. The Bible also gives us some advice about what to eat when we are dis-eased so we can help ourselves. Check out Ezekiel 47:12 and Daniel 1:8 for starters and then do some more research on your own.

- Day 12 -

In Chiropractic, there are 33 principles that explain the philosophy on which the profession was founded and how Chiropractic works. Principle number 6 is a tough one especially when you are in pain. Principle #6 states, "There is no process that does not require time." Doesn't everything in life follow that same principle?

Romans 12:12

rejoicing in hope; enduring in troubles; continuing steadfastly in prayer;

Galatians 6:9

Let us not be weary in doing good, for we will reap in due season, if we don't give up.

Ecclesiastes 7:9

Don't be hasty in your spirit to be angry, for anger rests in the bosom of fools.

Proverbs 25:15

By patience a ruler is persuaded. A soft tongue breaks the bone.

Patience really is a virtue. Holding our tongue instead of bursting out in anger, waiting for something you really want now, staying in prayer when you really want to just cry out for it to be done already, asking God for a healing in His time when you want the suffering to be over right now, or rejoicing when it appears that there is nothing to rejoice about yet... they all require supernatural patience. The only place real patience can come from is from God Almighty Himself. Stay close to God. Stay in Prayer and patience will be yours.

- Day 13 -

Today was an historic day as a new American president was inaugurated. There were several reactions to the event. Some were optimistic, some were appalled some were violent, some were civil, others were overjoyed and still others felt depressed to the point of weeping. The same event viewed by all but individuals reacted in so many different ways.

Philippians 4:6-7 In nothing be anxious, but in everything, by prayer and petition with thanksgiving, let your requests be made known to God. And the peace of God, which surpasses all understanding, will guard your hearts and your thoughts in Christ Jesus.

Proverbs 29:11 A fool vents all of his anger,   but a wise man brings himself under control.

Romans 12:15 Rejoice with those who rejoice. Weep with those who weep.

Joshua 1:9 Haven't I commanded you? Be strong and courageous. Don't be afraid. Don't be dismayed, for Yahweh your God is with you wherever you go."

Life is all about perspective. Each of us sees things through our own eyes and we react differently. We are called to pray and give thanks, not to exist in FEAR. FEAR is an acronym and stands for False Evidence Appearing Real. Many of the protests and anger expressed today was out of fear anticipating the worst and a lack of trust in God. Whether or not you like who got elected, remember that God does not call the equipped, He equips the called. Be strong enough and courageous enough to comfort those who weep and be happy for those that rejoice today and every day.

- Day 14 -

Women gathered today and marched across the country and across the world to make sure their voices are heard, their rights are protected and that freedom would prevail for all people. They gathered to march and it was shown that many of them gathered to pray not only for themselves but for all of us.

Matthew 18:19-20 Again, assuredly I tell you, that if two of you will agree on earth concerning anything that they will ask, it will be done for them by my Father who is in heaven. For where two or three are gathered together in my name, there I am in the middle of them."

1 Thessalonians 5:11 Therefore exhort one another, and build each other up, even as you also do.

Romans 15:5-6 Now the God of patience and of encouragement grant you to be of the same mind one with another according to Christ Jesus, that with one accord you may with one mouth glorify the God and Father of our Lord Jesus Christ.

Romans 12:12 rejoicing in hope; be patient in times of trouble; continuing steadfastly in prayer;

There is real power in numbers but the real power is when two or more are gathered in His name. There amongst them stood our Lord and Savior, Jesus Christ. It is Him, standing in and amongst the crowd representing the Good News which brings power to the voices gathered to be heard. It is His Word leading those voices which encourages us all to gather together, build one another up, rejoice in hope, be patient and pray without ceasing.

- Day 15 -

Each of us has suffered from a condition called "burn out". The definition of Burnout is very interesting. It can be ruin one's health or become completely exhausted through overwork. One other definition is very interesting as well...to be completely consumed and thus no longer aflame. That is interesting isn't it? Have you ever felt completely consumed and no longer aflame? If so, the Bible has some advice for you.

Matthew 11:28-30 "Come to me, all you who labor and are heavily burdened, and I will give you rest. Take my yoke upon you, and learn from me, for I am gentle and humble in heart; and you will find rest for your souls. For my yoke is easy, and my burden is light."

Exodus 20:8-10 "Remember the Sabbath day, to keep it holy. You shall labor six days, and do all your work, but the seventh day is a Sabbath to Yahweh your God. You shall not do any work in it,...

Galatians 6:2 Bear one another's burdens, and so fulfill the law of Christ.

Hebrews 12:1 Therefore let us also, seeing we are surrounded by so great a cloud of witnesses, lay aside every weight and the sin which so easily entangles us, and let us run with patience the race that is set before us,

The cure for burnout is entering into God's rest. We can even avoid future burnout by staying in God's Word and doing His will. Hey, not every day is going to be filled with unicorns and rainbows but through prayer and supplication, we are renewed with hope. It is with that Hope that we can relight the flame which was once fully consumed and fan it back into a warm roaring fire.

- Day 16 -

There are lots of reasons that we come up with not to share the Good News of Jesus Christ. You and I have both used them once or twice. You know, the fact that you are just not that good of a Christian, you don't know the Bible that well, you don't want to offend anyone, people will make fun of you or think you are a lunatic, or maybe you just don't know where to start.

Matthew 28:19 Go, and make disciples of all nations, baptizing them in the name of the Father and of the Son and of the Holy Spirit,

John 3:16 For God so loved the world, that he gave his one and only Son, that whoever believes in him should not perish, but have eternal life.

Acts 4:13 Now when they saw the boldness of Peter and John, and had perceived that they were unlearned and ignorant men, they marveled. They recognized that they had been with Jesus.

Philippians 2:15 that you may become blameless and harmless, children of God without defect in the middle of a crooked and perverse generation, among whom you are seen as lights in the world,

If you're still having a hard time figuring out where to begin, do so by just being a bright light in your community. I realized a long time ago that I was not a good "closer". That is, my gift was not getting a person to the point where they wanted to accept Jesus into their heart right there on the spot, say a prayer of salvation and baptize them. I have only done that once. But, what I am good at is sharing the message of the Bible. I once bought 150 Bibles from Christianbook.com and handed them out door to door. Others might have seen that as tough but I loved it and got a lot joy out of it. I continue to hand Bibles out to those that need one in my office to this day. Find what your gift of the spirit is and share the Good News using that God given gift. (Good Luck, I'll be praying for you.)

- Day 17 -

I really dislike watching the news but of late there is no escaping hearing about the craziness in the world. It seems to occupy every thought of people around me. The latest thing that's concerning everyone is immigration policy. Not taking one political side or the other, what does the Bible say about immigration?

Leviticus 19:33-34 "'If a stranger lives as a foreigner with you in your land, you shall not do him wrong. The stranger who lives as a foreigner with you shall be to you as the native-born among you, and you shall love him as yourself; for you lived as foreigners in the land of Egypt. I am Yahweh your God.

Matthew 25:35 for I was hungry, and you gave me food to eat. I was thirsty, and you gave me drink. I was a stranger, and you took me in.

Romans 13:1-6 Let every soul be in subjection to the higher authorities, for there is no authority except from God, and those who exist are ordained by God. Therefore he who resists the authority, withstands the ordinance of God; and those who withstand will receive to themselves judgment. For rulers are not a terror to the good work, but to the evil. Do you desire to have no fear of the authority? Do that which is good, and you will have praise from the same, for he is a servant of God to you for good. But if you do that which is evil, be afraid, for he doesn't bear the sword in vain; for he is a servant of God, an avenger for wrath to him who does evil. Therefore you need to be in subjection, not only because of the wrath, but also for conscience' sake. For this reason you also pay taxes, for they are servants of God's service, attending continually on this very thing.

OK, I'm sure not all of that is going to go over very well. Here is how I interpret what I read: You have to treat immigrants with love and as yourself and your neighbor. You are called to help those that are in need of any kind. BUT, and this may be a big butt for some to get past, we have to trust that those that have the authority to make decisions in our government are doing so to the best of their abilities and we need to respect their decisions and know that in the end, God is Large and In Charge. If the President or anyone in government makes a big mistake, we can trust that God will rectify it in the end.

- Day 18 -

Today I was listening to a sermon by Joyce Meyer. She made the point that anything we do with and for God is sanctified and holy. She gave the example of Moses standing next to the burning bush. Before Moses got the the bush is was just a bush but when he went there FOR God and was WITH God, the bush became holy and so did the very ground he walked on.

1 Peter 1:16 because it is written, "You shall be holy; for I am holy."

Leviticus 11:45 For I am Yahweh who brought you up out of the land of Egypt, to be your God. You shall therefore be holy, for I am holy.

Isaiah 6:3 One called to another, and said, "Holy, holy, holy, is Yahweh of Armies! The whole earth is full of his glory!"

1 Corinthians 1:30 Because of him, you are in Christ Jesus, who was made to us wisdom from God, and righteousness and sanctification, and redemption:

Once we decide to do everything we do FOR God and we are WITH God, essentially praying without ceasing, giving thanks for even the smallest things, God is in us and we are in God. That's deep! He is actually in us and we in Him. I mean, how much closer to Him could we get? We know that He is holy. No disputing that. And, if that's true then when He is in us, all we do is FOR His glory and becomes holy. Yes, even brushing your teeth is holy! Now think about that for a while and make sure you floss!

- Day 19 -

Perhaps now more than ever before, we need to trade fear for tranquility. We need to trade our apathy for love. We need to trade our anxiousness for peace. Really, it is all a matter of focus. What you think about, you will bring about in your life. Be careful what you are watching and listening to. Be mindful of what is coming out of your mouth when young impressionable minds are within earshot.

Romans 5:1 Being therefore justified by faith, we have peace with God through our Lord Jesus Christ;

Matthew 24:6 You will hear of wars and rumors of wars. See that you aren't troubled, for all this must happen, but the end is not yet.

2 Thessalonians 3:16 Now may the Lord of peace himself give you peace at all times in all ways. The Lord be with you all.

Matthew 15:11 That which enters into the mouth doesn't defile the man; but that which proceeds out of the mouth, this defiles the man."

OK, I realize those are a lot of scriptures and there are a lot of different pieces of advice they give. Let's recap God's Word for us today... 1. Faith in Jesus gives us peace even though everything we hear around us will indicate the world is a troubled place with wars and rumors of wars. 2. God is with us...Always. Isn't that cool and reassuring? 3. If you focus on the fleshy, materialistic things of this world, all there is to look forward to is death. If you focus on God, you can look forward to everlasting life and peace. 4. Don't listen to the potty mouths in the media and for heaven sakes, don't be a potty mouth yourself...people can smell the poop from a mile away. Focus on God the Father and on Jesus today by focusing on Tranquility, Love, and Peace and by outwardly demonstrating your faith through positive, clean speech and thoughts.

- Day 20 -

I was at a conference last weekend and I heard a great talk from my friend Peter Kevorkian. He talked about Pain. The essence of what I got out of his talk was that pain can be a GOOD thing. It is a message from the body to the brain that we need to pause and PAY ATTENTION. Often our bodies send us messages that we choose to ignore for a variety of excuses. We don't like pain but the truth is it is a gift.

Job 6:10 Be it still my consolation, yes, let me exult in pain that doesn't spare, that I have not denied the words of the Holy One.

Psalm 107:43 Whoever is wise will pay attention to these things. They will consider the loving kindnesses of Yahweh.

Hebrews 2:1 Therefore we ought to pay greater attention to the things that were heard, lest perhaps we drift away.

Psalm 69:29 But I am in pain and distress. Let your salvation, God, protect me.

Matthew 26:39 He went forward a little, fell on his face, and prayed, saying, "My Father, if it is possible, let this cup pass away from me; nevertheless, not what I desire, but what you desire."

Let's face it, pain is no fun! But, truly pain has a purpose. It causes us to pause and pay attention, to be fully present. Yes, before all the new age gurus, The Bible's advice was to be MINDFUL, to "pay attention" so that we do not "drift away" even when we are in pain. And, when we are in pain or about to go through a tough painful time, we can be consoled that even Jesus cried out asking that the cup pass away from Him. How can pain be good? For starters, it provided a way for our souls to be saved and it causes us to pay attention.

- Day 21 -

I just looked at my Cox Communications bill for January. It went up by $4.85. The service didn't increase or improve, it just went up without any notice. I have learned from experience if you just call and complain, somehow they are able to magically lower the price without changing the service. It doesn't seem fair. They raise the price hoping that you don't notice and just pay it. They have a lower price but you have to call and complain to get it. Not fair. There are lots of other things in life that are unfair as well.

James 4:17 To him therefore who knows the fair and just thing to do, and doesn't do it, to him it is sin.

Ezekiel 18:29 Yet the house of Israel says, "The way of the Lord is not fair." House of Israel, aren't my ways fair? Aren't your ways unfair?

Job 10:1 "My soul is weary of my life. I will give free course to my complaint. I will speak in the bitterness of my soul.
Leviticus 19:11 "'You shall not steal. "'You shall not lie. "'You shall not deceive one another.

Cox Communications was either knowingly or unknowingly trying to deceive me. Raising the bill slowly until they get to a rate that makes me irate is unfair to me but after all, life is occasionally unfair. They knew the right thing to do...give me the lowest rate but they chose not to do it without the complaint. To them that is sin. Cable TV is a very small thing, there are way more important things to consider in life. What other unimportant things are we preoccupying ourselves with these days that seem so unfair that they have taken our mind off of what is really important, like spending time with God in prayer for example?

- Day 22 -

We are constantly slipping and checking. On any journey, it's nearly impossible to stay on course 100% of the time. We are pulled off course in one direction or another all the time for a number of reasons. It's for that reason that we need to stop, look around, look at our map and check to make sure we didn't slip off course. In life we need to pause and check our bearings to be sure we are still on the path that God intended for us to follow.

Jeremiah 6:16 Yahweh says, "Stand in the ways and see, and ask for the old paths, 'Where is the good way?' and walk in it, and you will find rest for your souls. But they said, 'We will not walk in it.'
Proverbs 16:9 A man's heart plans his course, but Yahweh directs his steps.
Joel 2:7 They run like mighty men. They climb the wall like warriors. They each march in his line, and they don't swerve off course.
2 Corinthians 13:5 Examine your own selves, whether you are in the faith. Test your own selves. Or don't you know as to your own selves, that Jesus Christ is in you?—unless indeed you are disqualified.

Ezekiel 18:21 But if the wicked turn from all his sins that he has committed, and keep all my statutes, and do that which is lawful and right, he shall surely live, he shall not die.

If you've been traveling down the wrong path, no matter how far off course you've gotten or how long you've been off course, God's promise is still available to you. Make the decision today not to do the things that you know are wrong and not to go against God's commandments anymore, and instead ask Him for forgiveness. Once you have asked for forgiveness, ask Jesus into your heart. Light and life everlasting will be your reward. Have you checked yourself lately to ensure that you have not slipped off course?

- Day 23 -

There are over 110 million people that watch the Super Bowl on TV. That's a lot of people that take time and come together to view one event. There's also a lot of bad things that happen as a result of the Super Bowl. Lots of junk food will be consumed by people causing the day after the Super Bowl to require the sale of 20% more antacids than on any other day of the year. Did you know that God talks about 7 Super Bowls in the Bible and after the world sees those Super Bowls there won't be enough antacid in the world to calm everyone's stomach.

Revelation 16:1-4,8,10,12, 17 I heard a loud voice out of the temple, saying to the seven angels, "Go and pour out the seven bowls of the wrath of God on the earth!" The first went, and poured out his bowl into the earth, and it became a harmful and evil sore on the people who had the mark of the beast, and who worshiped his image. The second angel poured out his bowl into the sea, and it became blood as of a dead man. Every living thing in the sea died. The third poured out his bowl into the rivers and springs of water, and they became blood. The fourth poured out his bowl on the sun, and it was given to him to scorch men with fire. The fifth poured out his bowl on the throne of the beast, and his kingdom was darkened. They gnawed their tongues because of the pain,... The sixth poured out his bowl on the great river, the Euphrates. Its water was dried up, that the way might be prepared for the kings that come from the sunrise... The seventh poured out his bowl into the air. A loud voice came out of the temple of heaven, from the throne, saying, "It is done!"

Listen, tonight the Super Bowl on TV might seem pretty important but there are other "Super Bowls" that are truly important. The Super Bowls of Revelation teach us important lessons including the fact that sin can not be tolerated. Luckily, our sins have been paid for through the sacrifice of Jesus. Now THAT is worth cheering for!

- Day 24 -

Super Bowl 51 was certainly the greatest Comeback in Super Bowl history! The Red Sox world series comeback against the Yankees in 2004 was considered a 'miracle'. No doubt they were great comebacks but the Bible has some of the best Comebacks in the history The World! How about Joseph, Job, David, Saul (Paul) and Peter... Not to mention the Comeback God has planned for Jesus!

Genesis 37:28 Midianites who were merchants passed by, and they drew and lifted up Joseph out of the pit, and sold Joseph to the Ishmaelites for twenty pieces of silver. They brought Joseph into Egypt.
Genesis 41:41 Pharaoh said to Joseph, "Behold, I have set you over all the land of Egypt."
Job 2:7 So Satan went out from the presence of Yahweh, and struck Job with painful sores from the sole of his foot to his head.
Job 42:10 Yahweh turned the captivity of Job, when he prayed for his friends. Yahweh gave Job twice as much as he had before.
Acts 9:1 But Saul, still breathing threats and slaughter against the disciples of the Lord, went to the high priest,
1 Corinthians 9:22 Paul, formerly Saul, writes: To the weak I became as weak, that I might gain the weak. I have become all things to all men, that I may by all means save some.

Of course, Peter denies Jesus 3 times but then goes on to lead the Church. David goes from a scrawny shepherd boy to King. Joseph goes from being sold into slavery to ruler of Egypt. Job loses everything and begging for death to having twice what he had before. Saul goes from a murderer of Christians to arguably the best evangelist in history and the writer of most of the New Testament. And Jesus... WOW... from born in a manger to the King of kings, Lord of lords, Prince of peace. From cross to grave to seated at the right hand of God the Father And the Comeback that He has planned to judge the living and the dead will be the Comeback of ALL time.

- Day 25 -

What does it mean to be wealthy? Typically it means having a lot of money and a lot of stuff to go along with the money. To be rich can be an entirely different thing. Sometimes it is the poor person that lives the richest life filled with family, music, art, love, a job they love, travel and a relationship with God through Jesus which brings them a peace that surpasses all understanding.

Philippians 4:7 And the peace of God, which surpasses all understanding, will guard your hearts and your thoughts in Christ Jesus.
Psalm 112:3 Wealth and riches are in his house. His righteousness endures forever.
Proverbs 13:7 There are some who pretend to be rich, yet have nothing. There are some who pretend to be poor, yet have great wealth.
Proverbs 22:1 A good name is more desirable than great riches, and loving favor is better than silver and gold.

There's a lot to say about being wealthy. Today I will leave you with some words from the wise... Lottery: A tax on people who are bad at math – Ambrose Bierce. There is nothing wrong with [people] possessing riches. The wrong comes from riches possessing [people]- Billy Graham. When you are grateful, fear disappears and abundance appears – Tony Robbins. It's easy to make a buck. It's a lot tougher to make a difference – Tom Brokaw. Money is the barometer of a society's virtue – Ayn Rand. He who loses money, loses much; He who loses a friend, loses much more; He who loses faith, loses all – Eleanor Roosevelt. Money never made a man happy yet, nor will it. There is nothing in its nature to produce happiness. The more a man has, the more he wants. Instead of filling a vacuum, it makes one – Benjamin Franklin.

- Day 26 -

The Bible is not like any other book in the world. No matter how many times you read it, there's always a new message from God, a personal communication from Him to you. I can not think of a single other book that gets better and better each time you read it. Think you are a Bible scholar? Think you've read it and there's nothing left to learn? Do you remember the graves bursting open and some of the previously dead saints walking into town to say hello to friends and relatives when Jesus died on the cross? Doubt that happened? Check this out:

Matthew 27:50-54 Jesus cried again with a loud voice, and yielded up his spirit. Behold, the veil of the temple was torn in two from the top to the bottom. The earth quaked and the rocks were split. The tombs were opened, and many bodies of the saints who had fallen asleep were raised; and coming out of the tombs after his resurrection, they entered into the holy city and appeared to many. Now the centurion, and those who were with him watching Jesus, when they saw the earthquake, and the things that were done, feared exceedingly, saying, "Truly this was the Son of God."

What other book crosses every genre known to man? It is a drama with hundreds of characters going through conflicts and expressing emotions we can all relate to. It is an action- adventure like none other. It is a romance novel that defined Love and occasionally reads like a Harlequin novel. Some of its pages read like a horror and at times it paints word pictures that bring about emotions that are too difficult to express verbally. It is a self help book with advice from the wisest people to have ever lived. It is a non-fiction that often uses fiction through parables to teach important lessons. It is a guide to health, healing and travel. It is not a science text but it is scientifically accurate. It incorporates history, math and geometry. The Bible contains biographies, autobiographies and poetry...just to name a few. Think you've read the Bible and there are no more messages God wants to share with you? Think again! Pick up His Word again and Listen to Him speak directly to you as you begin to read the Bible today.

- Day 27 -

As a chiropractor, I'm blessed to often see miracles happen in my office. Some are big, some are small and some are literally mind blowing. Obviously, you don't need to be a chiropractor to see miracles happen in and around your life. It's always been my belief that God uses us to accomplish great things here on Earth to magnify and demonstrate His glory. I was wondering if it is biblically sound to say that 'God works through us'.

John 14:12 Most certainly I tell you, he who believes in me, the works that I do, he will do also; and he will do greater works than these, because I am going to my Father.

Matthew 5:14-16 You are the light of the world. A city located on a hill can't be hidden. Neither do you light a lamp, and put it under a measuring basket, but on a stand; and it shines to all who are in the house. Even so, let your light shine before men; that they may see your good works, and glorify your Father who is in heaven.

Philippians 2:12-13 So then, my beloved, even as you have always obeyed, not only in my presence, but now much more in my absence, work out your own salvation with fear and trembling. For it is God who works in you both to will and to work, for his good pleasure.

Philemon 7 For we have much joy and comfort in your love, because the hearts of the saints have been refreshed through you, brother.

So, yeah, He does work through us for sure. Sometimes He uses you as a light to shine the way to salvation for others. Sometimes He works through your vocation to help protect or heal his children. Sometimes He works through you to lift the hearts of those around you and to refresh them so that they can go on with their important work. And, sometimes, God will work through you to do works that are even greater than the works He did through Jesus. I know, that's hard to believe but Jesus Himself said it in the book of John and He's not capable of a lie. How has God worked through you in the past and what glorious works are ahead? How honored and blessed are we to have Him work through us?

- Day 28 -

Sin is not a topic that people love to discuss. Just the word makes me feel a little uncomfortable too. I recently spoke to someone that I love and respect and they spoke out quickly as if they had long pondered the question of sin and said, "there is no such thing as sin." I politely disagreed and said that I understood sin as anything that goes against the will of God. For now, we will have to disagree.

James 4:17 To him therefore who knows to do good, and doesn't do it, to him it is sin.
1 John 1:8-10 If we say that we have no sin, we deceive ourselves, and the truth is not in us. If we confess our sins, he is faithful and righteous to forgive us the sins, and to cleanse us from all unrighteousness. If we say that we haven't sinned, we make him a liar, and his word is not in us.

John 8:7-11 But when they continued asking him, he looked up and said to them, "He who is without sin among you, let him throw the first stone at her." Again he stooped down, and with his finger wrote on the ground. They, when they heard it, being convicted by their conscience, went out one by one, beginning from the oldest, even to the last. Jesus was left alone with the woman where she was, in the middle. Jesus, standing up, saw her and said, "Woman, where are your accusers? Did no one condemn you?" She said, "No one, Lord." Jesus said, "Neither do I condemn you. Go your way. From now on, sin no more."

No, not one of us has remained without sin in our lives. Without the saving grace of Jesus, the penalty for sin is death, an eternal separation from God. If your heart stopped beating are you at peace with God? Are you absolutely sure where you would spend eternity? If you're not absolutely sure, and you want a new beginning with a personal relationship with Jesus Christ, pray this simple prayer: Lord Jesus, I repent of my sins. Come into my heart. Wash me clean. I make you my Lord and Savior. If you said that prayer, you have been saved. Whoever calls on the name of the Lord will be saved and that is what you just did. Get a Bible, spend time talking to God through prayer, find a church that is Bible based and write today's date down. It is a date you will want to remember as a new beginning. Congratulations on your decision.

- Day 29 -

Valentine's Day is all about getting lovey dovey with your spouse or boyfriend/ girlfriend. That's all well and good but have you thought about what true love is? Have you thought about a kind of love that surpasses all understanding that is unconditional in every way? That is the love God has for each of us.

Deuteronomy 7:8 but because God loves you, and because he desires to keep the oath which he swore to your fathers, Yahweh has brought you out with a mighty hand, and redeemed you out of the house of bondage, from the hand of Pharaoh king of Egypt.
Deuteronomy 7:13 He will love you, bless you, multiply you. He will also bless the fruit of your body and the fruit of your ground, your grain and your new wine and your oil, the increase of your livestock and the young of your flock, in the land which he swore to your fathers to give you.
John 3:16 For God so loved the world, that he gave his one and only Son, that whoever believes in him should not perish, but have eternal life.
Revelation 1:5 and from Jesus Christ, the faithful witness, the firstborn of the dead, and the ruler of the kings of the earth. To him who loves us, and washed us from our sins by his blood;

Who or what do you love most? It is unimaginable that you would have to knowingly sacrifice that which you love most to save your other children. But that is precisely what God did with His Son Jesus. Sure, He knew that Jesus would defeat death but He had to look on as His Son suffered for US. Can you imagine how much He must love you to have gone through the agony of watching His Son suffer to save YOU? That is called Agape love. It is an unconditional everlasting love. Take a moment and pray a prayer of gratitude for His Agape love today.

- Day 30 -

Ever just sat around and had a pitty party for yourself? We've all done it. Once there was a man sitting by the pool at Bethesda. He was a cripple and had been for some time. Jesus asked the man if he wanted to be healed. The guy had some of the same excuses we've used in the past. I'm too slow, I'm not feeling too good, I can't do that on my own, I don't have anyone to help me, I'm not good enough...BLAH, BLAH, BLAH. So Jesus said something interesting to the man…

John 5:8-9 Jesus said to him, "Arise, take up your mat, and walk." Immediately, the man was made well, and took up his mat and walked.

That's not the only healing through the spoken word… Matthew 8:7-10 Jesus said to him, "I will come and heal him." The centurion answered, "Lord, I'm not worthy for you to come under my roof. Just say the word, and my servant will be healed. For I am also a man under authority, having under myself soldiers. I tell this one, 'Go,' and he goes; and tell another, 'Come,' and he comes; and tell my servant, 'Do this,' and he does it." When Jesus heard it, he marveled, and said to those who followed, "Most certainly I tell you, I haven't found so great a faith, not even in Israel.

Matthew 12:13 Then he told the man, "Stretch out your hand." He stretched it out; and it was restored whole, just like the other.

All those healings were pretty awesome and what they all had in common was faith and the spoken word. Jesus never touched them or anointed with any oil. Jesus just spoke a Word. They put their faith in Him and took one more step. An exercise in personal accountability. They made a leap of faith. They took up their mat, outstretched their hand and went home knowing that what Jesus said was immediately done without questioning it. Faith gives us the strength to overcome all our excuses and become all we were predestined by God to be. What excuses do you and I need to overcome?

- Day 31 -

I have always wondered if our dead relatives can communicate with us. When I was at my grandfather's funeral, I heard him loud and clear asking me to take care of my grandmother. I often have vivid dreams of my grandparents in my dreams and once in a meditation, my grandfather sent me a warning (which I heeded). So what's the deal?

Isaiah 8:19-20 When they tell you, "Consult with those who have familiar spirits and with the wizards, who chirp and who mutter:" shouldn't a people consult with their God? Should they consult the dead on behalf of the living? Turn to the law and to the testimony! If they don't speak according to this word, surely there is no light or life in them.

Psalm 119:105

Your word is a lamp to my feet, and a light for my path.

Ecclesiastes 5:3

For as a dream comes with a multitude of cares, so a fool's speech with a multitude of words.

Well, there is certainly nothing wrong with dreaming about our friends and relatives that have passed. It happens all the time. The real challenge comes with the curiosity of going to a necromancer- a person that conjures up spirits to predict the future or to answer questions. Me? Guilty as charged! I really didn't see any harm in it and found it interesting but the point in the Bible is that we should turn to the living God for answers, not to those that are dead. God really desires us to seek Him for direction, to light our path and He gives us that direction in His written Word, the Bible.

- Day 32 -

Who is Jesus? I think we overlook that question too much and assume that everyone knows who He is. I was raised in a family that was Jewish, Catholic as well as Greek Orthodox. That makes for a very confusing walk of faith. All those religions view Jesus very differently so who exactly is He?

Matthew 16:13-17 Now when Jesus came into the parts of Caesarea Philippi, he asked his disciples, saying, "Who do men say that I, the Son of Man, am?" They said, "Some say John the Baptizer, some, Elijah, and others, Jeremiah, or one of the prophets." He said to them, "But who do you say that I am?" Simon Peter answered, "You are the Christ, the Son of the living God." Jesus answered him, "Blessed are you, Simon Bar Jonah, for flesh and blood has not revealed this to you, but my Father who is in heaven.
John 4:25-26 The woman said to him, "I know that Messiah comes, he who is called Christ. When he has come, he will declare to us all things." Jesus said to her, "I am he, the one who speaks to you."
Mark 8:29-30 He said to them, "But who do you say that I am?" Peter answered, "You are the Christ." He commanded them that they should tell no one about him.
Mark 14:61-62 But he stayed quiet, and answered nothing. Again the high priest asked him, "Are you the Christ, the Son of the Blessed?" Jesus said, "I am. You will see the Son of Man sitting at the right hand of Power, and coming with the clouds of the sky."

So who was this man Jesus and who IS He? Was he just a nice guy and a prophet as I was taught in Hebrew school or was he the Son of God, part of the trinity of God consisting of Father, Son and Holy Spirit? I will tell you what I now have come to know. He is Almighty One, Alpha and Omega, Author and Perfecter of Our Faith, Bread of Life, Beloved Son of God, Bridegroom, Chief Cornerstone, Deliverer, Good Shepherd, Head of the Church, Holy Servant, I Am, Emmanuel, Judge, King of Kings, Lamb of God, Light of the World, Lion of the Tribe of Judah, Lord of All, Mediator, Messiah, Mighty One, One Who Sets Free, Our Hope, Peace, Prophet, Redeemer, Risen Lord, Rock, Sacrifice for Our Sins, Savior, Son of God, Son of the Most high, The Way, The Word, True, Truth, Victorious, Wonderful Counselor, Mighty God, Everlasting Father, Prince of Peace – And that's just for starters...

- Day 33 -

Have you ever had one of those inflatable stand up punching bags when you were a kid? You know the one. It looked like Bozo The Clown and when you hit it, it would flop over, touch the floor, bounce back and forth a few times then come back to upright again. No matter how hard you hit it, eventually it would stand upright again. You know why it did that? Because it had a solid foundation.

Matthew 7:24-27

"Everyone therefore who hears these words of mine, and does them, I will liken him to a wise man, who built his house on a rock. The rain came down, the floods came, and the winds blew, and beat on that house; and it didn't fall, for it was founded on the rock. Everyone who hears these words of mine, and doesn't do them will be like a foolish man, who built his house on the sand. The rain came down, the floods came, and the winds blew, and beat on that house; and it fell—and great was its fall."

Deuteronomy 32:4

"The Rock! His work is perfect, For all His ways are just; A God of faithfulness and without injustice, Righteous and upright is He.

At the very foundation of that inflatable punching bag we had as kids was a weight and that weight was much heavier than the rest of the entire bag. So no matter how hard you hit it, it would eventually come right back up. Listen, as the commercial says, "Life comes at you fast." Sometimes life will hit you harder than you ever imagined but if you have a foundation of Christ in your life and you have planted that foundation in your children, no matter how hard life hits you, eventually you and your family will come right back up. Build your spiritual foundation on a ROCK. Build it on God the Father and His Son Jesus Christ.

- Day 34 -

Sometimes I sit for over an hour waiting for inspiration from God for something to research in the Bible and share on this page. Often I sit with the computer in my lap until nearly midnight and my eyes get so heavy that I pass in and out of consciousness. Sometimes profound things just come to mind and other times, my mind is silent and empty. That's just how prayer works. Sometimes when we pray, we have profound revelations and other times we just sit quietly with God. Both are divine...

Psalm 54:2

Hear my prayer, God. Listen to the words of my mouth.

Psalm 4:1

Answer me when I call, God of my righteousness. Give me relief from my distress. Have mercy on me, and hear my prayer.

Matthew 21:22

All things, whatever you ask in prayer, believing, you will receive."

Luke 22:45

When he rose up from his prayer, he came to the disciples, and found them sleeping because of grief,

Acts 6:4

But we will continue steadfastly in prayer and in the ministry of the word."

Prayer is really just sitting quietly listening for inspiration from God while God simultaneously sits quietly listening to you. Sometimes, we hear Him speak to us through a feeling deep within our gut or through an epiphany. Other times, it is fine to just sit in silence and enjoy each other's presence. Often as we speak to God, we fall into a deep sleep and that's OK too. Let us strive to pray without ceasing from before the time we open our eyes in the morning to the time we rest our heads on our pillow to give thanks. Have you spoken to God today? Take the time now. You and He will be glad you did.

- Day 35 -

So, you may have guessed that we do a fair bit of praying in our family. One special type of prayer that I take very seriously is for travel mercies. When I know that a patient, friend or family member is traveling I take special time in my prayers to thank God for their safe passage to their destination and for their return. A friend emailed me today in response to an office email I sent out. I knew that she had been traveling so when I got her e-mail, before I replied, I said an additional prayer for her.

Deuteronomy 28:6 You shall be blessed when you come in, and you shall be blessed when you go out.

Psalm 121:7-8 Yahweh will keep you from all evil. He will keep your soul. Yahweh will keep your going out and your coming in, from this time forward, and forever more.

Psalm 5:12 For you will bless the righteous. Yahweh, you will surround him with favor as with a shield.

Proverbs 2:7-8 He is a shield to those who walk with integrity. He guards the paths of the just and protects those who are faithful to him.

Psalm 91:11 For he will put his angels in charge of you, to guard you in all your ways.

God has His eye on you in your going out and when you come in. He literally has his angels in charge of you to guard you in all your ways. So, why spend all that time in prayer? Because it honors God. It thanks Him for his mercy and goodness. We must also be mindful that not every journey ends the way we prayed it would. One day we will all take our final journey and we can take comfort in knowing that as believers our final destination is always into the loving arms of Jesus. As believers, when we part from one another on any journey, we know that it is never goodbye, it is until we meet again.

- Day 36 -

We have all heard the bible verse… "You have heard that it was said, 'An eye for an eye, and a tooth for a tooth.' But I tell you, don't resist him who is evil; but whoever strikes you on your right cheek, turn to him the other also." That's all well and good but what about fighting back? What about defending yourself?

Ecclesiastes 3:8
a time to love, and a time to hate; a time for war, and a time for peace.
Proverbs 21:15

It is joy to the righteous to do justice; but it is a destruction to the workers of iniquity.

Psalm 144:1

Blessed be Yahweh, my rock, who teaches my hands to war, and my fingers to battle:

James 4:1-2

Where do wars and fightings among you come from? Don't they come from your pleasures that war in your members? 2 You lust, and don't have. You murder and covet, and can't obtain. You fight and make war. You don't have, because you don't ask.

So, we have a decision to make. The Bible is clear that we should try to be the peacemaker first and foremost and try to avoid a fight. The Bible also says it's OK to defend yourself. As my old martial arts instructor once told us, "There is no shame in running from a fight. Run fast and run far. If they corner you, turn and ice them and then run as far and as fast as you can again." Sage advice which turns out to be biblical as well.

- Day 37 -

Who is God? That's a basic question but what is the answer? People have lots of answers but what does the Bible say about who God is?

John 4:24

God is spirit, and those who worship him must worship in spirit and truth."

John 14:6

Jesus said to him, "I am the way, the truth, and the life. No one comes to the Father, except through me.

Revelation 22:13

I am the Alpha and the Omega, the First and the Last, the Beginning and the End.

1 John 4:8

He who doesn't love doesn't know God, for God is love.

Exodus 3:14

God said to Moses, "I AM WHO I AM," and he said, "You shall tell the children of Israel this: 'I AM has sent me to you.'"

So, who is God? God is Spirit, The Way, The Truth, The Life, the Alpha and the Omega, the Beginning and the End. God is just simply I AM. He has always been, is now and will always be. But, most importantly, God is Love. Let us strive to be more like Him by being love and by loving both ourselves and those around us unconditionally.

- Day 38 -

How do we overcome our cravings? Cravings come in many types and often combating our cravings is an exercise in willpower. We are being pulled toward our cravings by our mind while our heart and spirit are trying to save us from ourselves. What is it that you most crave?

Galatians 5:16

But I say, walk by the Spirit, and you won't fulfill the lust of the flesh.

1 John 2:16

For all that is in the world, the lust of the flesh, the lust of the eyes, and the pride of life, isn't the Father's, but is the world's.

James 4:7

Be subject therefore to God. But resist the devil, and he will flee from you.

Ephesians 2:3

among whom we also all once lived in the lust of our flesh, doing the desires of the flesh and of the mind, and were by nature children of wrath, even as the rest.

Chocolate, potato chips, ice cream...what is your craving? Cigarettes, gambling, drinking... are these things pulling you in a direction you wish you were not heading in? A new car, a bigger bank account, a new house... all potential cravings. We all have these powerful desires for 'things' in our lives. Just know that although it's normal to have cravings and they seem like huge problems, God is BIGGER and will help you overcome them if you ask.

- Day 39 -

Another outstanding message at church today by Fr. Jared. In a heartfelt homily he pointed out that each and EVERY one of us carries a cross. Each of us has a secret burden, a weight we are carrying. Maybe from the outside we look like we have it all together but we are all dealing with unpleasant situations and responsibilities that we are forced to accept because we are unable to change them.

Matthew 16:24-25

Then Jesus said to his disciples, "If anyone desires to come after me, let him deny himself, and take up his cross, and follow me. For whoever desires to save his life will lose it, and whoever will lose his life for my sake will find it.

Galatians 6:2 Bear one another's burdens, and so fulfill the law of Christ.

James 5:16 Confess your offenses to one another, and pray for one another, that you may be healed. The insistent prayer of a righteous person is powerfully effective.

Matthew 11:28-30 "Come to me, all you who labor and are heavily burdened, and I will give you rest. Take my yoke upon you, and learn from me, for I am gentle and humble in heart; and you will find rest for your souls. For my yoke is easy, and my burden is light."

It's interesting that we all feel our burden or the "weight" we are carrying around is overwhelming but when we stop to help someone else, put our weight down and carry their cross to help them for a short while, we realize how light our own weight was after all. There is power in helping someone else carry their cross to ease their burdens for a while that makes our cross easier to bear. Bearing the weight of someone else's burden begins with a simple prayer for them. Who's burden can you lighten with prayer today?

- Day 40 -

Have you ever heard the phrase that, "We sow in tears and reap in joy"? Well, actually that's biblical. Tears are for cleansing the soul. They pour out when we are in pain or in angst. But tears also fall on those rare occasions in our lives when our heart's desires are so intense that we are brought to tears. With these tears, we are literally sowing into this dream. Tears are one of the most important tools to sow the seeds of our dreams.

Psalm 126:5-6

Those who sow in tears will reap in joy. He who goes out weeping, carrying seed for sowing, will certainly come again with joy, carrying his sheaves.

Luke 7:38

Standing behind at his feet weeping, she began to wet his feet with her tears, and she wiped them with the hair of her head, kissed his feet, and anointed them with the ointment.

Revelation 21:4

He will wipe away from them every tear from their eyes. Death will be no more; neither will there be mourning, nor crying, nor pain, any more. The first things have passed away."

It's tough to do the right thing. It's tough to go out every day and work hard to achieve your goals and dreams. I know you've been brought to tears along the way just trying to do your best. Remember those tears were cleansing your soul and watering your hopes and desires. It's God's promise that after the tears have fallen, Joy will come in time and you'll reap the harvest. Mary's tears fell on Jesus' feet and she was rewarded with the joy of finding the empty tomb on Easter morning. So too will God wipe away your tears, fill you with joy and fulfill your heart's desires. And as a bonus... death will be no more. Now that's something to be Joyful about!

- Day 41 -

Just recently I have heard from several people I know and they have told me that they are going to make a career change. Interestingly when I asked what they were doing they said they didn't know. They were just going to take some time off to "find themselves". In the Bible there is a story of a few guys that decided to have a career change.

Matthew 4:18-22

Walking by the sea of Galilee, he saw two brothers: Simon, who is called Peter, and Andrew, his brother, casting a net into the sea; for they were fishermen. He said to them, "Come after me, and I will make you fishers for men."

They immediately left their nets and followed him. Going on from there, he saw two other brothers, James the son of Zebedee, and John his brother, in the boat with Zebedee their father, mending their nets. He called them. They immediately left the boat and their father, and followed him.

I don't really think that you need to leave town or go away or take a trip to "find yourself". When people say they need to find themselves, what they really mean is that they are trying to find their calling, their destiny, their mission in life. You don't need to go "somewhere" to find that, you need to go to "someone"... you need to go to God in prayer to find that. You can do that anywhere including where you are right now and save the airfare. It is in the moments of quiet reflection and prayer that we find who we were predestined to be.

- Day 42 -

This from a friend in Christ: "God allows us to face difficulties so we grow, so we become stronger spiritually, to test us and to bring us closer to Him. The thought occurred to me that Jesus' Passion might not have been just for our sakes? Could it have served a second purpose to test Jesus? To prove to God the Father and to Jesus Himself that He was worthy to sit at the right Hand of the Father? That Jesus didn't just get that place from nepotism? That Jesus had to freely choose his Passion; knowing that He was going to earn his place at the right Hand of the Father thru choosing the suffering of His Passion? Even Jesus had to prove his devotion. We are all given the same test in a different way in our lives too. What do you think?"

John 1:1 In the beginning was the Word, and the Word was with God, and the Word was God.

Revelation 22:13 I am the Alpha and the Omega, the First and the Last, the Beginning and the End.

(Luke 4:1–13) and (Matthew 4:1–11) and (Mark 1:12-13) The three temptations of Jesus in the desert… read them on your own.

Luke 22:42 saying, "Father, if you are willing, remove this cup from me. Nevertheless, not my will, but yours, be done."

OK, listen, I'm not a Bible scholar, I'm a chiropractor but this is my take on it. Jesus didn't have to earn his spot at the right hand of God. It was His from the very beginning as all things were created with Him and through Him. So far as Jesus being tempted to prove Himself worthy, I don't think that was the purpose of the temptations. It was impossible for Jesus to sin even here on Earth. He was not tempted to see if He would fall. He was tempted to prove He could not fall. Thank you Jesus for proving that you would not and could not fall, for being our perfect sacrificial Lamb, for not succumbing to temptation and for providing life everlasting from the right hand of God the Father.

Ash Wednesday... you may have been wondering, What's the deal? There are many times in the Bible where people are sitting in ashes at the lowest point in their lives and they come to a turning point. When we wear the ashes on our forehead, we acknowledge that there is something wrong in this world, within ourselves. We look into our own heart and repent in dust and ashes.

Genesis 3:19 By the sweat of your face will you eat bread until you return to the ground, for out of it you were taken. For you are dust, and to dust you shall return."

Matthew 11:21   "Woe to you, Chorazin! Woe to you, Bethsaida! For if the mighty works had been done in Tyre and Sidon which were done in you, they would have repented long ago in sackcloth and ashes.

Job 42:6 Therefore I abhor myself, and repent in dust and ashes."

Daniel 9:3 I set my face to the Lord God, to seek by prayer and petitions, with fasting and sackcloth and ashes.

2 Corinthians 5:20-6:2 ...we beg you on behalf of Christ, be reconciled to God. ...Behold, now is the acceptable time. Behold, now is the day of salvation.

That desire to repent does not mean that we are 'so bad'. It means that we are acknowledging that we should be 'so good', that we were fearfully and wonderfully made and we have fallen short of our God given potential. The ashes are in the shape of a cross to signify that even in the midst of us falling short, Jesus claims us as His. So we wear the ashes as a sign that God believes that We (you and I) are worth dying for. The ashes mean we are a sinner but the cross means we have a savior. That is why we wear the ashes on Ash Wednesday.

- Day 44 -

What exactly is Lent? Well it is a 40 day period (not counting Sundays) between Ash Wednesday and Holy Saturday. It is 40 days long because it represents the 40 days Jesus spent in the wilderness enduring the temptations of the devil as he prepared to begin His ministry here on Earth. Sundays in Lent are not counted in the forty days because each Sunday represents a "mini-Easter" and the reverent spirit of Lent is tempered with joyful anticipation of the Resurrection. Lent is a time to get to know Jesus more intimately and to contemplate the sacrifice he made for us on the cross so that when Good Friday arrives, we can more fully receive the grace of God.

Matthew 4:1-2

Then Jesus was led up by the Spirit into the wilderness to be tempted by the devil. When he had fasted forty days and forty nights, he was hungry afterward.

Revelation 21:3

I heard a loud voice out of heaven saying, "Behold, God's dwelling is with people, and he will dwell with them, and they will be his people, and God himself will be with them as their God.

Ultimately lent doesn't just end in sadness, it points us to the hope of the resurrection. So, on Fridays during Lent you may want to hold the pepperoni on your pizza and have some salmon instead of steak. When we abstain from eating red meat, it is meant to be an act of penitence, in remembrance of the Friday Christ was crucified. It is just another way to draw ourselves closer to God and more fully understand His love for us through His sacrifice. Give it a try and see if that small sacrifice makes a big difference in your prayer life.

- Day 45 -

Reverend Robert H. Schuller really helped me develop the strong faith I have today as I watched and took notes every Sunday from his Hour of Power TV show. He told how he did not promote a religion, he promoted a relationship. He did not promote a doctrine, he promoted a relationship with Jesus Christ. It was this man that got me addicted to optimism and gave me a sensational faith.

Revelation 3:20

Behold, I stand at the door and knock. If anyone hears my voice and opens the door, then I will come in to him, and will dine with him, and he with me.

"Let the risen Jesus enter your life—welcome him as a friend, with trust: he is life! If up till now you have kept him at a distance, step forward. He will receive you with open arms. If you have been indifferent, take a risk; you won't be disappointed. If following him seems difficult, don't be afraid. Trust him, be confident that he is close to you, that he is with you, and he will give you the peace you are looking for and the strength to live as he would have you do." —The Joy of Discipleship by Pope Francis

Dr. Schuller had a dream given by God. To build a place and spend his entire life in one place doing something beautiful for God. He had no money to build that place. The message he wanted to give to the world was that If you can dream it, you can do it. If you can believe it, you can achieve it and with God, nothing is impossible. He most certainly built that place and did something beautiful for God. What can we do that is beautiful for God?

- Day 46 -

Have you ever heard the phrase that the road to hell is paved with good intentions? Another saying is, "Hell is full of good meanings, but Heaven is full of good works." Doing the wrong thing or even an evil thing is often masked by good intentions. Maybe we genuinely intend to do the "right thing" but never take action…that can be even worse.

Proverbs 16:2 All the ways of a man are clean in his own eyes; but God weighs the motives.

Proverbs 6:30 Men don't despise a thief, if he steals to satisfy himself when he is hungry:

Proverbs 14:12 There is a way which seems right to a man, but in the end it leads to death.

Galatians 6:7 Don't be deceived. God is not mocked, for whatever a man sows, that he will also reap.

"Most of the evil in this world is done by people with good intentions." T.S. Eliot

No one would remember the Good Samaritan if he'd only had good intentions; he had money as well. Margaret Thatcher

Hell isn't merely paved with good intentions; it's walled and roofed with them. Yes, and furnished too. Aldous Huxley

- Day 47 -

AMEN. What does the word mean? It means "So Be It". It is our outward expression of affirmation. We say it when we are in agreement with something. We say it at the end of prayers. We say it as we receive the host during communion. AMEN. Such a small word but a big sentiment.

1 Chronicles 16:36

Blessed be Yahweh, the God of Israel, from everlasting even to everlasting. All the people said, "Amen," and praised Yahweh.

Psalm 72:19

Blessed be his glorious name forever! Let the whole earth be filled with his glory! Amen and amen.

Matthew 6:13

Bring us not into temptation, but deliver us from the evil one. For yours is the Kingdom, the power, and the glory forever. Amen. '

Romans 15:33

Now the God of peace be with you all. Amen.

Revelation 7:12

saying, "Amen! Blessing, glory, wisdom, thanksgiving, honor, power, and might, be to our God forever and ever! Amen."

Isn't it wonderful that when we surrender our weakness to God, He fills us with His strength? Can I get an AMEN?

- Day 48 -

One of the biggest complaints wives have about their husbands is "Selective Hearing". You know what that means, right? It means that we as husbands only hear what we want to hear and what we don't want to hear immediately or soon after vanishes from our memory banks. That doesn't just happen when listening to our spouses.

Proverbs 1:5 that the wise man may hear, and increase in learning; that the man of understanding may attain to sound counsel:

Deuteronomy 28:2 All these blessings will come upon you, and overtake you, if you listen to Yahweh your God's voice.

Psalm 34:15 Yahweh's eyes are toward the righteous. His ears listen to their cry.

Proverbs 1:8 My son, listen to your father's instruction, and don't forsake your mother's teaching:

Luke 10:16 Whoever listens to you listens to me, and whoever rejects you rejects me. Whoever rejects me rejects him who sent me."

God realized we would have selective hearing when it came to our parents and we would also have selective hearing when it came to listening to His word. If we are to expect God to listen to us in prayer, we need to listen intently when He speaks to us through His Word which is the Bible. We are not to read the Bible with selective hearing, sifting out those things we don't like. We are to read it in it's entirety, accepting it's content as Truth even when we may not LIKE the entire message.

- Day 49 -

Confession. There are a lot of opinions about confession. There's quite a bit of dogma associated with confession. It seems that there are as many ways to confess your sins as there are different denominations in Christianity. That's all well and good but what does the Bible say about confession? Is there a right way and a wrong way? Do we need to confess through Jesus or a priest or a congregation of believers or can we bring our confession directly to God the Father?

1 John 1:9 If we confess our sins, he is faithful and righteous to forgive us the sins, and to cleanse us from all unrighteousness.

Joshua 7:19 Joshua said to Achan, "My son, please give glory to Yahweh, the God of Israel, and make confession to him. Tell me now what you have done! Don't hide it from me!"

Romans 10:10 For with the heart, one believes unto righteousness; and with the mouth confession is made unto salvation.

Hebrews 3:1 Therefore, holy brothers, partakers of a heavenly calling, consider the Apostle and High Priest of our confession, Jesus;

Mark 1:4-5 John came baptizing in the wilderness and preaching the baptism of repentance for forgiveness of sins. All the country of Judea and all those of Jerusalem went out to him. They were baptized by him in the Jordan river, confessing their sins.

Clearly, there's more than one way that's Biblically acceptable to confess our sins. There are examples of confessing directly to God, confessing through Jesus and confessing through a priest. There is no evidence that one has to confess in public or to the church. To the contrary, you should confess in private to the one you sinned against to get their forgiveness. No matter how you do it, choose a way to confess and get right with God. You'll be glad you did.

- Day 50 -

Mellifluous. Now that's a word you don't hear every day! Do you know what it means? It means (of a voice or words) sweet or musical; pleasant to hear. It is synonymous with Sweet-sounding, dulcet, honeyed, mellow, soft, liquid, silvery, soothing, rich, smooth, euphonious, harmonious, tuneful and musical. Wait, I've heard a sound like that described before...

Luke 2:13-14

Suddenly, there was with the angel a multitude of the heavenly army praising God, and saying, "Glory to God in the highest, on earth peace, good will toward men."

Psalm 98:4

Make a joyful noise to the Lord, all the earth! Burst out and sing for joy, yes, sing praises!

Psalm 100:1
Make a joyful noise unto the Lord, all ye lands.

Revelation 4:8
The four living creatures, each one of them having six wings, are full of eyes around and within. They have no rest day and night, saying, "Holy, holy, holy is the Lord God, the Almighty, who was and who is and who is to come!"

Holy, Holy, Holy. How sweet will the sound of all the heavenly host singing that all together sound? A Joyful noise is pleasing to God. Have you made a mellifluous noise to God today?

- Day 51 -

INEFFABLE. Now there is a biblical word that's not in the Bible, but it should be. It means: Too great or extreme to be expressed or described in words. Not to be uttered because of its sacredness. Does that sound like the way you would describe someone and something you might find in the Bible?

Job 37:23 We can't reach the Almighty. He is exalted in power. In justice and great righteousness, he will not oppress.

Ephesians 3:19 and to know Christ's love which surpasses knowledge, that you may be filled with all the fullness of God.

2 Corinthians 9:15 Now thanks be to God for his unspeakable gift!

2 Corinthians 12:4 how he was caught up into Paradise, and heard unspeakable words, which it is not lawful for a man to utter.

Throughout the Bible we are admonished not to utter God's name because it is so ineffable. "Thou shalt not take the Name of the Lord thy God in vain: for the Lord will not hold him guiltless that takes His Name in vain" (Exodus 20:7). And, "Our Father which art in heaven, Hallowed be thy Name" (Matt. 6:9). Instead of calling Him by name and risk using His name in vain, how about we call Him who He is? He is our "Father" in heaven and He is LOVE. Yes, true agape LOVE is also ineffable just like our Father in heaven.

Here's another quick thought for you today. Did you know that there is a pronunciation of God's name that is so secret and ineffable that no one will know it until Jesus returns? Yup, it's true... Revelation 19:12-13 His eyes are a flame of fire, and on his head are many crowns. He has names written and a name written which no one knows but he himself. He is clothed in a garment sprinkled with blood. His name is called "The Word of God."

- Day 52 -

Hiraeth. It is a concept that our souls are well acquainted with. What? Never heard of that word? Well, Hiraeth means: a homesickness for a home you can not return to OR an intense form of longing, nostalgia or wistfulness. It is said that we are spiritual beings having a human experience. During this experience, our soul longs to return home to be with God.

2 Corinthians 5:6-8

Therefore we are always confident and know that while we are at home in the body, we are absent from the Lord; for we walk by faith, not by sight. We are courageous, I say, and are willing rather to be absent from the body, and to be at home with the Lord.

1 Thessalonians 4:17

then we who are alive, who are left, will be caught up together with them in the clouds, to meet the Lord in the air. So we will be with the Lord forever.

Psalm 122:1

I was glad when they said to me, "Let's go to The Lord's house!"

We are but a mound of clay that was shaped and formed by The Lord God Almighty. It was His very breath that gave us life. We are, in many ways, just living on borrowed breath. It is in the use of that breath to praise God that we return home. It is with our dying breath that we truly return home to our Creator to be even more fully alive and experience life everlasting. We will forever experience Hiraeth until we come to stand before Jesus in that day in which there is no sunset and no dawning.

- Day 53 -

I heard a friend talk about serendipity. He felt it was serendipitous the way his life just seemed to all fall into place. He felt it was just a chance occurrence of events that came together in a beneficial way. I disagree. There is no serendipity or "coincidences", based on what I have read in the Bible, there are only "on purposes".

Romans 8:29

For whom he foreknew, he also predestined to be conformed to the image of his Son, that he might be the firstborn among many brothers.

Romans 8:30

Whom he predestined, those he also called. Whom he called, those he also justified. Whom he justified, those he also glorified.

Ephesians 1:5

having predestined us for adoption as children through Jesus Christ to himself, according to the good pleasure of his desire,

Jeremiah 29:11 (AMP)

For I know the plans *and* thoughts that I have for you,' says the Lord, 'plans for peace *and* well-being and not for disaster to give you a future and a hope.

The Bible indicates that God has seen your past and knows your future. True, we have free will but God already knows the choices we will make. God has great plans for us to live a peaceful life of well-being. God has planted seeds of hope within us from the time He breathed life into us. He predestined when those seeds would sprout into great things throughout our lives. But perhaps the most encouraging thing is that He assures us that ALL THINGS in our lives, even the ones we perceive as bad right now, will ultimately work together for good.

- Day 54 -

Today let's focus on the word ETHEREAL. That word means extremely delicate and light in a way that seems too perfect for this world. There are lots of things that come to mind when we think about ethereal things. The Bible teaches about things that are delicate and light and not of this world...

John 8:23
He (Jesus) said to them, "You are from beneath. I am from above. You are of this world. I am not of this world.
James 1:17

Every good gift and every perfect gift is from above, coming down from the Father of lights, with whom can be no variation, nor turning shadow.

John 15:19

If you were of the world, the world would love its own. But because you are not of the world, since I chose you out of the world, therefore the world hates you.

Philippians 3:20-21

For our citizenship is in heaven, from where we also wait for a Savior, the Lord Jesus Christ; who will change the body of our humiliation to be conformed to the body of his glory, according to the working by which he is able even to subject all things to himself.

What can be more delicate and light than LIGHT itself? Light comes from above the Earth which makes it not of this world. The Bible teaches us that Jesus IS the Light. And we, by the gift of grace, will one day be ethereal as well when we are conformed to the body of His glory.

- Day 55 -

Ever had an EPIPHANY? Of course you have. We all have had an epiphany at one point in our lives or another. We have all experienced the moment when several thoughts or circumstances all come together at once and we come to a moment of sudden revelation. The Bible describes several moments of epiphany as well. Paul describes one of his epiphanies in his letter (epistle) to the Ephesians...

Ephesians 3:2-6

2 if it is so that you have heard of the administration of that grace of God which was given me toward you; 3 how that by revelation the mystery was made known to me, as I wrote before in few words, 4 by which, when you read, you can perceive my understanding in the mystery of Christ; 5 which in other generations was not made known to the children of men, as it has now been revealed to his holy apostles and prophets in the Spirit; 6 that the Gentiles are fellow heirs, and fellow members of the body, and fellow partakers of his promise in Christ Jesus through the Good News,

There are some key phrases in this passage of Ephesians written by the Apostle Paul. First, what he spoke of was brought to him by a revelation. An epiphany of sorts where in a moment, he was changed from Saul to Paul through a divine intervention. Secondly, he refers to the "mystery of Christ". The Greek word mysterion refers to a secret which is now open. The mysterion of Christ is that salvation is not just for the Jews but for all people through Christ. Now, listen, you don't need to be struck down in the middle of the road and blinded like Paul to have an epiphany but it does help if your heart and mind are open, your mouth is closed and you prepare yourself through prayer to hear God's voice through a feeling in your gut or through a strong thought that brings you to an epiphany.

- Day 56 -

FRUITION- pronounced froo͞ˈiSH(ə)n/ is the point at which a plan or project is realized. God has a plan for us for sure! In fact, He has a plan for the entire world and it will come to fruition.

Philippians 1:6
being confident of this very thing, that he who began a good work in you will complete it until the day of Jesus Christ.

Revelation 21:1-4

I saw a new heaven and a new earth: for the first heaven and the first earth have passed away, and the sea is no more. I saw the holy city, New Jerusalem, coming down out of heaven from God, prepared like a bride adorned for her husband. I heard a loud voice out of heaven saying, "Behold, God's dwelling is with people, and he will dwell with them, and they will be his people, and God himself will be with them as their God. He will wipe away from them every tear from their eyes. Death will be no more; neither will there be mourning, nor crying, nor pain, any more. The first things have passed away."

Just as God has an individual work He will complete in you, He has a work He will complete in the world. God has already forethought a new earth and a new heaven. God has already prepared a New Jerusalem where He will dwell among those of us that are saved. He has a plan to end death, to end suffering and bring an everlasting life to fruition for us all.

Day 57

On St. Patrick's Day, we're usually overcome with the pageantry that includes parades, the wearing of green, the adoption of the Irish heritage, and green beer. What we may overlook are the two letters before his name, St. which of course stand for Saint. We often overlook what exactly he did to acquire that status like overcoming huge odds and obstacles to evangelize the entirety of Ireland. What does the Bible have to say about Saints?

Psalm 16:3
As for the saints who are in the earth, they are the excellent ones in whom is all my delight.
Psalm 50:5
"Gather my saints together to me, those who have made a covenant with me by sacrifice."
Revelation 14:12
Here is the patience of the saints, those who keep the commandments of God, and the faith of Jesus."
Ephesians 4:11-13

He gave some to be apostles; and some, prophets; and some, evangelists; and some, shepherds and teachers; for the perfecting of the saints, to the work of serving, to the building up of the body of Christ; until we all attain to the unity of the faith, and of the knowledge of the Son of God, to a full grown man, to the measure of the stature of the fullness of Christ;

The Bible would lead us to believe that there is no 5 step process to becoming a saint or some canonization ritual that's needed to confirm sainthood. Instead the Bible would have us understand that it requires patiently keeping the commandments of God, faith in Jesus Christ, putting that faith into action through service, selfless sacrifices in His name and spreading the Good News that death was conquered and there is life everlasting available to all that believe. God tells us through the Bible that Saints are on Earth even today. What can we do to become more holy and virtuous and follow in the footsteps of the saints?

- Day 58 -

Yesterday I was asked an interesting question. If God is all knowing and all powerful, why would he create humans that he knew were going to sin and spend an eternity in hell? Why would He create people that He would kill in the Old Testament? Why would he have even created people in the first place if He knew there would be suffering? Isn't that immoral? WOW, those are some good questions for sure. To answer these questions we need to look at the Bible... a lot... so here are a few more verses than usual...

Isaiah 55:8-9 "For my thoughts are not your thoughts, and your ways are not my ways," says The Lord. "For as the heavens are higher than the earth, so are my ways higher than your ways, and my thoughts than your thoughts.

Deuteronomy 29:29 The secret things belong to Yahweh our God; but the things that are revealed belong to us and to our children forever, that we may do all the words of this law.

Revelation 4:11 "Worthy are you, our Lord and God, the Holy One, to receive the glory, the honor, and the power, for you created all things, and because of your desire they existed, and were created!"

Psalm 115:3 But our God is in the heavens. He does whatever he pleases.

Isaiah 43:7 everyone who is called by my name, and whom I have created for my glory, whom I have formed, yes, whom I have made.'"

Matthew 7:13-14 "Enter in by the narrow gate; for wide is the gate and broad is the way that leads to destruction, and many are those who enter in by it. How narrow is the gate, and restricted is the way that leads to life! Few are those who find it.

(to be continued...)

- Day 59 -

Yes, two days, one topic...

Deuteronomy 30:19

I call heaven and earth to witness against you today, that I have set before you life and death, the blessing and the curse. Therefore choose life, that you may live, you and your descendants;

Joshua 24:15

If it seems evil to you to serve God, choose today whom you will serve; whether the gods which your fathers served that were beyond the River, or the gods of the Amorites, in whose land you dwell; but as for me and my house, we will serve God."

2 Peter 3:9

The Lord is not slow concerning his promise, as some count slowness; but is patient with us, not wishing that any should perish, but that all should come to repentance.

OK, let's recap. Our finite mind can never perceive what an infinite mind can perceive. Humans were created by an act of God's free will to receive and respond to His glory. God has given every person an equal opportunity to choose heaven, to have not created them in the first place would have been even more immoral or "unfair". God's attributes place Him and Him only in a position to choose which world and who in it would be best. I would like to end with a quote from C.S. Lewis: "There are only two kinds of people in the end: those who say to God, 'Thy will be done,' and those to whom God says, in the end, '*Thy* will be done.' All that are in Hell, choose it"

- Day 60 -

To TRANSCEND means to go beyond the limits, to surpass. God has no limits but His glory continues to rise above anything we could possibly understand. The Bible talks about God transcending even our greatest expectations.

Romans 5:20
The law came in besides, that the trespass might abound; but where sin abounded, grace abounded more exceedingly;
Ephesians 3:20
Now to him who is able to do exceedingly abundantly above all that we ask or think, according to the power that works in us,
1 Timothy 1:14
The grace of our Lord abounded exceedingly with faith and love which is in Christ Jesus.

Ephesians 3:19

and to know Christ's love which surpasses knowledge, that you may be filled with all the fullness of God.

Philippians 4:7

And the peace of God, which surpasses all understanding, will guard your hearts and your thoughts in Christ Jesus.

His Love Transcends all things. Offering eternal life where there ought to be punishment for breaking His law…that blows me away and I am filled with gratitude. He is exceedingly, abundantly above and beyond anything we could ever ask or think of. Just thinking about it fills us with the Peace which surpasses all our understanding.

- Day 61 -

There are times when it seems like God is asking us to do more than He equipped us to do or He is asking us to bear more than we can handle. Is it true that He never gives us more than we can handle or does He occasionally allow us to be weighed down to the point that we can feel as though we are breaking? Ever been in that position and had a well meaning friend give you the biblically inaccurate quote that "God will never, ever give you more than you can handle"? How did that make you feel?

1 Corinthians 10:13 No temptation has taken you except what is common to man. God is faithful, who will not allow you to be tempted above what you are able, but will with the temptation also make the way of escape, that you may be able to endure it.

Psalm 46:1-3 God is our refuge and strength, a very present help in trouble. Therefore we won't be afraid, though the earth changes, though the mountains are shaken into the heart of the seas; though its waters roar and are troubled, though the mountains tremble with their swelling. Selah.

2 Corinthians 1:8-9 For we don't desire to have you uninformed, brothers, concerning our affliction which happened to us in Asia, that we were weighed down exceedingly, beyond our power, so much that we despaired even of life. Yes, we ourselves have had the sentence of death within ourselves, that we should not trust in ourselves, but in God who raises the dead,

Listen, it's true that the Bible says that we'll never be given a temptation we can't overcome but the Bible DOESN'T say we'll never be given more than we can bear. It most certainly happens and it happened to Paul too. Life's not always fair. Rain falls on the righteous and unrighteous alike. The difference is that when suffering falls on the faithful, we don't turn inward for answers, we turn to God for comfort. By doing so, we find the strength to carry on. God will most certainly give you more than you can handle but suffering will not have the last word. "For this light momentary affliction is preparing for us an eternal weight of glory beyond all comparison" (2 Cor. 4:17).

- Day 62 -

Father Matthew Glover was ON FIRE for the Lord this morning (at 7 AM no less) during his homily. He told a story of a prospector that bought a very expensive mule because it was advertised as "the most obedient mule in the world". 15 minutes after he bought it he banged on the door of the person that sold it to him. The seller answered the door and asked what the problem was. The prospector said he wanted his money back because it was definitely not the most obedient mule in the world. He had been trying to get the mule to move for 15 minutes but he would not budge. The seller went into the yard, found a 2x4, walloped the mule across the head and told the mule to start walking, which it did right away. The prospector was appalled and asked, "What did you do that for? I thought this was the most obedient mule in the world!" The seller told the prospector, "This is indeed the most obedient mule in the world but before it will obey, you have to get his attention."

Acts 9:1-9, 17-18 (abridged) But Saul, still breathing threats and slaughter against the disciples of the Lord, went …he got close to Damascus, and suddenly a light from the sky shone around him. He fell on the earth, and heard a voice saying to him, "Saul, Saul, why do you persecute me?" He said, "Who are you, Lord?" The Lord said, "I am Jesus, whom you are persecuting. Rise up, and enter into the city, and you will be told what you must do."… Saul arose from the ground, and when his eyes were opened, he saw no one. They led him by the hand, and brought him into Damascus. He was without sight for three days, and neither ate nor drank… Ananias departed, and entered into the house. Laying his hands on him, he said, "Brother Saul, the Lord, who appeared to you on the road by which you came, has sent me, that you may receive your sight, and be filled with the Holy Spirit." Immediately something like scales fell from his eyes, and he received his sight. He arose and was baptized.

Sometimes God has to hit us over the head with a spiritual 2X4. After Saul was "hit over the head with a blinding light", he became known as Paul, evangelized the rest of his life and went on to write most of the New Testament. What could you accomplish if you were obedient to God's call in your life?

- Day 63 -

EPHEMERAL- an adjective meaning to last for a very short time. Some of the most beautiful things only last a very short time. The bubble you blew when you were a child that mesmerized you and reflected all the colors of the rainbow only lasted a very short time. The vacation you looked forward to for an entire year seemed to pass in just moments and you were back to work. What does the Bible say about things that last just a short time?

Psalm 30:5
For his anger is but for a moment. His favor is for a lifetime. Weeping may stay for the night, but joy comes in the morning.

1 Corinthians 15:51-53

Behold, I tell you a mystery. We will not all sleep, but we will all be changed, in a moment, in the twinkling of an eye, at the last trumpet. For the trumpet will sound, and the dead will be raised incorruptible, and we will be changed. For this perishable body must become imperishable, and this mortal must put on immortality.

James 4:14

Whereas you don't know what your life will be like tomorrow. For what is your life? For you are a vapor, that appears for a little time, and then vanishes away.

So, some pretty important things only last for a short time. Luckily God's anger only lasts a short time. The change from this, our earthly perishable body, to our incorruptible, imperishable, immortal body will happen in a moment (and a moment is indeed a very short time). Also, the life we lead here in these earthly bodies is like a vapor, it only lasts for a very short time. The real question becomes what will we do with the precious little time we have to glorify God? How will we leave our mark on this world to make it a better place?

- Day 64 -

My grandmother was a great woman. She had a mastery of the English language that she was very proud of. A phrase she loved to use was "an eloquent sufficiency". If you asked her if she was still hungry or if she wanted a second helping, she would say, "No, thank you. I have had an eloquent sufficiency." That meant that she had just exactly the right amount, in fact the perfect amount.

2 Corinthians 3:5
not that we are sufficient of ourselves, to account anything as from ourselves; but our sufficiency is from God;
2 Corinthians 9:8
And God is able to make all grace abound to you, that you, always having all sufficiency in everything, may abound to every good work.
2 Corinthians 12:9
He has said to me, "My grace is sufficient for you, for my power is made perfect in weakness." Most gladly therefore I will rather glory in my weaknesses, that the power of Christ may rest on me.
Exodus 4:10
Moses said to Yahweh, "O Lord, I am not eloquent, neither before now, nor since you have spoken to your servant; for I am slow of speech, and of a slow tongue."

Eloquent usually means being able to clearly express yourself in writing or in speech. Moses didn't think of himself as eloquent but God reassured him that what he possessed was sufficient to get the job done. In fact, God's power was made perfect in his weakness. God was able to prove through Moses that we are not sufficient by ourselves, but our sufficiency is through Him. I don't think though, that we could ever have an "eloquent sufficiency" of God or His Word until that day that we become part of the body of Christ. What could you acknowledge today that you do not have an "eloquent sufficiency" of? Take a moment to pray to God to make you sufficient.

- Day 65 -

I saw an interesting post this morning. It was from a friend that re-posted a post that stated that they "do have a problem being asked to not show my religion too much! I have a problem with the media and anyone else who leaves out words like Christ or God because they may be afraid to offend someone. It offends me!" The post went on to accuse NBC and MSN of editing out of the interview the words of the grieving navy seal widow when she said that her late husband's greatest legacy to his children was his love of the Lord Jesus Christ. I checked it out for myself and replied to her post that they, in fact, did not cut out that statement. Another Christian quickly replied, "Supply the link so we can all be the judge."

Matthew 7:1-3 Judge not, that ye be not judged. For with what judgment ye judge, ye shall be judged: and with what measure ye mete, it shall be measured to you again. And why beholdest thou the mote that is in thy brother's eye, but considerest not the beam that is in thine own eye?

2 Chronicles 20:12 Our God, will you not judge them? For we have no might against this great company that comes against us; neither know we what to do, but our eyes are on you."

Romans 14:13 Therefore let's not judge one another any more, but judge this rather, that no man put a stumbling block in his brother's way, or an occasion for falling.

The post requested that if you loved Christ that you re-post it which is precisely why my friend unwittingly re-posted it. I am certain she loves Jesus. If it is true that what the original post said was untrue, there could only be one reason it was typed; to spread a lie that was designed to cause Christians to stumble. Hey, let's face it, it satisfies a carnal need to find a guilty party, judge them and have them punished. But, before we act as the judge, jury and executioner, let's first listen to the advice of Jesus Christ himself who admonished us to love deeply and forgive completely when He taught us how to pray.

- Day 66 -

There's a song by Carrie Underwood called Jesus Take The Wheel. The song describes a tired, stressed, struggling young mother trying to drive herself and her baby to her parent's home on Christmas Eve. She was running low on Faith and Gasoline just trying to make it after a long hard year. She hits a patch of black ice on this cold dark night and the car begins to spin out of control like her life. She see's her child and her life flash before her eyes, realizing that she can't fix this on her own, she throws her hands up in the air and asks Jesus to take the wheel.

Isaiah 40:29-31 He gives power to the weak. He increases the strength of him who has no might. Even the youths faint and get weary, and the young men utterly fall; But those who wait for Yahweh will renew their strength. They will mount up with wings like eagles. They will run, and not be weary. They will walk, and not faint.

Matthew 11:28-29 Come to me, all you who labor and are heavily burdened, and I will give you rest. Take my yoke upon you, and learn from me, for I am gentle and humble in heart; and you will find rest for your souls.

John 16:33 I have told you these things, that in me you may have peace. In the world you will have pain and trouble; but cheer up! I have overcome the world."

We have all been in a position like the young mother in the song where we needed to be saved from the road we were on. Maybe we are on one of those roads right now. Perhaps it is time to do as this young mother did and put our hands together in prayer and ask, "Jesus, take the wheel. Take it from my hands. 'Cause I can't do this on my own. I'm letting go. So give me one more chance and save me from this road I'm on. Jesus, take the wheel." Surrendering to God means we are asking Him to fulfill His will through us and that we trust His plan. I pray we all have the strength to do that when the time comes.

- Day 67 -

Someone used an interesting word in the office today that I haven't heard in awhile. BEFUDDLED. It means to make someone unable to think clearly, to confuse or perplex. I'm sure we can all recall a time when we felt befuddled. Being unable to think clearly can lead to us making decisions that are not in our best interests or in the best interests of those around us.

Acts 2:6
When this sound was heard, the multitude came together, and were bewildered, because everyone heard them speaking in his own language.

1 Corinthians 14:33
for God is not a God of confusion but of peace, as in all the churches of the saints.

Deuteronomy 7:23

But Yahweh your God will deliver them up before you, and will confuse them with a great confusion, until they are destroyed.

2 Corinthians 4:8

We are pressed on every side, yet not crushed; perplexed, yet not to despair;

Our God is indeed a God of peace and love. God can cause those that attack you to become befuddled so that they become harmless to you. I have seen that happen in my own life. God can bring people together to glorify His kingdom in ways that would cause someone to be befuddled. But most importantly, when we feel pushed in on every side by life's stresses, He protects us from being crushed under their sheer weight. We become perplexed and befuddled yet we do not despair... that is a gift indeed.

I recently heard the word Atonement and although I wanted to look smart and pretended I knew what it was, in fact, I wasn't quite sure. When I looked it up, it was a little different than what I originally thought it was. It actually means: reparation for a wrong or injury, reparation or expiation for sin and it can also mean the reconciliation of God and humankind through Jesus Christ. So how are these definitions used in the Word?

Numbers 5:7

then he must confess his sin that he has committed and must make full reparation, add one fifth to it, and give it to whomever he wronged.

Proverbs 14:9

Fools mock at making atonement for sins, but among the upright there is good will.

2 Corinthians 5:18
But all things are of God, who reconciled us to himself through Jesus Christ, and gave to us the ministry of reconciliation;
John 3:16
For God so loved the world, that he gave his one and only Son, that whoever believes in him should not perish, but have eternal life.

Atonement, based upon the Bible is both a heart thing and a justice thing. The person doing the atonement is making a good faith offering to make right what went wrong. It offers both the sinner and the one who was sinned against opportunities to have their trespasses forgiven as well as to forgive those that have trespassed against them. Atonement also reminds us that we are all sinners, in other words, none of us could possibly uphold God's law without breaking it except one man and one man only- Jesus Christ. And, that one man willingly gave His own life to save ours and provide reconciliation between us and God. What do WE need to atone for? Give it a try.

- Day 69 -

My friend Bill is a man of great faith. He came to the office and gave me his personal typed up notes from his Bible studies and the sermons he's listened to. Among the notes was a summary of a great book called Crazy Love. It says, "God is Love. Crazy, relentless, all-powerful love. And, God is calling you to a passionate love relationship with himself."

Luke 10:27

He answered, "You shall love the Lord your God with all your heart, with all your soul, with all your strength, and with all your mind; and your neighbor as yourself."

1 John 5:1
Whoever believes that Jesus is the Christ has been born of God. Whoever loves the Father also loves the child who is born of him.
1 Corinthians 8:3
But if anyone loves God, the same is known by him.
Proverbs 8:17

I love those who love me. Those who seek me diligently will find me.

If you give it some thought, it's CRAZY how much He loves us. "The God of the Universe- the Creator of nitrogen and pine needles, galaxies and E-minor- loves us with a radical, unconditional, self-sacrificing love. And what is our response?" God isn't waiting for you to become more 'religious' or to do something or stop doing something. He is waiting for you to fall in love with Him. And when you do, your life will never be the same. The sun seems brighter, the air smells sweeter, food tastes better, music sounds more harmonious, and you will find that what you touch is not nearly as important as those things that touch your heart. Are you ready to love God back with a Crazy love?

- Day 70 -

It's true that this world is filled with billions of people but it seems that we are more isolated now than we were 20 years ago. A friend of mine commented that she reaches out to people but they don't respond. She goes on to say, "It is almost like I'm invisible. I almost feel I am alone in a crowded room."

2 Timothy 4:16-17

At my first defense, no one came to help me, but all left me. May it not be held against them. But the Lord stood by me, and strengthened me...

Matthew 28:20

teaching them to observe all things that I commanded you. Behold, I am with you always, even to the end of the age." Amen.

Matthew 10:14 Whoever doesn't receive you, nor hear your words, as you go out of that house or that city, shake off the dust from your feet.

1 Thessalonians 5:14 (CEV)
"Encourage anyone who feels left out, help all who are weak, and be patient with everyone."

It's true that in this age when everyone is consumed by one type of media or another be it social media or TV, we often forget to turn off the computer or television to look up and carry on a conversation with those we love. We forget to return phone calls to hear each other's voice in favor of just texting to save time. In this age of disconnection, we call for help from those we know but "no one came to help me, but all left me. May it not be held against them." One thing is for certain though, The Lord is always with you, He will never leave you, He will strengthen you, and never forsake you. Truly, we are never alone when we are in Christ and Christ is in us. Instead of focusing on those that have neglected us, let us use the Light of Christ to shine on others so that they do not feel neglected.

- Day 71 -

I think that most people have heard the verse in the Bible that says that "It's easier for a camel to get through the eye of a needle than for a rich man to get into heaven." That's all well and good but our spiritual bodies are imprisoned within these physical bodies which lust for physical things in this world. A big house, an expensive car, jewelry, an unending flow of cash to buy all the creature comforts, expensive meals out, fancy trips around the world, traveling first class, enough money in the bank to never have to work again, a limousine, etc... What material things would you want if you had unlimited resources?

Hebrews 13:5 Be free from the love of money, content with such things as you have, for he has said, "I will in no way leave you, neither will I in any way forsake you."
1 John 2:16 For all that is in the world, the lust of the flesh, the lust of the eyes, and the pride of life, isn't the Father's, but is the world's.

Ecclesiastes 5:10 He who loves money will not be satisfied with money, nor he who loves wealth with his income; this also is vanity.
1 Timothy 6:10 For the love of money is a root of all kinds of evil. Some have been led astray from the faith in their greed, and have pierced themselves through with many sorrows.

We are, after all, human made of flesh and blood. From time to time we'll be tempted, frustrated by and even lustful of the things of this world. BUT, it is actually the things of this world that overcome people in ruin and destroy them. Truly Rich is the person that is content with their relationship with God and the manna they are given for the day. You found out what material things you most wanted in the first question. Here's a better question: "What would you give to be loved unconditionally, to be completely and totally at Peace, and to know that physical death would not separate you from those you love who trust in the Lord?" Seek Him and ask God into your heart, do it now and all this will be added unto you. (Matthew 6:33) Wealth is of utmost importance until you come across a problem that money won't fix

- Day 72 -

There's a great book that was brought to my attention today by my friend Clarence. The book is called Emotionally Healthy Spirituality. The book makes the case for the fact that it's impossible to be spiritually mature if you are emotionally immature. The author lists 10 signs you may be suffering from emotionally unhealthy spirituality. They include using God to run from God, ignoring the emotions of anger, sadness and fear, dying to the wrong things, denying the past's impact on the present, dividing our lives into secular and sacred compartments, doing for God instead of being with God, spiritualizing away conflict, covering over brokenness, weakness and failure, living without limits and judging other people's spiritual journey. WOW! That's a lot to think about but let's go to the Bible...

Psalm 139:7-10 (Don't try to use God to run from God) Where shall I go from your Spirit? Or where shall I flee from your presence? If I ascend to heaven, you are there! If I make my bed in Sheol, you are there! If I take the wings of the morning and dwell in the uttermost parts of the sea, even there your hand shall lead me, and your right hand shall hold me.
John 11:33-35 (even Jesus Himself did not ignore His emotions) When Jesus therefore saw her weeping, and the Jews weeping who came with her, he groaned in the spirit, and was troubled, and said, "Where have you laid him?" They told him, "Lord, come and see." Jesus wept.

Mark 3:25 (you can not divide yourself, sacred from secular) If a house is divided against itself, that house cannot stand.

There's way too much to go through and share with Bible verses on this one. You'll have to pick up Peter Scazzaro's book and check it out for yourself. The bottom line is however, that if you truly want to be spiritually healthy, you have to be emotionally healthy and vice versa. The only way to be either is to have a strong, healthy relationship with Jesus. When we do this, we open ourselves to more fully experience life, our emotions and our relationships as Jesus did during His life. What can our first step towards an emotionally healthy spirituality be?

- Day 73 -

Today I'd like to touch on two very important parts of the gospels, asking for forgiveness and granting forgiveness. None of us are without sin and I will go so far as to say that every one of us has said or done something to another human being that we are not proud of. Perhaps it was decades ago but it has weighed heavily on us to this very day. Maybe it was just yesterday that we offended someone. Maybe it was even someone we care deeply about but got caught up in the moment and let something out of our mouths or wrote something in a text or e-mail we wish we could take back. It's not too late to ask for forgiveness. In Matthew 5, The Lord advises us to "Leave", "Go" and "BE RECONCILED".

Matthew 5:23-24

"If therefore you are offering your gift at the altar, and there remember that your brother has anything against you, LEAVE your gift there before the altar, and GO your way. First BE RECONCILED to your brother, and then come and offer your gift.

Matthew 18:21-22

Then Peter came and said to him, "Lord, how often shall my brother sin against me, and I forgive him? Until seven times?"

Jesus said to him, "I don't tell you until seven times, but, until seventy times seven.

Sincerely admitting you were wrong, saying that you are very, very sorry, and asking please, please can you find it in your heart to forgive me can be very very healing even if the other person does not grant the forgiveness. However, as a Christian, if someone that has offended you asks for forgiveness, we are admonished not only to forgive them if they offend you once, but you are to forgive them 490 times. When we truly grant forgiveness, we turn our Enmity (feelings of hostility) into Amnesty (an act of forgiveness). So what are you waiting for? Leave, Go, Be Reconciled.

- Day 74 -

How does the Bible define wisdom? Secularly, wisdom is defined as the quality of having experience, knowledge, and good judgment; the quality of being wise. The Bible has a little different take on that. Here are several verses about wisdom. The ones from Proverbs were written by the wisest man to ever have lived.

Proverbs 1:7 The fear of Yahweh is the beginning of knowledge; but the foolish despise wisdom and instruction.

Proverbs 2:7 He lays up sound wisdom for the upright. He is a shield to those who walk in integrity;

Proverbs 3:13 Happy is the man who finds wisdom, the man who gets understanding.

Proverbs 4:7 Wisdom is supreme. Get wisdom. Yes, though it costs all your possessions, get understanding.
Proverbs 9:10 The fear of Yahweh is the beginning of wisdom. The knowledge of the Holy One is understanding.
Ecclesiastes 2:26 For to the man who pleases him, God gives wisdom, knowledge, and joy;...
James 3:17 But the wisdom that is from above is first pure, then peaceful, gentle, reasonable, full of mercy and good fruits, without partiality, and without hypocrisy.

So, Wisdom is given to those who please God along with knowledge, joy, peace, and other desirable qualities. The Bible also alludes that the beginning of knowledge is the fear of God. That fear is not one of a fear of torture but one of a child to his parent as described by Luther as "filial" fear. It is the healthy fear of not wanting to disappoint his father who is the source of security and love. So, in a good way, the fear of God is the beginning of wisdom. It is also through this filial fear that we are motivated to be reconciled with God through Christ. Do you have a filial fear of God?

- Day 75 -

The faith of a mustard seed placed in the person of Jesus has life changing power.

Have you ever considered a mustard seed. It is one of the smallest seeds on the earth. They are only about 1 or 2 millimeters in diameter. They are called by many interesting names which include Eye of Newt and was called by that name in Shakespeare's famous play Macbeth. Even though these seeds are tiny, they grow into large shrubs with only a 3-10 day germination. A very interesting seed indeed. The Bible has some stuff to say about mustard seeds as well.

Matthew 13:31 He set another parable before them, saying, "The Kingdom of Heaven is like a grain of mustard seed, which a man took, and sowed in his field;

Matthew 17:20 He said to them, "Because of your unbelief. For most certainly I tell you, if you have faith as a grain of mustard seed, you will tell this mountain, 'Move from here to there,' and it will move; and nothing will be impossible for you.

Mark 4:31 It's like a grain of mustard seed, which, when it is sown in the earth, though it is less than all the seeds that are on the earth,

Luke 13:19 It is like a grain of mustard seed, which a man took, and put in his own garden. It grew, and became a large tree, and the birds of the sky live in its branches."

Luke 17:6 The Lord said, "If you had faith like a grain of mustard seed, you would tell this sycamore tree, 'Be uprooted, and be planted in the sea,' and it would obey you.

So, how much faith does it take to move a mountain, uproot a huge tree and have it plant itself again by the water and to be able to to make the impossible become possible? It only takes faith the size of a mustard seed. You see, just like the mustard seed, even the smallest amount of faith can grow into something huge. Just as the mustard seed grows into a large shrub, our faith can grow into huge works that can change the world. Do you possess faith as a grain of a mustard seed?

- Day 76 -

I have looked into the eyes of many people that were overwhelmed by life this week. Some have lost a current job, some have been given a bad medical report, others find it nearly impossible to juggle working, being a parent and being a spouse. Some people still choose to watch the news on TV and feel the world is out of control. In this world there's heartache and pain and suffering all around us. What are we to do?

Isaiah 12:2 Behold, God is my salvation. I will trust, and will not be afraid; for Yahweh, is my strength and song; and he has become my salvation."

John 16:33 I have told you these things, that in me you may have peace. In the world you have oppression; but cheer up! I have overcome the world."
John 1:5 The light shines in the darkness, and the darkness hasn't overcome it.

1 John 4:4 You are of God, little children, and have overcome them; because greater is he who is in you than he who is in the world.
Psalm 34:17 The righteous cry, and Yahweh hears, and delivers them out of all their troubles.
Romans 12:12 rejoicing in hope; enduring in troubles; continuing steadfastly in prayer;

Though the weight of your troubles in this world may seem overwhelming, you have more strength to overcome these troubles than you may have thought. For greater is He who is in YOU, than he who is in this world. God promises in His Word that He hears you cry and He will deliver you from your troubles. Your only job is to focus and rejoice in HOPE and to steadfastly pray. And for those of us that have friends or family who are in a dark place right now, be the light in their lives to help them overcome the darkness through prayer and faith, lending a listening ear and by doing good works. Who can you be the light for today?

The light shines in the darkness, and the darkness hasn't overcome it. Be the light.

- Day 77 -

I happened upon a most interesting word- Sonder. "Sonder- n. -the realization that each random passerby is living a life as vivid and complex as your own—populated with their own ambitions, friends, routines, worries and inherited craziness—an epic story that continues invisibly around you like an anthill sprawling deep underground, with elaborate passageways to thousands of other lives that you'll never know existed, in which you might appear only once, as an extra sipping coffee in the background, as a blur of traffic passing on the highway, as a lighted window at dusk."

Psalm 139:14
I will give thanks to you, for I am fearfully and wonderfully made. Your works are wonderful. My soul knows that very well.
1 Corinthians 12:25-28

that there should be no division in the body, but that the members should have the same care for one another. When one member suffers, all the members suffer with it. Or when one member is honored, all the members rejoice with it. Now you are the body of Christ, and members individually. God has set some in the assembly: first apostles, second prophets, third teachers, then miracle workers, then gifts of healings, helps, governments, and various kinds of languages.

It's an interesting thing isn't it? Millions of people living their lives right this very moment and each of them are just as important as you are to God. God, The Author of all life, made each and every one of us fearfully and wonderfully in His image. Each one of us has an important job and talent He has bestowed upon us. It would be impossible for us to know the complexities of every person in the world's life. And yet nothing is impossible for Him. Take a moment to look into the eye of a friendly passer by, give them a warm smile and consider the complexity of their life.

- Day 78 -

A Reproof is a criticism for a fault. As parents, we are called to reproof our children so that they may grow up to be better adults. There is a right way and a wrong way to reproof one another. Reproofing is not to be done in a condescending way. The best way is to do so in private with a loving and caring tone.

Proverbs 15:32

He who refuses correction despises his own soul, but he who listens to reproof gets understanding.

2 Timothy 3:16

Every Scripture is God-breathed and profitable for teaching, for reproof, for correction, and for instruction in righteousness,
Job 20:3
I have heard the reproof which puts me to shame. The spirit of my understanding answers me.
Zephaniah 3:1-2

Woe to her who is rebellious and polluted, the oppressing city! She didn't obey the voice. She didn't receive correction. She didn't trust in Yahweh. She didn't draw near to her God.

Receiving correction is actually a blessing. When someone cares enough to call us aside and respects us enough to take the time to help us reduce our faults, we should be grateful. "The trouble with most of us is that we would rather be ruined by praise than saved by criticisms." --Norman Vincent Peale

- Day 79 -

The cross is not just two pieces of wood nailed together. It was the solution to a dilemma. God needed a way to reconcile sinners to Himself while still remaining perfectly just. The penalty for sin was death and it's not perfect justice for God to just randomly forgive sin. Jesus dying on the cross for our sins as the perfect sacrifice, gave us a way to obtain grace and to be reconciled to God without causing God to be unjust. During the days preceding Good Friday, the enormity of that sacrifice, the true meaning of the cross and it's purpose come more clearly into focus.

John 19:28-31

After this, Jesus, seeing that all things were now finished, that the Scripture might be fulfilled, said, "I am thirsty." Now a vessel full of vinegar was set there; so they put a sponge full of the vinegar on hyssop, and held it at his mouth. When Jesus therefore had received the vinegar, he said, "It is finished." He bowed his head, and gave up his spirit.

Therefore the Jews, because it was the Preparation Day, so that the bodies wouldn't remain on the cross on the Sabbath (for that Sabbath was a special one), asked of Pilate that their legs might be broken, and that they might be taken away.

Wow- they totally missed the boat. Here God's Son, Jesus the Christ was just crucified and died for their sins and their main concern was to get the bodies off the cross for the Sabbath. They were concerned about not breaking the Jewish laws and committing a sin when right before their eyes The Savior just gave his life to cover their sins. They were so concerned about getting home for the big Passover meal, that they completely missed the gift that was before them. This Good Friday and Easter, let's not get so caught up in the dying of eggs, chocolate bunnies or where we will eat our Easter brunch that we forget the sacrifice our Savior made on the Cross for us.

- Day 80 -

Right this very moment, as you are reading this, there are some people that are in a light mist. Some people are being rained on and some of you are in the middle of a terrible storm in your life. You may even feel like you are in a boat, miles offshore with high winds, heavy rain, waves well overhead and what looks like no possible way you can make it out alive.

Matthew 14:22-32 immediately Jesus made the disciples get into the boat, and to go ahead of him to the other side, while he sent the multitudes away. After he had sent the multitudes away, he went up into the mountain by himself to pray. When evening had come, he was there alone. But the boat was now in the middle of the sea, distressed by the waves, for the wind was contrary. In the fourth watch of the night, Jesus came to them, walking on the sea. When the disciples saw him walking on the sea, they were troubled, saying, "It's a ghost!" and they cried out for fear. But immediately Jesus spoke to them, saying "Cheer up! It is I! Don't be afraid." Peter answered him and said, "Lord, if it is you, command me to come to you on the waters." He said, "Come!" Peter stepped down from the boat, and walked on the waters to come to Jesus. But when he saw that the wind was strong, he was afraid, and beginning to sink, he cried out, saying, "Lord, save me!" Immediately Jesus stretched out his hand, took hold of him, and said to him, "You of little faith, why did you doubt?" When they got up into the boat, the wind ceased.

Wow, there's a lot of stuff going on here. First, Jesus Commanded them to get into the boat knowing they were heading into a storm. Second, He waited about 12 hours before he went out to help them knowing they were scared. Third, Peter didn't just go out to Jesus, he asked Him to 'command' him to do it. Fourth, Peter was able to do something ordinarily impossible when he walked on water UNTIL he took his eyes off of Jesus. Listen, God will sometimes send you into a storm to strengthen you but He always has you in the palm of His hand. Peter shows us that in the middle of your storm, if you ask for God to direct (command) you, He will show you the way out. And if you keep your eyes on God, and do His will, you will be able to do things that would seem impossible. How can you apply this to your life now?

- Day 81 -

Good Friday. There was nothing 'good' about the Friday Jesus died on the cross the day it happened. It only becomes 'good' when we look back and realize the significance of what happened that day some 2000 years ago. In that day, after His death, His loss must have been devastating to His disciples, family and friends. The silence must have been deafening. In the Catholic tradition, when we remember the stations of the cross in a special service on Good Friday. When we get to the station of the death of Jesus, we pause, kneel and remain in silence for quite some time.

Deuteronomy 27:9
Moses and the priests the Levites spoke to all Israel, saying, "Be silent, and listen, Israel! Today you have become the people of Yahweh your God.

Psalm 62:5
My soul, wait in silence for God alone, for my expectation is from him.

Ecclesiastes 3:7
a time to tear, and a time to sew; a time to keep silent, and a time to speak;

Psalm 46:10
"Be still, and know that I am God. I will be exalted among the nations. I will be exalted in the earth."

What exactly is it about the silence that makes it reverent? Could it be that in our times of silence, we sit still and listen intently for God to speak to us and simultaneously God is also intently listening to us speak to Him through prayer? Could it be that silence is the tool that God uses to speak to our hearts and during these times of reflection, the revelations we receive are directly from Him? Have you sat silently in His presence today?

While praying, never mistake the silence as God's absence. He is with you always.

- Day 82 -

I once heard a story in church about a young boy named Paul who usually kept to himself and had trouble communicating with the other children. He was constantly teased but kept a sunny disposition. One day in the early Spring, the Sunday school teacher brought in empty Easter eggs and asked the kids to go into the church yard and put something in the egg that represented life and come back into the class. The teacher opened the eggs one at a time. There were eggs with grass, flowers, moss, a caterpillar and even a butterfly. Nervously, the teacher picked up Paul's egg afraid that Paul had not understood the assignment. She opened the egg and it was empty. She looked at Paul with disapproval and the class began to laugh at him.

Luke 24:1-7

But on the first day of the week, at early dawn, they and some others came to the tomb, bringing the spices which they had prepared. They found the stone rolled away from the tomb. They entered in, and didn't find the Lord Jesus' body. While they were greatly perplexed about this, behold, two men stood by them in dazzling clothing. Becoming terrified, they bowed their faces down to the earth.

They said to them, "Why do you seek the living among the dead? He isn't here, but is risen. Remember what he told you when he was still in Galilee, saying that the Son of Man must be delivered up into the hands of sinful men, and be crucified, and the third day rise again?"

With tears in his eyes, Paul looked up at his teacher and said, "The egg is EMPTY, just like the tomb. The only reason we have LIFE is because the tomb was EMPTY." Silence fell upon the class and the teacher walked over to wipe the tears from Paul's eyes. "YES", she declared, "Your egg most represents LIFE of all the eggs we opened." This Easter, let us remember that it's the EMPTY TOMB and our Risen Savior who provides for us LIFE and LIFE EVERLASTING.

- Day 83 -

Ever felt powerless? The last recorded thing that Jesus says to his disciples before ascending into heaven may change your mind. He came back on the third day after his death and stayed with them for forty days more. On the fortieth day He sat them down outside and gave them one last talk. He said to them, and effectively to you and me, that we are not powerless. Quite the contrary, He reminded them that the Holy Spirit was with them and because of that we are more powerful than we think.

Acts 1:7-9

He said to them, "It isn't for you to know times or seasons which the Father has set within his own authority. But you will receive power when the Holy Spirit has come upon you. You will be witnesses to me in Jerusalem, in all Judea and Samaria, and to the uttermost parts of the earth." When he had said these things, as they were looking, he was taken up, and a cloud received him out of their sight.

John 14:16-17

I will pray to the Father, and he will give you another Counselor, that he may be with you forever,— the Spirit of truth, whom the world can't receive; for it doesn't see him, neither knows him. You know him, for he lives with you, and will be in you.

You may be feeling powerless right now. We all do from time to time, but Jesus promised us that we will receive power from the Holy Spirit. What exactly is the power of the Holy Spirit? It is the power of God. It is the same power that created the world and everything in it. Jesus promised the Holy Spirit would be with you always and thus His guidance, His teaching, His Salvation, His comfort and yes, the unspeakable power of God is with you always, now and forever. So, when you feel powerless know you are being deceived by the enemy! The truth is that He who is in you is powerful beyond measure and works through you. Go forth, with your God-given talents, and serve the world by spreading light where there is darkness.

- Day 84 -

Was it really God's plan for Jesus to come to Earth, live a sinless life and be the perfect sacrifice for our sins? In more easily understood questions, did God really send Jesus to die for us? Was that really God's plan? I recently read a blog that implied that if God really sent Jesus to die for us and it was His plan, that in effect God sent Jesus on a "suicide" mission. Although that is an incredibly shallow and distorted view of what actually happened, it is a most disrespectful interpretation of the actual meaning of the life and sacrifice of our Lord and Savior.

Psalm 41:9 (1000 years before Jesus was betrayed) Yes, my own familiar friend, in whom I trusted, who ate bread with me, has lifted up his heel against me.

Zechariah 11:12 (500 years before Judas took the 30 pieces of silver. Zechariah also talks about a good shepherd whose service was brought to an end.) I said to them, "If you think it best, give me my wages; and if not, keep them." So they weighed for my wages thirty pieces of silver.

Isaiah 53:7 (700 years later it happened in Matthew 27:12-14) He was oppressed, yet when he was afflicted he didn't open his mouth. As a lamb that is led to the slaughter, and as a sheep that before its shearers is silent, so he didn't open his mouth.

I could go on and on with over 100 references to show that Jesus came to fulfill the prophesies of the Old Testament. God and Jesus both knew the mission at hand and it was certainly NOT a suicide mission. It was a Rescue Mission. From the beginning of time, but most certainly at least 1000 years before it occurred, God knew what had to be done before Jesus came to Earth and gave the ultimate sacrifice. Christ died for our sins in accordance with scriptures. The punishment for sin is death which is God's perfect justice. God promised He would send a Savior to defeat the serpent to provide Grace for us (Genesis 3:15) but that promise required an innocent sacrifice. God's perfect Son fulfilled God's perfect requirement of God's perfect law. It is perfectly brilliant in its simplicity. "God made Him (Christ), who knew no sin, to be sin for us that we might become the righteousness of God in Him" (2 Corinthians 5:21).   THANKS BE TO GOD.

- Day 85 -

Miracles are defined as a surprising and welcome event that is not explicable by natural or scientific laws and is therefore considered to be the work of a divine agency. There are two types of people. Those that believe in miracles and those that can't believe or don't want to believe in miracles. Believing in miracles requires a great faith and trust in our Creator to know when to and when not to grant a miracle.

Galatians 3:5
He therefore who supplies the Spirit to you, and does miracles among you, does he do it by the works of the law, or by hearing of faith?

Acts 19:11
God worked special miracles by the hands of Paul,

Acts 8:13
Simon himself also believed. Being baptized, he continued with Philip. Seeing signs and great miracles occurring, he was amazed.

Acts 4:22
For the man on whom this miracle of healing was performed was more than forty years old.

Psalm 105:27
They performed miracles among them, and wonders in the land of Ham.

I think we have all prayed for a miracle at one point in our lives or another. I have a friend that told me he could not believe in miracles because he could not accept that God grants miracles to one person and withholds miracles from another family desperately begging for a miracle. While I sympathize with my friend and all those whose miracles did not arrive, the Word clearly states that God does indeed perform miracles. The toughest part for us, the faithful, is to give thanks when God's plan does not include the miracle we have prayed for. In the end, believing in miracles requires great faith. Praying for miracles and trusting in God's plan simultaneously requires the greatest faith of all.

- Day 86 -

Today I went car shopping with my son who needs an inexpensive car to commute a short distance to his first job. We traveled nearly 45 minutes to see a car that "looked good" in the Craig's list ad. When we arrived, what we found was a bit more than was described. They failed to mention that it had a check engine light that was on, an abs light that was on, a rear fender that was nearly off and several other "surprises". The mileage was true, the sides of the car that were shown in the picture were accurate but those really didn't tell the whole story.

Romans 3:12-13 There is no one who does good, no, not so much as one." "Their throat is an open tomb. With their tongues they have used deceit." "The poison of vipers is under their lips";

Jeremiah 17:9 The heart is deceitful above all things, and it is exceedingly corrupt: who can know it?

Proverbs 12:22 Lying lips are an abomination to Yahweh, but those who do the truth are his delight.

James 4:17 To him therefore who knows to do good, and doesn't do it, to him it is sin.

I don't think the cars we looked at today had people that were outright lying to us to get us to take a look at their car. I think they were just omitting some of the facts. Considering their obvious omissions, it becomes cause for us to reflect on how we interact with those around us. Do we answer questions directly and completely and honestly or do we answer incompletely omitting key facts. Do we know what the good and just thing to do is and fail to do it? More importantly, does the content of our character and integrity of our actions cause people to ask us where we gain our strength from so that we can share the gospel with them?

- Day 87 -

If you haven't seen The Kindness Diaries on Netflix, you're really missing out. An ex-stockbroker leaves his unfulfilling job and sets out on a vintage motorcycle to circumnavigate the globe without any money in hand. He relies solely on the kindness of strangers to provide gas for his motorcycle, food for him to eat and shelter for him at night. I was surprised that the Bible has 216 references to kindness. Here are a few:

Genesis 21:23
Now, therefore, swear to me here by God that you will not deal falsely with me, nor with my son, nor with my son's son. But according to the kindness that I have done to you, you shall do to me, and to the land in which you have lived as a foreigner."

Job 10:12 You have granted me life and loving kindness. Your visitation has preserved my spirit.

Psalm 23:6 Surely goodness and loving kindness shall follow me all the days of my life, and I will dwell in Yahweh's house forever.

Proverbs 3:3 Don't let kindness and truth forsake you. Bind them around your neck. Write them on the tablet of your heart.

Colossians 3:12 Put on therefore, as God's chosen ones, holy and beloved, a heart of compassion, kindness, lowliness, humility, and perseverance;

Could we live out our life relying solely on the kindness of others? Could we have enough faith to go anywhere in the world and know that God, through his children, would care for us and provide for all our needs? Even more importantly, can God rely on us to provide for all His children we come across and help provide for their needs instead of looking the other way? What have we done lately to directly help another human being who is in need?

- Day 88 -

During the summer, a group of boats will come together offshore so that they can tie up together to share food, drink and stories of the big fish that got away. The idea is that the first boat there drops anchor and the other boats essentially anchor to the first by tying up to it. They key is the first boat has to be anchored or the whole group will drift away. It is the same with people who gather on Sunday at church. Pastors, priests, ministers, reverends and anyone that preaches the Gospel must be anchored or the whole church with all its parishioners will soon drift away from the truth.

Hebrews 6:19 This hope we have as an anchor of the soul, a hope both sure and stedfast and entering into that which is within the veil;
James 3:1   Let not many of you be teachers, my brothers, knowing that we will receive heavier judgment.

John 14:6 Jesus said to him, "I am the way, the truth, and the life. No one comes to the Father, except through me.
John 17:17 Sanctify them in your truth. Your word is truth.
Isaiah 9:16 For those who lead this people lead them astray; and those who are led by them are destroyed.

We must be so very careful to choose a church that has as it's pastor, priest or minister, a preacher that teaches us the TRUTH directly from the Word which is God's Word. We must seek out a church leader that is Anchored to the TRUTH because as BJ Palmer once said, "Who can anchor to an unanchored mind?" Anchor to God, Stay in the Word and make sure that the lessons you learn in church are coming Through your pastor, priest or minister, not From them.

- Day 89 -

Everyone experiences the highs and lows of life. In our walk with Christ, we get to see so many inspirational things such as births, baptisms, weddings, and the occasional miracle that could only have come from God. We will all eventually experience the inevitable lows of life like the loss of a loved one, illnesses, failures, disappointments, and heartbreak. The Bible has something to say about the highs and lows of life.

Matthew 6:25-34
Therefore I tell you, don't be anxious for your life: what you will eat, or what you will drink; nor yet for your body, what you will wear. Isn't life more than food, and the body more than clothing? See the birds of the sky, that they don't sow, neither do they reap, nor gather into barns. Your heavenly Father feeds them. Aren't you of much more value than they? "Which of you, by being anxious, can add one moment to his lifespan? …

The take home message here is that we will all have highs and lows in life. That's a given. Just stay in faith, keep your eyes on God and keep serving Him with the talents He gave you. Don't become anxious about anything- what good will that do? Just trust that all your needs will be taken care of in the tough times remembering that tough times never last but tough people do.

- Day 90 -

So many people walk around wishing they had what other people have and feel jealous. They think about what could have been had they only made different choices in their lives. Did you know that this breaks the 10th commandment? Commandments are a big deal and they got even tougher to follow after Jesus began teaching what they really meant.

Exodus 20:17

"You shall not covet your neighbor's house. You shall not covet your neighbor's wife, nor his male servant, nor his female servant, nor his ox, nor his donkey, nor anything that is your neighbor's."

Matthew 5:17-19

"Don't think that I came to destroy the law or the prophets. I didn't come to destroy, but to fulfill. For most certainly, I tell you, until heaven and earth pass away, not even one smallest letter or one tiny pen stroke shall in any way pass away from the law, until all things are accomplished. Whoever, therefore, shall break one of these least commandments, and teach others to do so, shall be called least in the Kingdom of Heaven; but whoever shall do and teach them shall be called great in the Kingdom of Heaven.

Listen, the 10th commandment was God's way of showing us that the things of this world are seductive but lead to destruction. There is no quenching the flesh's desire for things of this world. Be it money, power, possessions or even other people's lives, it always looks greener on the other side of the fence. Take a moment and access what you have to be grateful for in this life. Take a moment to put a value on your relationship with God. Is anything of this world worth risking your relationship with Him? Take a moment to say a prayer of thanksgiving for all you have because of your relationship with God

- Day 91 -

In this world everyone seems to be stressed out about politics and the threat of warfare but that's not what we really should be worried about. The real danger is the invisible war that is being waged on all of us. There's a very real war going on but it's not visible to the naked eye. It is the spiritual war satan has waged on us. Sometimes the battle is fought outside of us, sometimes it's fought inside of us but the battle is very real. That's the bad news. Here is the GOOD NEWS: You have everything you need to be victorious and win this battle!

Ephesians 6:13-18

Therefore put on the whole armor of God, that you may be able to withstand in the evil day, and, having done all, to stand. Stand therefore, having the utility belt of truth buckled around your waist, and having put on the breastplate of righteousness, and having fitted your feet with the preparation of the Good News of peace; above all, taking up the shield of faith, with which you will be able to quench all the fiery darts of the evil one. And take the helmet of salvation, and the sword of the Spirit, which is the word of God; with all prayer and requests, praying at all times in the Spirit, and being watchful to this end in all perseverance and requests for all the saints:

We have everything we need to win each and every spiritual battle in our lives but we have the responsibility of putting on the spiritual armor that God has provided for us. When the enemy tries to convince you that there are things that are beyond God's control, when he tries to convince you that you are powerless, that you are weak and you have no chance of being victorious, REBUKE that lie with the shield of truth. When the enemy tries to get you to stop praying for your miracle, defend yourself with the breastplate of righteousness. Do not allow the enemy to steal your HOPE with deception. Know this- we serve a mighty God. All things are possible with Him.

- Day 92 -

Today I returned to a place that I hadn't been in 20 years and thought was my "favorite place in the world". 20 years have made me wiser...

Proverbs 18:22
Whoever finds a wife finds a good thing, and obtains favor of Yahweh.

Philippians 4:12

I know how to be humbled, and I know also how to abound. In everything and in all things I have learned the secret both to be filled and to be hungry, both to abound and to be in need.

3 John 4 I have no greater joy than this, to hear about my children walking in truth.

Deuteronomy 26:11
And you shall rejoice in all the good that the Lord your God has given to you and to your house, you, and the Levite, and the sojourner who is among you.

For the last 20 years I have been thinking that my favorite place on Earth was Muir Woods in California. Just the thought of it brought me joy because I remember carrying my son and daughter through the redwood forest with my wife at my side at one of the most peaceful times in my life. Today when I went back, the smell of the redwoods was awesome, the sound of the stream was tranquil and the redwoods were too grand for words but I realized that Muir Woods is not my favorite place in the world. Today something was missing in the park, my wife and kids. Wisdom has taught me that "my favorite place in the world" is wherever my family is gathered. Today let's give thanks to God for blessing us with family and let us rejoice in the knowledge that everything we most desire we already have without having to leave home.

- Day 93 -

In this world that's becoming more and more "politically correct" we are called to teach our children many things that are not congruent with the way this world operates now. Even at a very young age the world teaches them things that seem OK on the outside but leaves them unprepared for the real world and ultimately, they are unprepared for the Kingdom of Heaven. If we give every child a trophy, how will they learn how to deal with loss later in life?

1 Corinthians 9:24
Don't you know that those who run in a race all run, but one receives the prize? Run like that, that you may win.
Proverbs 16:9

A man's heart plans his course, but God directs his steps.

Psalm 147:3
He heals the broken in heart, and binds up their wounds.
Hebrews 12:1

Therefore let us also, seeing we are surrounded by so great a cloud of witnesses, lay aside every weight and the sin which so easily entangles us, and let us run with patience the race that is set before us,

Hey, we are going to win a few and we are going to lose a few but we must trust that when we are called to His purpose, ALL THINGS including winning and losing work to good and are part of His plan and we need to teach this to our children as well. Let's face it, losing stinks but God reminds us that only one person can win a race but He is there to heal our wounds which are often in the heart. He also reminds us that life is a marathon not a sprint and if we are patient and trust in Him that we will have the chance to always win the race that really matters... the one that ends in His arms.

- Day 94 -

One of the hymns we sing in church is "Create in me a clean heart". It's actually from one of the Psalms written by David. It goes on to say "create a right spirit in me". So what's that all about? A clean heart? A right spirit? What does that mean?

Psalm 51:10

Create in me a clean heart, O God. Renew a right spirit within me.

Ezekiel 36:25-27

I will sprinkle clean water on you, and you shall be clean: from all your filthiness, and from all your idols, will I cleanse you. I will also give you a new heart, and I will put a new spirit within you; and I will take away the stony heart out of your flesh, and I will give you a heart of flesh. I will put my Spirit within you, and cause you to walk in my statutes, and you shall keep my ordinances, and do them.

Acts 15:9

He made no distinction between us and them, cleansing their hearts by faith.

David, the writer of the Psalms, was known as one who was "a man after God's own heart". But, let me tell you, he did some seemingly terrible and unforgivable things. We should be grateful that the Bible doesn't cover up or hide righteous people's faults and sins. It shows us that we are not alone in the need for grace. David recognized his sins and asked God to 'Create' in him a clean heart, not merely restore him to before he sinned. In essence he asked for a 'new heart', a 'new birth', a 'new life'. Today we have that opportunity for a New Life through a Rebirth that results in a new clean heart simply by asking God for forgiveness of our sins, by asking Jesus to come into our hearts and by making Him our Lord and Savior.

- Day 95 -

Have you ever considered the meaning of the word Sympathy? To truly have sympathy means that you actually suffer with another person when you hear of their misfortune. When people lose a loved one, you feel as though you have lost a loved one yourself. When their heart is broken, your heart aches too. If you knew the penalty for sin was death, and you truly felt sympathy for those who were going to die an eternal death, what would you do if you knew you had the power to help them?

Romans 6:23 For the wages of sin is death, but the free gift of God is eternal life in Christ Jesus our Lord.

Isaiah 63:9 In all their affliction he was afflicted, and the angel of his presence saved them. In his love and in his pity he redeemed them. He bore them, and carried them all the days of old.

John 11:35 Jesus wept.

Hebrews 10:12 but he, when he had offered one sacrifice for sins forever, sat down on the right hand of God;

WOW! Jesus felt such sympathy for those that were unsaved, that He offered one perfect sacrifice, His own body, His own life. I mean, just think about that. He was so sympathetic to our plight, that he made the ultimate sacrifice so that we would be saved from an eternity in hell and an eternity of separation from God. It was because of His sympathy for us and His obedience to God that He allowed His body to be broken and His blood to be spilled so that we might escape the pain and torment of hell and instead rejoice with Him and in Him as the body of Christ for all eternity.

- Day 96 -

I heard a great question from a friend this morning that I really needed to pray on before I wrote this Bible minute. The question was, "How do we know what Jesus said when He was alone?" In other words, how did the things that Jesus said when he was alone get recorded in the gospels? That's a great question and here's an example and a few biblical explanations:

Matthew 4:1-25 Then Jesus was led up by the Spirit into the wilderness to be tempted by the devil. When he had fasted forty days and forty nights, he was hungry afterward. The tempter came and said to him, "If you are the Son of God, command that these stones become bread." But he answered, "It is written, 'Man shall not live by bread alone, but by every word that proceeds out of the mouth of God.'"...

John 14:26 But the Counselor, the Holy Spirit, whom the Father will send in my name, he will teach you all things, and will remind you of all that I said to you.

2 Timothy 3:16 Every Scripture is God-breathed and profitable for teaching, for reproof, for correction, and for instruction in righteousness,

Historically, the Bible wasn't written as the events happened, they were written down much later but John and Matthew were eyewitnesses to the events and Luke and John spoke directly to eye witnesses. All of them carefully investigated the truth before writing their accounts and all the writers were inspired by the Holy Spirit as described in John 4:26. Another possibility is that Jesus told His disciples what happened during the years they were together and filled them in on the rest after his resurrection in the 40 days He spent with them as described in Acts 1:3. Lastly, there really can't be absolute proof and definitive evidence about how the Bible writers were able to know what Jesus said and did in private. Part of the answer has to be based on Faith. It's faith that's at the heart of Christianity. After all, Faith is the substance of things hoped for and the evidence of things not seen- Hebrews 11:1

- Day 97 -

Floc·ci·nau·ci·ni·hil·i·pil·i·fi·ca·tion pronounced as fläksənôsənīhiləpiləfikāSHən/ is a noun and means: the action or habit of estimating something as worthless. (The word is used chiefly as a curiosity.). Gold, silver, riches and all that glitters seem pretty attractive to the flesh but compared to our God and our Lord and Savior, they are really worthless.

Acts 4:11
He is 'the stone which was regarded as worthless by you, the builders, which has become the head of the corner.'\
Jeremiah 2:5
Yahweh says, "What unrighteousness have your fathers found in me, that they have gone far from me, and have walked after worthless vanity, and have become worthless?
Psalm 119:37
Turn my eyes away from looking at worthless things. Revive me in your ways.

Things of this world will come and go but the life given us by our Lord and Savior is everlasting. Gold will be completely worthless in heaven, after all, the streets are paved with it. The only thing of worth in this life is a relationship with God. Take a minute to sit down and cultivate that relationship with Him today through prayer...it will be totally Worth It.

- Day 98 -

So, what's the difference between human nature and sin nature? Are they the same? Well, in the beginning, God Created humans... and He said it was "very good". Human nature was originally perfect by virtue of being created by God. Unfortunately that "goodness" was messed up by Adam and Eve when they allowed the enemy to tempt them to go against God's will. That began what is known as the Sin Nature of man.

Genesis 1:27 & 31 God created man in his own image. In God's image he created him; male and female he created them. God saw everything that he had made, and, behold, it was very good. There was evening and there was morning, a sixth day.

Genesis 3:1 Now the serpent was more subtle than any animal of the field which Yahweh God had made. He said to the woman, "Has God really said, 'You shall not eat of any tree of the garden?'"

Ecclesiastes 7:20 Surely there is not a righteous man on earth, who does good and doesn't sin.

2 Corinthians 5:17 & 21 Therefore if anyone is in Christ, he is a new creation. The old things have passed away. Behold, all things have become new. & For him who knew no sin he made to be sin on our behalf; so that in him we might become the righteousness of God.

Therefore, there's Good News, There's Bad News and then there's Really Good news. The Good news is that God created us in His image, sinless and perfect and that was how Human Nature was supposed to be. The bad news is that Satan tempted and continues to tempt humans and that lead to our Sin Nature. The really Good News is that once we accept Jesus Christ as our Lord and Savior, our sins are forgiven and THAT is indeed "Very Good".

- Day 99 -

As a first responder to an accident, sometimes we come across people that are really injured very badly. It can become obvious that if they don't stay conscious and actively, mentally fight to stay alive, their chances of surviving diminish. We don't want the injured person to look at themselves and see an injury that could be too much for them to handle and we need to keep them focused. Often a first responder will get right in the face of the injured person and yell, "Look at me in the eyes! Listen to me! You are going to be OK. Stay with me. Don't look away. Keep looking at me right in the eyes!"

Psalm 141:8

For my eyes are on you, Yahweh, the Lord. In you, I take refuge. Don't leave my soul destitute.

Psalm 46:1

God is our refuge and strength, a very present help in trouble.

Proverbs 4:25-27

Let your eyes look straight ahead. Fix your gaze directly before you. Make the path of your feet level. Let all of your ways be established. Don't turn to the right hand nor to the left. Remove your foot from evil.

Fix your eyes on the Lord. Focus solely and intensely on Him. Our minds like to wander off and focus on things that are ungodly but we must catch ourselves and regain focus on Him. Just as the injured person needs to stay focused on the first responder there to save him, We must stay focused on Jesus for He is here to save us.

- Day 100 -

Adam? Adam? Oh, Adam, where are you? Did you ever wonder why God calls out for Adam in the Garden of Eden? Do you really think that the Creator of Heaven and Earth, the all knowing, everlasting and eternal creator of all things really didn't know where Adam was? Perhaps He misplaced His GPS that day or He couldn't see behind the bush that Adam and Eve were hiding behind. Or maybe He was asking a question other than what Adam's geographical location was. Perhaps God was asking about something entirely different...

Genesis 3:9-13
God called to the man, and said to him, "Where are you?" The man said, "I heard your voice in the garden, and I was afraid, because I was naked; and I hid myself." God said, "Who told you that you were naked? Have you eaten from the tree that I commanded you not to eat from?" The man said, "The woman whom you gave to be with me, she gave me fruit from the tree, and I ate it." Yahweh God said to the woman, "What have you done?"

God didn't somehow lose Adam. Quite the contrary, He knew exactly where Adam was. Have you ever felt God asking where YOU are? God most certainly didn't lose you either. God never asks a question He doesn't know the answer to. He merely wants you to know the condition you're in and for you to give thought to what caused it. When God asks you a question through scripture or with a feeling right down in the pit of your stomach, He is trying to start a conversation with you that will help you find a way out of your difficulties. So, Where are YOU?

- Day 101 -

Forgiveness is so very healing. Not just the act of asking for forgiveness but the act of granting forgiveness is healing as well. The thing about forgiveness is that it works best when it's complete and unconditional whether it is being asked for or being granted.

James 5:16 Confess your faults one to another, and pray one for another, that ye may be healed. The effectual fervent prayer of a righteous man availeth much.

1 John 1:9 If we confess our sins, he is faithful and just to forgive us our sins, and to cleanse us from all unrighteousness.

Proverbs 28:13 He that covereth his sins shall not prosper: but whoso confesseth and forsaketh them shall have mercy.

Luke 17:3-4 Be careful. If your brother sins against you, rebuke him. If he repents, forgive him. If he sins against you seven times in the day, and seven times returns, saying, 'I repent,' you shall forgive him."

Colossians 3:13 bearing with one another, and forgiving each other, if any man has a complaint against any; even as Christ forgave you, so you also do.

Listen, the Lord's prayer says "Forgive us our trespasses as we forgive those who have trespassed against us", not "Forgive me for most of the stuff I've done because the rest of the stuff wasn't so bad and it was totally called for AND I will forgive most of the stuff that others did to me but some of the stuff was so bad that there is no way I will forgive them". Confess your sins completely and sincerely to God and one another. Grant forgiveness sincerely and completely as Christ did for you "so ye both may be healed".

- Day 102 -

Sometimes it appears as if we're walking around in the darkness of this world. The nightly news is no longer a place to get information about our world in an objective way that portrays both the good and the bad. Only shock, horror and fear sell advertisements so the news predominantly talks about the darkness. It's easy to be fooled into believing that you must therefore be in this darkness but that's merely the enemy whispering lies in your ear.

1 John 1:5-6

This is the message which we have heard from him and announce to you, that God is light, and in him is no darkness at all. If we say that we have fellowship with him and walk in the darkness, we lie, and don't tell the truth.

John 8:12

Again, therefore, Jesus spoke to them, saying, "I am the light of the world. He who follows me will not walk in the darkness, but will have the light of life."

It's impossible for a follower of Christ to be in the darkness. "Where is the light when all I see is darkness?", you may ask. The light is upon you all the time. That is a promise from God, through Jesus, to you in His Word. The problem is that you let the enemy distract you and turn your head away from God. In doing so, he turned your eyes away from the light and towards the darkness. If you are a believer and feel like the light has disappeared, it's merely shining on your back... simply turn around and face Him again.

- Day 103 -

Although I'm not a big fan of holidays created by the card companies, I am completely in favor of a special day to honor our mothers. Whether the person whom we identify as our mother was our biological mother or a surrogate mother, they deserves a big hand and a moment of praise and thanks. Whether they gave birth to us or raised us as children, we owe them a debt of gratitude.

Proverbs 31:25-30

Strength and dignity are her clothing. She laughs at the time to come. She opens her mouth with wisdom. Faithful instruction is on her tongue. She looks well to the ways of her household, and doesn't eat the bread of idleness. Her children rise up and call her blessed. Her husband also praises her: "Many women do noble things, but you excel them all." Charm is deceitful, and beauty is vain; but a woman who fears Yahweh, she shall be praised.

Deuteronomy 5:16

Honor your father and your mother, as the Lord your God commanded you, that your days may be long, and that it may go well with you in the land that the Lord your God is giving you.

Every day, but more so today, take time to honor your mother. Whether she was the one that rocked you to sleep, carried you in her womb, fed you, kissed you when you were hurt, sent you to school and made sure you did your homework or was adopted into that role to the extent that you felt compelled to call her your mother, take time to honor her. Depending on where you are in life, give her respect by cleaning your room, respecting your curfew, calling on the phone to check in or by making sure her needs are met when she can no longer meet them herself. Even if your mother has not perfectly fulfilled the role as you may have hoped she would, see your way through to recognizing, respecting and honoring the important role she had in making you the person you are today.

- Day 104 -

Have you ever been so "in the spirit" that it felt as if the words were coming through you instead of from you? Often we, as Christians, are afraid to tell others about the Good News because we don't think we'll have the right words to share the gospel properly. We're concerned that if they ask deep questions, we won't be able to remember the chapter and verse to answer the question (as if that was the most important thing- NOT).

Matthew 10:20

For it is not you who speak, but the Spirit of your Father who speaks in you.

Luke 12:12

for the Holy Spirit will teach you in that same hour what you must say."

Isaiah 59:21 "As for me, this is my covenant with them," says Yahweh. "My Spirit who is on you, and my words which I have put in your mouth, shall not depart out of your mouth, nor out of the mouth of your offspring, nor out of the mouth of your offspring's offspring," says Yahweh, "from henceforth and forever."

Our job is to create within us a clean empty vessel for God to fill with His Word. My prayer before getting into bed and before rising is, "Lord God, empty me of me, fill me with you. Empty me of me, fill me with you." It is His promise to us that the words which He placed in our mouth will never depart us. His promise includes the fact that when we need to speak on His behalf, the Holy Spirit will speak for us and exactly the right words will come through us at exactly the right time. Don't be afraid to step up and share your faith and spread the gospel, God will be with you though the Holy Spirit...He says so in the Bible and He is incapable of lying so it must be true.

- Day 105 -

Have you ever felt badly when someone teased you about something personal. Maybe it's your 'snort laugh', or your sweaty palms or your hairstyle or your weight. The Bible encourages us not to listen to the Words of these fools. God knows who you are and that's all that matters.

Matthew 5:11-12 "Blessed are you when people reproach you, persecute you, and say all kinds of evil against you falsely, for my sake. Rejoice, and be exceedingly glad, for great is your reward in heaven. For that is how they persecuted the prophets who were before you.

Proverbs 26:18-19 Like a madman who shoots torches, arrows, and death, is the man who deceives his neighbor and says, "Am I not joking?"

1 Peter 5:10 But may the God of all grace, who called you to his eternal glory by Christ Jesus, after you have suffered a little while, perfect, establish, strengthen, and settle you.

Matthew 5:22 But I say to you that everyone who is angry with his brother will be liable to judgment; whoever insults his brother will be liable to the council; and whoever says, 'You fool!' will be liable to the hell of fire.

If a fool slings insults at you, remember the source from which it came. They may try to insult you but you don't have to receive it. If someone offers you a gift but you don't accept it, who then does the gift belong to? To the giver still, of course. Likewise if someone offers you an insult and you don't receive it, the insult belongs to them, not you. Remember always who you are and whose you are. God loves you and that will never change.

- Day 106 -

The Bible says that we will become part of the body of Christ. Isn't that an interesting thing? So what is the Bible talking about here? I find it fascinating! Is the Bible talking about us becoming part of a single 'Organism' as a cell which makes up the actual body of Christ? Or, is the Bible talking about us becoming part of a single 'Organization' such as the Church of Christ often referred to as the body of Christ?

1 Corinthians 12:27 Now you are the body of Christ, and members individually.

Romans 12:4-5 For even as we have many members in one body, and all the members don't have the same function, so we, who are many, are one body in Christ, and individually members one of another.

Ephesians 4:4 There is one body, and one Spirit, even as you also were called in one hope of your calling;

Ephesians 2:19-22 So then you are no longer strangers and foreigners, but you are fellow citizens with the saints, and of the household of God, being built on the foundation of the apostles and prophets, Christ Jesus himself being the chief cornerstone; in whom the whole building, fitted together, grows into a holy temple in the Lord; in whom you also are built together for a habitation of God in the Spirit.

Confused? Don't worry, you're not alone. Even the scholars debate about this going back to the original language in the original scrolls. For me, after long study, both make sense. Right now, it makes sense that we are to be part of the Organizational body of Christ, which is His church and we are to go forth and proclaim the Good News. But, one day, we will shed this earthly body and we will become part of the perfect Organism which is the body of Christ and dwell through Him, with Him and In Him in unity with the Holy Spirit. As part of His body, the unity of all people in one body will be restored and we will give all glory and honor to our Almighty Father forever and ever.

- Day 107 -

When we look at the world it appears as a relatively dark place dotted by lots of bright lights. It's just like looking at the night sky. As we look up into the night sky and peer at the universe, we are faced with a very dark sky which is dotted by countless bright stars. What does the Bible say about the darkness and the light?

John 1:5

The light shines in the darkness, and the darkness hasn't overcome it.

Genesis 1:4
God saw the light, and saw that it was good. God divided the light from the darkness.

John 3:19
This is the judgment, that the light has come into the world, and men loved the darkness rather than the light; for their works were evil.

Ephesians 5:8

For you were once darkness, but are now light in the Lord. Walk as children of light,

John 8:12

Again, therefore, Jesus spoke to them, saying, "I am the light of the world. He who follows me will not walk in the darkness, but will have the light of life."

No matter how dark it appears around us here in the world and out into the universe, remember that the light will always prevail. More importantly remember that You are a bright light when you follow Christ and there is no darkness that can overcome you. Be aware that there are many people around you that have been overcome by darkness. Share the light of LIFE with them so that they too can triumph over the darkness and defeat it. You can make a difference.

- Day 108 -

It's nearly impossible to stop watching the news these days. If you intentionally don't watch the news on TV, they sneak it in while you are getting your e-mail on the computer. If you don't use a computer, friends and family feel compelled to say, 'Oh my God, did you see what happened in Washington today?" You begin to notice that everything that happens in politics, is said or is promised as an appeal to the flesh.

1 John 2:15-16

Don't love the world or the things that are in the world. If anyone loves the world, the Father's love isn't in him. For all that is in the world, the lust of the flesh, the lust of the eyes, and the pride of life, isn't the Father's, but is the world's.

Romans 8:6-8

For the mind of the flesh is death, but the mind of the Spirit is life and peace; because the mind of the flesh is hostile towards God; for it is not subject to God's law, neither indeed can it be. Those who are in the flesh can't please God.

No matter where you get your news, it's painfully clear that if you want to get elected in politics, you need to appeal to the flesh. However, if you want to be elected to an everlasting life in Heaven, you need to appeal to God through Jesus. Psalms 34:15 reminds us that God is waiting to hear from us and that He is attentive to our prayers. So turn off the bad news, tune into the Good News, and pray.

- Day 109 -

The morning is a great time especially if you wake a little early before anyone else has the chance to disturb the quiet. There's something special about the morning. It's a new beginning, a new chance to accomplish something special. Like all journeys there must be a first step. What you do first thing in the morning is your first step for that day.

Psalm 5:3

Lord God, in the morning you shall hear my voice. In the morning I will lay my requests before you, and will watch expectantly.

Lamentations 3:22-23
It is because of Yahweh's loving kindnesses that we are not consumed, because his compassion doesn't fail. They are new every morning; great is your faithfulness.
Mark 1:35
Early in the morning, while it was still dark, he rose up and went out, and departed into a deserted place, and prayed there.
John 8:2
Now very early in the morning, he came again into the temple, and all the people came to him. He sat down, and taught them.

Big things happen in the morning while most everyone is asleep. Don't lament over the fact that you like to wake up a little later, just don't squander what morning hours you have left. Take a moment to pray before you put your feet on the ground. Praying first thing in the morning will help you keep a positive, peaceful attitude throughout the day. Start your day by giving thanks to God and place your requests before Him and then wait expectantly as you serve His Children throughout the day.

- Day 110 -

These days you hear a lot about people having a secular part of their life and a spiritual part of their life. They pray at night and maybe over a meal or two, they go to church, sit through the sermon and the service and that's the spiritual part of their life. The same person goes to work and proceeds to use unethical means to increase their wealth and it's "OK" because that's "just business" and it's the "secular" part of their life. Well, God never intended for there to be a "spiritual" and a "secular" part of our lives. It's certainly not biblical...

1 Corinthians 10:31 Whether therefore you eat, or drink, or whatever you do, do all to the glory of God.

Colossians 3:17 Whatever you do, in word or in deed, do all in the name of the Lord Jesus, giving thanks to God the Father, through him.

Matthew 5:16 Even so, let your light shine before men; that they may see your good works, and glorify your Father who is in heaven.

James 2:26 For as the body apart from the spirit is dead, even so faith apart from works is dead.

I get a huge laugh out of trying to pull out of the church parking lot after church. I find it funny that most people just heard an hour long sermon about being more Christ-like and yet they intentionally don't make eye contact with you when you're trying to pull out of your parking spot to leave. They will do almost anything not to allow anyone to come before themselves. We can't be "spiritual" in church and "secular" "biblical mules" when we exit the building. We must eat, drink, work, drive, etc. all to the glory of God inside AND outside the Church.

- Day 111 -

The Bible is pretty clear that if you pass a hungry man on the street and don't stop to feed him (as we have all been guilty of at one time or another), and you pray for forgiveness...you are forgiven. The question is, are you required to go back and feed him if you know he is still there?

Job 22:5-9 Isn't your wickedness great? Neither is there any end to your iniquities. For you have taken pledges from your brother for nothing, and stripped them naked of their clothing. You haven't given water to the weary to drink, and you have withheld bread from the hungry. But as for the mighty man, he had the earth. The honorable man, he lived in it. You have sent widows away empty, and the arms of the fatherless have been broken.

Matthew 25:41-43 Then he will say also to those on the left hand, 'Depart from me, you cursed, into the eternal fire which is prepared for the devil and his angels; for I was hungry, and you didn't give me food to eat; I was thirsty, and you gave me no drink; I was a stranger, and you didn't take me in; naked, and you didn't clothe me; sick, and in prison, and you didn't visit me.'

Acts 3:19 "Repent therefore, and turn again, that your sins may be blotted out, so that there may come times of refreshing from the presence of the Lord,

1 John 1:9 If we confess our sins, he is faithful and righteous to forgive us the sins, and to cleanse us from all unrighteousness.

It really comes down to 2 questions... Must you? And Should you? After you repent for having not fed the hungry or clothed the naked or given drink to the thirsty or sheltered the homeless or visit the lonely, God forgives you. MUST you go back and feed the hungry person on the corner to obtain this grace? Must you? -No. Should you? -Yes. Lord God, give us the strength to do what we should do, not just what we must do.

- Day 112 -

Here's a biblical question for you: Is there a difference between BETRAYAL and DENIAL as far as God is concerned? Both are sins and we know the penalty for sin but think about the acts of BETRAYAL and DENIAL. Jesus was both Betrayed and Denied.

Matthew 26:23-25 He answered, "He who dipped his hand with me in the dish, the same will betray me. The Son of Man goes, even as it is written of him, but woe to that man through whom the Son of Man is betrayed! It would be better for that man if he had not been born." Judas, who betrayed him, answered, "It isn't me, is it, Rabbi?" He said to him, "You said it."
Matthew 27:3-5 Then Judas, who betrayed him, when he saw that Jesus was condemned, felt remorse, and brought back the thirty pieces of silver to the chief priests and elders, saying, "I have sinned in that I betrayed innocent blood." But they said, "What is that to us? You see to it." He threw down the pieces of silver in the sanctuary, and departed. He went away and hanged himself.

Matthew 26:34 Jesus said to him, "Most certainly I tell you that tonight, before the rooster crows, you will deny me three times."

Matthew 26:75 Peter remembered the word which Jesus had said to him, "Before the rooster crows, you will deny me three times." He went out and wept bitterly.
Matthew 16:18 I also tell you that you are Peter, and on this rock I will build my assembly, and the gates of Hades will not prevail against it.

So, one of the disciples Betrayed Jesus and the other Denied Him. One disciple winds us remorseful and confesses his sins to the chief priests but winds up taking his own life. The other wept remorsefully but was called to repentance by the risen Jesus Christ, was forgiven his sins and was restored. The tragedy of Judas was that he wasn't around to receive the message of the Good News from the arisen Christ and instead tried to save himself. When you look in the mirror, judge yourself by God's law and find yourself a sinner but don't despair as Judas did, be restored as Peter was.

- Day 113 -

Medical malpractice comes in two 'flavors', acts of commission and acts of omission. Acts of commission are things that are done which are harmful. Acts of omission are things that are not done which could have been helpful. Spiritual malpractice come in two 'flavors' as well…

James 4:17

To him therefore who knows to do good, and doesn't do it, to him it is sin.

1 John 3:17-18

But whoever has the world's goods, and sees his brother in need, and closes his heart of compassion against him, how does the love of God remain in him? My little children, let's not love in word only, or with the tongue only, but in deed and truth.

Matthew 26:74

Then he began to curse and to swear, "I don't know the man!"

Immediately the rooster crowed.

Matthew 15:18-19

But the things which proceed out of the mouth come out of the heart, and they defile the man. For out of the heart come evil thoughts, murders, adulteries, sexual sins, thefts, false testimony, and blasphemies.

In the case of our spiritual malpractice, at the end of our trial, we will all be found guilty as charged. Whether it be something we did or something we should have done but did not, the verdict will be the same. Guilty. But, if we recognize our sin, repent and ask for His forgiveness, Jesus intercedes on our behalf and grants grace where there should be justice. Can I get a Hallelujah?

Day 114

Legalism is when someone abstracts the law of God from it's original intent. Some Christians become so obsessed with following the rules that they wind up turning Christianity into a set of do's and don'ts. Sometimes this turns Christianity into a cold set of moral principles which miss the mark entirely.

Matthew 12:9-14 World English Bible (WEB)

9 He departed there, and went into their synagogue. 10 And behold there was a man with a withered hand. They asked him, "Is it lawful to heal on the Sabbath day?" that they might accuse him.

11 He said to them, "What man is there among you, who has one sheep, and if this one falls into a pit on the Sabbath day, won't he grab on to it, and lift it out? 12 Of how much more value then is a man than a sheep! Therefore it is lawful to do good on the Sabbath day." 13 Then he told the man, "Stretch out your hand." He stretched it out; and it was restored whole, just like the other. 14 But the Pharisees went out, and conspired against him, how they might destroy him.

It's true that Christianity is concerned with morality, righteousness and ethics but we must guard ourselves from turning our passionate concern for upholding God's law into legalism. Perhaps it is law that we rest on the Sabbath day but on that Sabbath day, if we find a person in need of help, let's do the right thing. With God's help, hopefully we will be able to do the right thing in accordance with His will.

- Day 115 -

Does it upset you when others offer you their criticism? Some people try to offer correction but it comes across as criticism and it can sting like a bee. Are we called to correct or to criticize each other or should we just leave well enough alone to spare each other's feelings? What is God's advice on this subject?

Galatians 5:15

But if you bite and devour one another, be careful that you don't consume one another.

Matthew 7:1-3

"Don't judge, so that you won't be judged. For with whatever judgment you judge, you will be judged; and with whatever measure you measure, it will be measured to you. Why do you see the speck that is in your brother's eye, but don't consider the beam that is in your own eye?

Luke 6:37 Don't judge, and you won't be judged. Don't condemn, and you won't be condemned. Set free, and you will be set free.

1 Peter 3:16 having a good conscience; that, while you are spoken against as evildoers, they may be disappointed who curse your good way of life in Christ.

The Bible is clear about criticism...Don't do it. From time to time, someone we know may need correction but the Bible is also clear on how to correct them. Correction should be done wisely, with love, non-argumentatively, kind, patient, gentle, and based upon God's Word. So if you are being criticized, yes, it's OK to be 'pissed off'. But, if someone is concerned about you and your welfare and is attempting to correct you lovingly in a kind and gentle way that's Biblically sound, listen quietly, pray, make the necessary changes and be sure to thank them.

Learning to control the tongue is not an easy task. The Bible teaches that the tongue can be a destructive power. The tongue can pour out blessings and curses, healings and afflictions.

Proverbs 18:21
Death and life are in the power of the tongue; those who love it will eat its fruit.

James 3:6,8

And the tongue is a fire. The world of iniquity among our members is the tongue, which defiles the whole body, and sets on fire the course of nature, and is set on fire by Gehenna. But nobody can tame the tongue. It is a restless evil, full of deadly poison.

James 3:9-10

With it we bless our God and Father, and with it we curse men, who are made in the image of God. Out of the same mouth comes blessing and cursing. My brothers, these things ought not to be so.

Proverbs 12:18
There is one who speaks rashly like the piercing of a sword, but the tongue of the wise heals.

As we become more spiritually mature, we gain control over our tongue. But, even in our spiritual maturity, we are not perfect. Our tongue may 'slip' and we may speak words we aren't proud of. The truly wise person, after having spoken words that cut to the core, will gain control of their tongue and offer words of apology to heal the very same wounds. It doesn't cost a dime to speak words of praise and healing or continued health over someone. Who will you praise today?

- Day 117 -

I know a couple who are some of the kindest, most loving and generous people on the planet. In a recent conversation with them, they were concerned that perhaps they weren't giving 'enough'. They were actually feeling guilty that they were so blessed and perhaps they had not done their part to share those blessings.

1 John 1:9

If we confess our sins, he is faithful and righteous to forgive us the sins, and to cleanse us from all unrighteousness.

2 Timothy 2:15

Give diligence to present yourself approved by God, a workman who doesn't need to be ashamed, properly handling the Word of Truth.

Philippians

Not that I speak in respect to lack, for I have learned in whatever state I am, to be content in it.

Guilt is the fact or state of having committed an offense, crime, violation, or wrong, especially against moral or penal law; and a feeling of responsibility or remorse for some offense, crime, wrong, etc., whether real or imagined. Often we have done our best yet feel guilty that there was more that could have been done. God reminds us that we have done all we can do and if we have not, He has already forgiven us.

- Day 118 -

OK, so if God is in charge of who's elected to be in heaven with Him and He has already predetermined who is elected and who will not be elected, why is it necessary to share the gospel? I mean, if it's all predestined to happen before the beginning of time, what's the point of going out and evangelizing? Aren't there things we can do that would be a better use of our time?

Matthew 28:19-20 Go, and make disciples of all nations, baptizing them in the name of the Father and of the Son and of the Holy Spirit, teaching them to observe all things that I commanded you. Behold, I am with you always, even to the end of the age." Amen.

Psalm 96:3 Declare his glory among the nations, his marvelous works among all the peoples.

Mark 16:15 He said to them, "Go into all the world, and preach the Good News to the whole creation.

Matthew 24:14 This Good News of the Kingdom will be preached in the whole world for a testimony to all the nations, and then the end will come.

The answer to this one is pretty simple. We go out and share the Good News also called the gospel because God and Jesus told us to. That alone should be enough. But, who's to say that even though God chose someone to be elect that WE were not the instrument He chose to use to call them into His Kingdom? If we are to be used by God for His good, we must first become obedient to His will and answer His call to go forth and proclaim the gospel.

- Day 119 -

Here's an interesting question: Do you really think that Satan wanted to be "the devil"? That's not what the Bible says that he wanted. Even more importantly, did God create the devil?

Isaiah 14:12-15

How you have fallen from heaven, morning star, son of the dawn! How you are cut down to the ground, who laid the nations low! You said in your heart, "I will ascend into heaven! I will exalt my throne above the stars of God! I will sit on the mountain of assembly, in the far north! I will ascend above the heights of the clouds! I will make myself like the Most High!" Yet you shall be brought down to Sheol, to the depths of the pit.

Ezekiel 28:14-17

You were the anointed cherub who covers: and I set you, so that you were on the holy mountain of God; you have walked up and down in the middle of the stones of fire. You were perfect in your ways from the day that you were created, until unrighteousness was found in you. By the abundance of your traffic they filled your insides with violence, and you have sinned: therefore I have cast you as profane out of the mountain of God; and I have destroyed you, covering cherub, from the middle of the stones of fire. Your heart was lifted up because of your beauty; you have corrupted your wisdom by reason of your brightness: I have cast you to the ground; I have laid you before kings, that they may see you.

God created the angel Lucifer which means "light-bringing" or "Morning star". He was created beautiful, perfect and sinless. Because of free will, Lucifer sought to be 'higher than God' and was unrighteous. So, in his disobedience, Lucifer himself really created 'Satan' which means resister. God didn't create the devil, He merely created the angel Lucifer that fell from grace and became Satan.

- Day 120 -

Seems as though as we grow older, so many of our friends and family become susceptible to disease. We find ourselves praying intercessory prayers for them. Quietly we may think the worst when the doctor's reports are not good. How are we to stay positive and optimistic about them (or us) healing?

Jeremiah 33:6

Behold, I will bring to it health and healing, and I will heal them and reveal to them abundance of prosperity and security.

Psalm 103:3

Who forgives all your iniquity, who heals all your diseases,

Exodus 23:25

You shall serve the Lord your God, and he will bless your bread and your water, and I will take sickness away from among you.

Psalm 107:20

He sent out his word and healed them, and delivered them from their destruction.

The best way to stay positive and optimistic is to study the Bible. God promises us that He will heal us, deliver us from evil, He will bless us, He will forgive us and He will grant us an abundance of prosperity and security. Now that's a promise that we can stay optimistic about!

- Day 121 -

What happens if you take a can of pure white paint and put a drop or two of black paint into it and mix it up? No matter how you look at it, the paint is no longer white...It's gray.

Daniel 7:9
I saw until thrones were placed, and one who was ancient of days sat: his clothing was white as snow, and the hair of his head like pure wool; his throne was fiery flames, and its wheels burning fire.

Philippians 4:8

Finally, brothers, whatever things are true, whatever things are honorable, whatever things are just, whatever things are pure, whatever things are lovely, whatever things are of good report; if there is any virtue, and if there is any praise, think about these things.

Matthew 5:8
Blessed are the pure in heart, for they shall see God.

1 Peter 1:22

Seeing you have purified your souls in your obedience to the truth through the Spirit in sincere brotherly affection, love one another from the heart fervently:

If you have pure water, would you drink it? If I put just a single drop of deadly poison into the water, would you still drink it? We are called to have a pure heart and soul through obedience to His Word. Just a 'drop' of disobedience is like adding poison to our heart and soul. Thank God that through Jesus we can be forgiven, the poisonous sin is washed away and we are made pure again.

- Day 122 -

While on vacation, my wife and I were walking down the street and a beggar looked me in the eye across from the Subway sandwich shop and said, "Hey mister, I'm hungry. I don't want any money. I just want some food." We passed him by but a few steps later we turned around, brought him into Subway and he proceeded to order a sandwich. It was about 8 dollars. It looked like the girl was about to make the sandwich and had the roll in her hand. Instead of sticking around with him while he ate, I handed him a $10 bill and we left.

Matthew 25:35

for I was hungry, and you gave me food to eat. I was thirsty, and you gave me drink. I was a stranger, and you took me in.

Isaiah 58:10 and if you pour out your soul to the hungry, and satisfy the afflicted soul: then your light will rise in darkness, and your obscurity will be as the noonday;

Proverbs 12:22 Lying lips are an abomination to God, but those who do the truth are his delight.

So, you may have noticed the last verse was about lying, not feeding the hungry. About a half a block down, I had a funny feeling in the pit of my stomach. I turned around and the same guy was back out in front of Subway looking for another sucker to bait into handing him money without any intention of actually buying a sandwich. Ouch! That hurt! We were lied to. Then we thought about it. 1- we should have handed the money to the sandwich maker to make sure he was fed and stayed to pray with him, but we were "too busy" and trusted him. 2- It's not about what happened when we left, it was about our intention to feed a fellow man that said he was hungry. If it happened to you, given the opportunity, would you do it all over again?

- Day 123 -

How we choose to share our blessings can be different every day. Today we woke early, caught a bus to the Cathedral Basilica of Philadelphia and went to the 7:30 AM mass. The Basilica is a massive building which reminded me, in many ways, of St. Patrick's Cathedral in NYC. As the basket was passed around before the bread and wine were consecrated to God, our offering was given to the church.

Acts 20:28 Take heed, therefore, to yourselves, and to all the flock, in which the Holy Spirit has made you overseers, to shepherd the church of the Lord and God which he purchased with his own blood.

2 Chronicles 31:4-5 Moreover he commanded the people who lived in Jerusalem to give the portion of the priests and the Levites, that they might give themselves to Yahweh's law. As soon as the commandment came abroad, the children of Israel gave in abundance the first fruits of grain, new wine, and oil, and honey, and of all the increase of the field; and the tithe of all things brought they in abundantly.

John 6:35 Jesus said to them, "I am the bread of life. He who comes to me will not be hungry, and he who believes in me will never be thirsty.

Today we chose to trust the church to feed it's sheep in this city. I have never seen this much poverty in any city I have ever visited. Today we chose to give back to the church that sustains us and gives us strength. I was struck that several homeless people took seats at the back of the church during mass so that as we left they could stand near the door to ask for money for food. Conspicuously, they did not get up to accept communion. I wondered if they knew the significance of the Bread of Life. Today we give thanks that we will not be hungry and never be thirsty because we are in Christ. We continue to pray for His children that are among the hungry and thirsty.

- Day 124 -

Today I took time to reflect on the meaning of brotherly love. Wikipedia describes it as the following: "Brotherly love in the biblical sense is an extension of the natural affection associated with near kin, toward the greater community of fellow believers, that goes beyond the mere duty in Leviticus 19:18 to "love thy neighbour as thyself", and shows itself as "unfeigned love" from a "pure heart", that extends an unconditional hand of friendship that loves when not loved back, that gives without getting, and that ever looks for what is best in others."

Psalm 51:10
Create in me a clean heart, O God. Renew a right spirit within me.

Romans 12:10

In love of the brothers be tenderly affectionate to one another; in honor preferring one another;

1 Thessalonians 4:9

But concerning brotherly love, you have no need that one write to you. For you yourselves are taught by God to love one another,

Hebrews 13:1

Let brotherly love continue.

What if every city became the city of brotherly love? What would the world look like if we truly loved for the sake of loving, served for the sake of serving and gave for the sake of giving so that others may live their lives more abundantly? What would our community look like if we just began to walk the talk of brotherly love described in the Bible, and in Wikipedia?

- Day 125 -

As a culture, our most valued possession is no longer money, it's TIME. The result of which is that we rush from one place to another trying to "save time". Our lives have become all about rushing to get to the destination instead of enjoying the journey.

John 10:10

The thief only comes in order to steal, kill, and destroy. I came that they may have life and enjoy it, and may have it in abundance (to the full, till it overflows). (AMP version)

Ecclesiastes 5:18

Behold, that which I have seen to be good and proper is for one to eat and to drink, and to enjoy good in all his labor, in which he labors under the sun, all the days of his life which God has given him; for this is his portion.

Proverbs 17:22

A cheerful heart makes good medicine, but a crushed spirit dries up the bones.

1 Thessalonians 5:16

Rejoice always.

God wants you to live in the moment, to enjoy your life right now, not when you get to some arbitrary point in time. Make a decision today to enjoy your life and to enjoy the journey. We have been directed to "Rejoice Always", not just when we are on vacation or get off work or become retired or when_____. While you're running around today, remember that THIS is the day the LORD has made, REJOICE and be GLAD in it.

- Day 126 -

Truly everything has it's time. The Bible teaches us that there is a plan for our life. There are appointed times for all things in our lives. There will be ups and there will be downs. There will be good and there will be bad. There is a season for all things.

Ecclesiastes 3:1-8 For everything there is a season, and a time for every purpose under heaven: a time to be born, and a time to die; a time to plant, and a time to pluck up that which is planted; a time to kill, and a time to heal; a time to break down, and a time to build up; a time to weep, and a time to laugh; a time to mourn, and a time to dance; a time to cast away stones, and a time to gather stones together; a time to embrace, and a time to refrain from embracing; a time to seek, and a time to lose; a time to keep, and a time to cast away; a time to tear, and a time to sew; a time to keep silence, and a time to speak; a time to love, and a time to hate; a time for war, and a time for peace.

If you are mourning, know that you are being prayed for and that God mourns with you. If you are rejoicing, know that God rejoices with you. But, no matter where you are in life, know that your steps are ordered by God and when you stumble, you will not fall because He is there to catch you. (Pslam 37: 23-24)

- Day 127 -

I had a great conversation with a Pastor Paul from Curtis Corner Baptist Church. It sounds like he's planning an awesome sermon for Father's day. He shared actual Bible verses in his blog Paulechapman.com This man is always so excited and enthusiastic for the Lord. God literally shines through him. The revelation that got him so excited was that our Father in heaven shares the title 'father' with fathers on earth and he expressed it in his blog this way: "What a privilege that God shares this lofty title with earthly fathers!"

Matthew 6:1 "Be careful that you don't do your charitable giving before men, to be seen by them, or else you have no reward from your Father who is in heaven.

Matthew 6:4 so that your merciful deeds may be in secret, then your Father who sees in secret will reward you openly.

Matthew 6:6 But you, when you pray, enter into your inner room, and having shut your door, pray to your Father who is in secret, and your Father who sees in secret will reward you openly.

Matthew 6:9 Pray like this: 'Our Father in heaven, may your name be kept holy.

This also from his blog- "God shares glory with earthly fathers. We must seize this precious gift and do our best to live up to the high place God has given us in our children's hearts. Are you a father? Pray daily for the strength and wisdom to fulfill your noble role. Walk in the Spirit each day. Are you a child? Reach out to your Dad today letting him know how much you love and respect Him. May we never forget the glory of fatherhood!"

- Day 128 -

I know, I know, technically Sunday is the first day of the week but to most Americans, Monday is the first day of the week. It's at least the first day of the work week for most people. For some reason people have a hard time getting started on Mondays. There's so much to be positive about on Mondays though. We can use this day to have a positive impact on those around us. Imagine waking up one morning and saying, "Hey, let's create the universe today."

Genesis 1

In the beginning, God created the heavens and the earth. The earth was formless and empty. Darkness was on the surface of the deep and God's Spirit was hovering over the surface of the waters.

God said, "Let there be light," and there was light. God saw the light, and saw that it was good. God divided the light from the darkness. God called the light "day", and the darkness he called "night". There was evening and there was morning, the first day.

John 1:1-3

In the beginning was the Word, and the Word was with God, and the Word was God. The same was in the beginning with God. All things were made through him. Without him was not anything made that has been made.

On a Monday God created the heavens and the Earth and light...that's a hard act to follow for sure but still, we have today to do something special. Notice that He literally spoke everything into existence. What can we do today to make a difference and make a positive change in this world? Perhaps it will be just a kind word to someone who needs it. Don't squander this day. Use your talents to Serve God By Serving Man through your unique abilities.

- Day 129 -

Everyone loves a party, right? So what does the Bible say about celebrating holidays? When it comes to celebrating holidays, some interpret it as unbiblical, some interpret it as biblical so what are we to do?

Colossians 2:16

Let no one therefore judge you in eating, or in drinking, or with respect to a feast day or a new moon or a Sabbath day,

Romans 14:5-6

One man esteems one day as more important. Another esteems every day alike. Let each man be fully assured in his own mind. He who observes the day, observes it to the Lord; and he who does not observe the day, to the Lord he does not observe it. He who eats, eats to the Lord, for he gives God thanks. He who doesn't eat, to the Lord he doesn't eat, and gives God thanks.

When we interpret the Bible for everyday use here in the 21st century, it's a little different than reading and interpreting the Bible a dozen centuries ago. Give consideration as to whether what you are celebrating allows us to thank God for what we observe in a holiday OR whether the holiday we are celebrating might promote immorality or false doctrine. IF you and your family have searched your hearts and prayed over it and have found that the celebration allows you to give more thanks to God… Party on my friends.

- Day 130 -

While watching a popular TV talent show, I saw one of the judges vote 'NO' against having a performer move on to the next round of the show. The performer gave a compelling reason why the judge should reconsider and to everyone's surprise, the judge changed his mind. When things are not going our way or things are not going the way we had hoped, are there compelling arguments we can bring to God in prayer to have Him reconsider what's best for us and have Him bring us to the destiny we desire?

Jeremiah 26:3 (NLT) Perhaps they will listen and turn from their evil ways. Then I will change my mind about the disaster I am ready to pour out on them because of their sins.

Psalm 110:4 God has sworn, and will not change his mind: "You are a priest forever in the order of Melchizedek."

Exodus 32:12-14 Why should the Egyptians speak, saying, 'He brought them out for evil, to kill them in the mountains, and to consume them from the surface of the earth?' Turn from your fierce wrath, and repent of this evil against your people. Remember Abraham, Isaac, and Israel, your servants, to whom you swore by your own self, and said to them, 'I will multiply your offspring as the stars of the sky, and all this land that I have spoken of I will give to your offspring, and they shall inherit it forever.'" Yahweh repented of the evil which he said he would do to his people.

God is Immutable, in that He is the same now as He was and will be unchanged forever more. God is Omniscient in that He knows everything that has happened and will happen. Throughout time God has changed His mind but there was one important factor each time in the Bible that He does so. He only changes His attitude when people change their behavior. In other words, a change in our conduct changes God's judgement. Remember though, just because God can change His mind does not mean he will. He always knows what's best for us in the end. Will you trust that today?

- Day 131 -

I had a friend write to me today to share a song called "Trust and Obey". In reference to that song he admitted that he struggles with control. I imagine that wanting to be in control is a struggle many people have. Our culture has made us believe that if we are "In Control", we wield more power, we feel less pain, we have a less chaotic life, we attract more friends, we don't have to answer to anybody else, etc. The truth is that all the control we think we have is just an illusion. We are not in control, He is…

Proverbs 19:21 There are many plans in a man's heart, but God's counsel will prevail.

Jeremiah 29:11 For I know the thoughts that I think toward you, says Yahweh, thoughts of peace, and not of evil, to give you hope and a future.

Matthew 19:26 Looking at them, Jesus said, "With men this is impossible, but with God all things are possible."

Proverbs 16:9 A man's heart plans his course, but Yahweh directs his steps.

Isaiah 14:24 The LORD of hosts hath sworn, saying, Surely as I have thought, so shall it come to pass; and as I have purposed, [so] shall it stand:

The irony is that the only way to gain control is to give up control and give it back to God. When we learn to let go and "Let God" take over we come to more fully understand that He knows what's best for us as in the verse from Jeremiah above. Each morning and night I have repeated this prayer for as long as I can remember- "Lord God, Empty me of me, fill me with You. Empty me of me, fill me with You. Empty me of me, fill me with You."

- Day 132 -

The other day I asked a friend if he was sure that if he died today that he would go to heaven. He looked me in the eye and said confidently, "I'm a good person. I do good things for other people. I'm peaceful and I love everyone. Of course I'm going to heaven." Then I asked if he ever took time to repent of his sins and asked Jesus into his heart. "I don't have anything to repent for", he said. "And I don't know how I feel about that 'Jesus thing' but I'm definitely going to heaven", he added.

John 14:6 Jesus said to him, "I am the way, the truth, and the life. No one comes to the Father, except through me.

Romans 10:9 that if you will confess with your mouth that Jesus is Lord, and believe in your heart that God raised him from the dead, you will be saved.

Ephesians 2:8-9 for by grace you have been saved through faith, and that not of yourselves; it is the gift of God, not of works, that no one would boast.

Revalation 21:18-23 The construction of its wall was jasper. The city was pure gold, like pure glass. The foundations of the city's wall were adorned with all kinds of precious stones. The first foundation was jasper; the second, sapphire; the third, chalcedony; the fourth, emerald; the fifth, sardonyx; the sixth, sardius; the seventh, chrysolite; the eighth, beryl; the ninth, topaz; the tenth, chrysoprasus; the eleventh, jacinth; and the twelfth, amethyst. The twelve gates were twelve pearls. Each one of the gates was made of one pearl. The street of the city was pure gold, like transparent glass. I saw no temple in it, for the Lord God, the Almighty, and the Lamb, are its temple. The city has no need for the sun, neither of the moon, to shine, for the very glory of God illuminated it, and its lamp is the Lamb.

Heaven, it seems like a pretty nice place indeed. A city made of gold so pure that it's like glass and there's no need for the sun because the glory of God literally lights the place up. Do a checklist to see if you've ever broken one of the Ten Commandments. If you have, you may want to check out that 'Jesus thing'.

- Day 133 -

In our busy lives it's easy to get so caught up in our work, our day to day lives, our obligations and in our commitments that we forget to "take time to smell the roses". We can be in the car rushing to get somewhere and pass by something beautiful that God has made for us to enjoy without even noticing it. Our eyes may be open but we do not see the huge yellow forsythia or a spectacular sunrise or sunset.

Psalm 19:1 The heavens declare the glory of God. The expanse shows his handiwork.

Job 37:5 God thunders marvelously with his voice.   He does great things, which we can't comprehend.

Matthew 6:28-29 Why are you anxious about clothing? Consider the lilies of the field, how they grow. They don't toil, neither do they spin, yet I tell you that even Solomon in all his glory was not dressed like one of these.

Ecclesiastes 3:11 He has made everything beautiful in its time. He has also set eternity in their hearts, yet so that man can't find out the work that God has done from the beginning even to the end.

When we are overwhelmed by our hustle bustle lives, we need only listen to God's Word which is filled with peace and tranquility. When our day to day obligations seem to rob us of our joy, we need only look out the window to be reminded of the beauty that God has created for us to enJOY. When we feel lost and alone in the 'thick of thin things', we need only slow down for a moment to feel the presence of God who is always with us.

Day 134

Do you come from a "dysfunctional family"? Seems today that is the new norm. A dysfunctional family is defined by Wikipedia as a family in which conflict, misbehavior, and often child neglect or abuse on the part of individual parents occur continually and regularly, leading other members to accommodate such actions. Children sometimes grow up in such families with the understanding that such an arrangement is normal.

Proverbs 11:29 He who troubles his own house shall inherit the wind. The foolish shall be servant to the wise of heart.

Philippians 2:3-4 doing nothing through rivalry or through conceit, but in humility, each counting others better than himself; each of you not just looking to his own things, but each of you also to the things of others.

1 Corinthians 13:11 When I was a child, I spoke as a child, I felt as a child, I thought as a child. Now that I have become a man, I have put away childish things.

Ephesians 6:4 You fathers, don't provoke your children to wrath, but nurture them in the discipline and instruction of the Lord.

God instructs us as to have a "functional family" in the Bible. God gives clear instructions as to how we are to treat each other in a family. God's plan is that husbands are to assume the responsibility of being the head of the household and are to be respected in that role. Husbands and wives are to love each other in the same way that Christ loves His church. Children are to obey their parents. How many family problems would be solved if husbands, wives, and children simply followed those basic rules?

- Day 135 -

We proclaim that we are serving the 'living' God. That is also a declaration that He is alive and with us. But, let's face it, when was the last time you heard the audible voice of God? Does God still speak to us?

Exodus 3:14 God said to Moses, "I AM WHO I AM," and he said, "You shall tell the children of Israel this: 'I AM has sent me to you.'"

2 Timothy 3:16 Every Scripture is God-breathed and profitable for teaching, for reproof, for correction, and for instruction in righteousness,

Hebrews 1:1-2 God, having in the past spoken to the fathers through the prophets at many times and in various ways, has at the end of these days spoken to us by his Son, whom he appointed heir of all things, through whom also he made the worlds.

Romans 8:26-27   In the same way, the Spirit also helps our weaknesses, for we don't know how to pray as we ought. But the Spirit himself makes intercession for us with groanings which can't be uttered. He who searches the hearts knows what is on the Spirit's mind, because he makes intercession for the saints according to God.

As for me personally, I've never heard God's voice audibly but as these Bible verses teach us, God speaks to us in several ways. He speaks to us through prayer, through circumstances, through His Spirit, through other believers, through music, through His creation and animals, through His Son Jesus Christ, and through the Bible which is His living Word. Ever felt an uneasy feeling in the pit of your stomach before you were about to make a bad decision? ...Yup, it might have been Him. Listen prayerfully for His voice. You will be amazed at what He has to say to you even if it's in the form of deafening silence.

- Day 136 -

I had a great conversation with a patient of mine this afternoon. He owns an excavation business but on the back of each of his trucks is the Bible verse... Colossians 3:23-24 Whatever you do, work at it with all your heart, as working for the Lord, not for human masters, since you know that you will receive an inheritance from the Lord as a reward. It is the Lord Christ you are serving. And, though he and his family work hard for God through his work, he still was quick to point out that God doesn't want our sacrifice, He wants our love and gratitude...

Hosea 6:6 (TLB)

"I don't want your sacrifices—I want your love; I don't want your offerings—I want you to know me.

Psalm 51:16-17

For you don't delight in sacrifice, or else I would give it. You have no pleasure in burnt offering. The sacrifices of God are a broken spirit. A broken and contrite heart, O God, you will not despise.

1 Samuel 15:22

Samuel said, "Has Yahweh as great delight in burnt offerings and sacrifices, as in obeying Yahweh's voice? Behold, to obey is better than sacrifice, and to listen than the fat of rams.

It's true that every day we are given opportunities to sacrifice our own wants and needs to advance the kingdom of God and that's good. But, remember that His Son Jesus made the ultimate sacrifice on our behalf already. What God seems to be trying to tell us through His Word in scripture is that what he really wants is our undivided love, joy, gratitude, obedience and He wants to have relationship with us through prayer. Do you love Him? Take a moment to tell Him.

- Day 137 -

Yesterday, at our local Bible study, an interesting question came up: "Will we be sad if we get to heaven and find out that some of our loved ones are not there and some people we 'hoped would not be there' ARE there? OR will we be so overwhelmed by God's Shekinah glory that we won't notice who is there and who is not there?"

Revelation 21:4 He will wipe away from them every tear from their eyes. Death will be no more; neither will there be mourning, nor crying, nor pain, any more. The first things have passed away."

Revelation 4:8 The four living creatures, each one of them having six wings, are full of eyes around and within. They have no rest day and night, saying, "Holy, holy, holy is the Lord God, the Almighty, who was and who is and who is to come!"

Psalm 16:11 You will show me the path of life. In your presence is fullness of joy. In your right hand there are pleasures forever more.

Psalm 95:2 Let's come before his presence with thanksgiving. Let's extol him with songs!

Sure, it would be great if we knew that everyone we cared about in our life was going to heaven but that's probably not going to happen unless everyone we know also admitted they were sinners, asked for forgiveness, asked Jesus to be their Lord and Savior. Although that's true, we are going to be so overcome by the beauty of the most perfect, spectacular light we have ever seen that our only reaction will be to fall to our knees and extol Him with songs. Holy, holy, holy...

Check out this video called Overwhelmed by Big Daddy Weave...
https://youtu.be/A_Bgz90isFk

- Day 138 -

As I sit here in the hotel room on the 3rd floor in Long Island at 9:45 at night, it sounds like the revolutionary war is being fought outside the window. Through the window we can see at least 4 towns putting on a fireworks display in the distance. I tried to go to sleep at least 3 times but each time, after a short a period of silence, it begins again and I am drawn to the window to see the beautiful display of colors in the sky. Each time it stops for a minute, I think it's done but back it starts and I pop out of bed to go to the window because I want to miss the Grand Finale.

John 1:5 The light shines in the darkness, and the darkness hasn't overcome (can't comprehend) it.

Matthew 5:14 You are the light of the world. A city located on a hill can't be hidden.

Matthew 5:16 Even so, let your light shine before men; that they may see your good works, and glorify your Father who is in heaven.

Revelation 21:6 He said to me, "It is done! I am the Alpha and the Omega, the Beginning and the End. I will give freely to him who is thirsty from the spring of the water of life.

God encourages us to be the light in the darkness. We are to be bright lights, all of us. We are to stand on top of the hilltop and allow everyone to see His light shining through us. And when 'it is done', Oh what a glorious finale that will be. Way better than the grand finale of any fireworks display we've ever seen.

- Day 139 -

Weddings are an incredibly beautiful thing. The uniting of two people in holy matrimony is something very special. When two people are truly meant to be together and they have found true love, their desire to love each other for life is what marriage is all about. Marriage is the outward expression of the couple's love in the presence of God, their family and friends.

Ephesians 4:2 (NLT) Always be humble and gentle. Be patient with each other, making allowance for each other's faults because of your love.

Genesis 2:22-24 Yahweh God made a woman from the rib which had taken from the man, and brought her to the man. The man said, "This is now bone of my bones, and flesh of my flesh. She will be called 'woman,' because she was taken out of Man." Therefore a man will leave his father and his mother, and will join with his wife, and they will be one flesh.

Proverbs 18:22 Whoever finds a wife finds a good thing, and obtains favor of Yahweh.

Matthew 19:4-6 He answered, "Haven't you read that he who made them from the beginning made them male and female, and said, 'For this cause a man shall leave his father and mother, and shall join to his wife; and the two shall become one flesh?' So that they are no more two, but one flesh. What therefore God has joined together, don't let man tear apart."

As I looked into my brother and sister-in-law's eyes during their wedding ceremony. I was overcome by the depth of their love. It was so obvious that they had found their perfect mate, their perfect love. And it is marriage before God and man that joined them as one flesh. If you are married, take a moment to thank God for the special love you share with your mate. If you are not married, thank God for the person who will come at the perfect time.

- Day 140 -

I heard a phrase once that 'home' is where you hang your hat. In other words, home is wherever you are right now. We put so much importance on our home, as in the house or apartment or the condo that we live in. When it comes to 'home' what is it that God tells us about homes in the Bible?

2 Corinthians 5 (WEB)

5 For we know that if the earthly house of our tent is dissolved, we have a building from God, a house not made with hands, eternal, in the heavens. 2 For most certainly in this we groan, longing to be clothed with our habitation which is from heaven; 3 if so be that being clothed we will not be found naked. 4 For indeed we who are in this tent do groan, being burdened; not that we desire to be unclothed, but that we desire to be clothed, that what is mortal may be swallowed up by life. 5 Now he who made us for this very thing is God, who also gave to us the down payment of the Spirit.

6 Therefore we are always confident and know that while we are at home in the body, we are absent from the Lord; 7 for we walk by faith, not by sight. 8 We are courageous, I say, and are willing rather to be absent from the body, and to be at home with the Lord. 9 Therefore also we make it our aim, whether at home or absent, to be well pleasing to him.

God's not talking about the brick and wood house we live in when He talks about our home. He's talking about our bodies as being our temporary home here on Earth. And although while we are here for 'a moment', we are to treat this body like a temple, this earthly body is only a temporary home. For one day, we will leave this 'home' and we will be fully present with The Lord God Almighty.

- Day 141 -

Have you ever wondered about the difference between 'happiness' and 'joy'? Happiness depends on circumstances but Joy is a gift from God. Happiness may only last for a while but Joy is everlasting. Joy is intense because God has granted it to us and no one can take it away from us no matter what our circumstance may be.

James 1:2-4 Count it all joy, my brothers, when you fall into various temptations, knowing that the testing of your faith produces endurance. Let endurance have its perfect work, that you may be perfect and complete, lacking in nothing.

Romans 5:3-5 Not only this, but we also rejoice in our sufferings, knowing that suffering produces perseverance; and perseverance, proven character; and proven character, hope: and hope doesn't disappoint us, because God's love has been poured out into our hearts through the Holy Spirit who was given to us.

1 Peter 4:13 But because you are partakers of Christ's sufferings, rejoice; that at the revelation of his glory you also may rejoice with exceeding joy.

Philippians 4:4-7 Rejoice in the Lord always! Again I will say, "Rejoice!" Let your gentleness be known to all men. The Lord is at hand. In nothing be anxious, but in everything, by prayer and petition with thanksgiving, let your requests be made known to God. And the peace of God, which surpasses all understanding, will guard your hearts and your thoughts in Christ Jesus.

Here's the take home message. All the 'stuff' we thought we needed to be happy pale in comparison to the joy that can be found in the Lord. All the things we thought we needed last year to be 'happy' seem unimportant this year. But, Joy, true Joy from God is everlasting. Even as we are being persecuted and as we are going through a tough time in our lives, we still carry the joy of knowing that even if we lose EVERYTHING here on Earth, we gain EVERYTHING in the end when we are finally in the presence of Jesus.

- Day 142 -

Dependency isn't a 'cool' thing these days. No one wants to be dependent on anyone but themselves. People even give advice saying, "You just can't depend on anyone these days." And while that may be true of human beings, there is one person it's OK to be dependent on.

John 15:5

I am the vine. You are the branches. He who remains in me, and I in him, the same bears much fruit, for apart from me you can do nothing.

John 3:16

For God so loved the world, that he gave his one and only Son, that whoever believes in him should not perish, but have eternal life.

Hebrews 13:6

So that with good courage we say, "The Lord is my helper. I will not fear. What can man do to me?"

There is one time when it can be advantageous to become dependent. It's completely OK to become dependent on God and His sovereign will. I've found over the last 50 years of my life that when I place my complete trust and dependence in God, I always have enough manna for the day. In other words, when we let God direct our steps we always walk on the right path in the right direction towards our predestined destination.

- Day 143 -

There's a feeling that's hard to describe when you are with family. It's a feeling of comfort and love and wholeness. I think it's particularly intense when the family has not been together for a while. It is truly hard to describe the feeling you get when your adult parents come to visit for the first time in a while or when your adult children come home for the holidays and all of you sit at the dinner table and you look around and realize how very fortunate you are.

Joshua 24:15 If it seems evil to you to serve God, choose today whom you will serve; whether the gods which your fathers served that were beyond the River, or the gods of the Amorites, in whose land you dwell; but as for me and my family, we will serve The Lord."

1 Timothy 5:8 But if anyone doesn't provide for his own, and especially his own household, he has denied the faith, and is worse than an unbeliever.

Exodus 20:12 "Honor your father and your mother, that your days may be long in the land which The Lord your God gives you.

Psalm 127:3 Behold, children are a heritage from the Lord, the fruit of the womb a reward.

2 Corinthians 6:18 And I will be a father to you, and you shall be sons and daughters to me, says the Lord Almighty."

No family is perfect. Just as we are all individually flawed in one way or another, so it is with every family. But, just as each part of our body collectively makes us whole, when our family is together (no matter how dysfunctional it may be), we feel whole. Someday we will be part of the body of Christ and we will be one with Him. Imagine how good that will feel when the imperfections and flaws are left behind with our mortal bodies and we are together with our family, inseparable forever and united with agape love. Have you told your family how much you love them today?

- Day 144 -

My will or His? My timing or His? When we are making small decisions, how important is it to be sure that the decisions we make are congruent with His will and are done in His time? If it's an important, big decision, how much MORE important is it to be sure the decision is in His will and in His time?

Proverbs 3:5-6 Trust in The Lord with all your heart, and don't lean on your own understanding. In all your ways acknowledge him, and he will make your paths straight.

Psalm 37:4-5 Also delight yourself in The Lord, and he will give you the desires of your heart. Commit your way to The Lord. Trust also in him, and he will do this:

Acts 16:6-10 When they had gone through the region of Phrygia and Galatia, they were forbidden by the Holy Spirit to speak the word in Asia. When they had come opposite Mysia, they tried to go into Bithynia, but the Spirit didn't allow them. Passing by Mysia, they came down to Troas. A vision appeared to Paul in the night. There was a man of Macedonia standing, begging him, and saying, "Come over into Macedonia and help us." When he had seen the vision, immediately we sought to go out to Macedonia, concluding that the Lord had called us to preach the Good News to them.

When you're a person of faith, Making important decisions can become even more difficult. Just remember to obey what you already know to be His will, seek godly advice, listen intently for His spirit, and pay close attention to your circumstances. If your ego or heart desires something that is not in His will or in His timing, you'll meet up with circumstances and obstacles that clearly demonstrate what His plan is for you. God is pretty good at opening doors that are in your best interest to pass through and closing doors that should not be passed through...or at least, not be passed through yet.

- Day 145 -

When I awoke today it was a typical foggy New England morning. It gets this way at the coastline most mornings during the summer. It is as we say here, "As thick as pea soup."

Proverbs 3:5-6

Trust in The Lord with all your heart, and don't lean on your own understanding. In all your ways acknowledge him, and he will make your paths straight.

Psalm 32:8

I will instruct you and teach you in the way which you shall go. I will counsel you with my eye on you.

Psalm 48:14

For this God is our God forever and ever. He will be our guide even to death.

Isaiah 58:11

and The Lord will guide you continually,...

Sure, it might seem foggy right now both outside and perhaps inside our lives but God has you in the palm of His hand. He will guide your steps even when you can't see your own hand in front of your face. Take a deep breath, trust in The Lord and move forward according to His will. Before you know it, the sun will burn through the fog and it will expose a beautiful day.

- Day 146 -

I've made an interesting observation recently. I've concluded that the best way to change the world for the better is just to love the people closest to you. If we only focused on loving the people we come in contact with during the day, this world would be a better place. When given the choice to 'like' a comment on Facebook, or 'love' it... choose 'LOVE'. I mean, why not?

John 13:34

A new commandment I give to you, that you love one another. Just as I have loved you, you also love one another.

1 John 4:19-21

We love him, because he first loved us. If a man says, "I love God," and hates his brother, he is a liar; for he who doesn't love his brother whom he has seen, how can he love God whom he has not seen? This commandment we have from him, that he who loves God should also love his brother.

Song of Solomon 2:15

Take us the foxes, the little foxes, that spoil the vines: for our vines have tender grapes.

It's truly the 'little foxes' that can spoil the grapes. In other words it's the little things that can make the biggest differences. It's in the small act of a kind word or a genuine act of love that we make the biggest difference in the world. The Word says that it is in loving your brother (not a gender thing...that goes for sister too) that you truly love God and THAT makes all the difference in this world and the world to come.

- Day 147 -

Pneu·ma·tol·o·gy pronounced: n(y)oōmə' tälejē is the branch of Christian theology concerned with the Holy Spirit. WOW... you learn something new every day! I think the Holy Spirit is often the overlooked part of the Holy Trinity. God and Jesus get 'a lot of press' but the Holy Spirit doesn't seem to be spoken about as much.

John 14:26
But the Comforter, which is the Holy Ghost, whom the Father will send in my name, he shall teach you all things, and bring all things to your remembrance, whatsoever I have said unto you.
Psalm 51:11
Cast me not away from thy presence; and take not thy holy spirit from me.
Matthew 12:32
Whoever speaks a word against the Son of Man, it will be forgiven him; but whoever speaks against the Holy Spirit, it will not be forgiven him, neither in this age, nor in that which is to come.
Mark 3:29
but whoever may blaspheme against the Holy Spirit never has forgiveness, but is subject to eternal condemnation."

As you may have gathered, the Holy Spirit is a BIG DEAL. The Holy Spirit taught and comforted and protected the disciples after Jesus ascended to heaven and the Holy Spirit does the same for us today. We are baptized in the Holy Spirit and we are filled with the Holy Spirit. But, it's not a good idea to mess with the Holy Spirit. The 'unforgivable sin' concerns the Holy Spirit and the same warning is found in nearly all the gospels. Never, ever, under any circumstance blaspheme against the Holy Spirit...that won't end well for you...

- Day 148 -

You may have heard the phrase "God is Good" to which the reply is "All the time". The second person may even say afterward, "And all the time" to which the reply would be, "God is Good".

Exodus 33:19

He said, "I will make all my goodness pass before you, and will proclaim The Lord's name before you. I will be gracious to whom I will be gracious, and will show mercy on whom I will show mercy."

Mark 10:18

Jesus said to him, "Why do you call me good? No one is good except one—God.

James 1:17

Every good gift and every perfect gift is from above, coming down from the Father of lights, with whom can be no variation, nor turning shadow.

Everything I have I owe to Him. Everything I am I was led to by Him. My thanks in prayer to Him seems inadequate to fully describe how grateful I am that He has blessed me with so much joy in my life. God is Good all the time and All the time...

- Day 149 -

Yet another great sermon at church tonight Father Jared! He told a story of a pastor that was traveling down a road and came upon the most beautiful farm he had ever seen so he pulled over to take a closer look. Lush crops, beautiful plants, flowers everywhere and all perfectly groomed. The farmer was on the tractor taking care of the front yard. As the farmer got close to where the pastor was standing admiring the farm, he stopped to speak to the pastor. The pastor remarked to the farmer, "God has certainly blessed you with a magnificent farm!"...

Matthew 13:3-8

He spoke to them many things in parables, saying, "Behold, a farmer went out to sow. As he sowed, some seeds fell by the roadside, and the birds came and devoured them. Others fell on rocky ground, where they didn't have much soil, and immediately they sprang up, because they had no depth of earth. When the sun had risen, they were scorched. Because they had no root, they withered away. Others fell among thorns. The thorns grew up and choked them. Others fell on good soil, and yielded fruit: some one hundred times as much, some sixty, and some thirty.

Philippians 2:13

For it is God who works in you both to will and to work, for his good pleasure.

The farmer wiped the sweat off his face and turned to take a good long look around his beautiful farm. He then looked back at the pastor and replied, "Yes, He certainly has blessed us and we're grateful. But, you should have seen this place when He had it all to himself." The world may look pretty messed up right now, like the farm before the farmer got there but if we work the land and spread the Good News, the fields will be white for the harvest before we know it. "Our food is to do the will of Him who sent us, and to accomplish His work."- JESUS

- Day 150 -

What are we to do when we're asked by other people to be someone whom we are not or to do something which we don't feel we can do? We know who God created us to be and what our spiritual gifts are. Even if you don't know exactly, you probably have a pretty good idea. What happens if we pretend to be someone we are not or agree to do something that we don't feel comfortable doing to appease someone else?

Philippians 2:13

For it is God who works in you both to will and to work, for his good pleasure.

1 John 3:19-20

And by this we know that we are of the truth, and persuade our hearts before him, because if our heart condemns us, God is greater than our heart, and knows all things.

Galatians 1:10

For am I now seeking the favor of men, or of God? Or am I striving to please men? For if I were still pleasing men, I wouldn't be a servant of Christ.

The only one we need to appease is God and God alone. Never allow anyone to pressure you into being someone that God did not create you to be. Never allow anyone to guilt or coerce you into doing anything that is not within the set of gifts God has given you. Know who you are, Who's you are and what you were created to do. If you do not know yet, pray without ceasing on it.

- Day 151 -

Here's a word for you... Zeal. It means to have great energy or enthusiasm in pursuit of a cause or an objective. Seems people have a zeal for fine food, sports, social media, money, fame, and worldly possessions. All those things are temporary and in the long run they're meaningless.

Romans 10:2

For I testify about them that they have a zeal for God, but not according to knowledge.

Titus 2:14

Who gave himself for us, that he might redeem us from all iniquity, and purify for himself a people for his own possession, zealous for good works.

Psalm 69:9

For the zeal of your house consumes me. The reproaches of those who reproach you have fallen on me.

Romans 12:11

not lagging in zeal; fervent in spirit; serving the Lord;

When it comes to having great enthusiasm and energy for a cause, I can think of no cause greater than serving The Lord God Almighty. We see people stand up and cheer at the top of their lungs at a ball game. What if we had THAT kind of ZEAL for serving The Lord? What if we had THAT kind of Enthusiasm every time we shared the gospel or saved another soul for God? What are you demonstrating Zeal for in your life?

- Day 152 -

Seems everyone wants to be a leader today. It's not as 'cool' to be the follower. I once heard that "If you're not the lead dog, the view never changes." So why would you want to be the follower?

Luke 5:11
When they had brought their boats to land, they left everything, and followed him.
Matthew 4:25
Great multitudes from Galilee, Decapolis, Jerusalem, Judea and from beyond the Jordan followed him.
Matthew 19:21
Jesus said to him, "If you want to be perfect, go, sell what you have, and give to the poor, and you will have treasure in heaven; and come, follow me."
1 Peter 2:21
For to this you were called, because Christ also suffered for us, leaving you an example, that you should follow his steps,

When it comes right down to it, if you decide not to be a follower of God, then by default you will end up following Satan. That's not my opinion, that's biblical...Matthew 12:30. Perhaps in this world it's not in vogue to be a follower but as for me and my house, we will follow The Lord.

- Day 153 -

Here's a question that 'MATTERs': Is Quantum Physics compatible with a belief in God and what the Bible teaches? I mean, can you be smart enough to understand Quantum Physics, develop these theories and laws and still believe in God? You may be surprised at the answer. In fact, a famous experiment called the double slit experiment proves that matter can behave like waves and particles, solid and not solid At The Same Time. Kinda like…

John 20:19-20 When therefore it was evening, on that day, the first day of the week, and when the doors were locked where the disciples were assembled, for fear of the Jews, Jesus came and stood in the middle, and said to them, "Peace be to you." When he had said this, he showed them his hands and his side. The disciples therefore were glad when they saw the Lord.

John 20:26 After eight days again his disciples were inside, and Thomas was with them. Jesus came, the doors being locked, and stood in the middle, and said, "Peace be to you."

Mark 9:23 Jesus said unto him, If thou canst believe, all things [are] possible to him that believeth.

Matthew 14:29 He said, "Come!" Peter stepped down from the boat, and walked on the waters to come to Jesus.

Jesus passed through a door or a wall at least two times, walked on water and Peter was able to walk on water until he got scared and stopped believing he could. Jesus told us if we believe, all things are possible even stuff that's not solid actually being solid at the same time. Oh, yea, one last thing. John Polkinghorne, the guy who discovered the sub-nuclear particles known as quarks, a critical part of the quantum model became an Anglican priest. Quantum physics is totally compatible with the Bible's teachings about God and may even explain a little bit about how God accomplished some of His creative works. Check this out to learn a little more about the double slit experiment: http://bit.ly/1zPkJJd

- Day 154 -

The Bible makes some interesting claims about time and space. Einstein's theory of relativity states that at the speed of light, there is no time. If you ARE the Light and the Way, time could literally stand still for you. Though that sounds pretty unbelievable, the science is there to prove it and it makes some of the verses in the Bible seem a little more understandable...

Luke 4:5

The devil, leading him up on a high mountain, showed him all the kingdoms of the world in a moment of time.

1 Corinthians 15:51-53

Behold, I tell you a mystery. We will not all sleep, but we will all be changed, in a moment, in the twinkling of an eye, at the last trumpet. For the trumpet will sound, and the dead will be raised incorruptible, and we will be changed. For this perishable body must become imperishable, and this mortal must put on immortality.

Being shown all the countries of the world in one moment? Hanging out eating lunch one moment with this earthly body and in the next moment if you gave your life to Christ you'll be kneeling before God in an imperishable body with unspeakable joy? Yup. And the science is there to prove it. Not that God is confined by time, space or science as we know it but even by those parameters, it's possible. So when will this moment arrive? It will come like a thief in the night... you'll never know. All we know is that it will be very soon, but then again, time is relative to God. Are you ready? Why not get ready right now?

- Day 155 -

It's popular for people to take time off or travel so that they can 'find themself'. You hear this more and more today among young and old people alike. The question begs, where and when did they lose themself?

Matthew 10:39

He who seeks his life will lose it; and he who loses his life for my sake will find it.

I think Peterson's interpretation in The Message captures the essence of this verse best: *"If your first concern is to look after yourself, you'll never find yourself. But if you forget about yourself and look to me, you'll find both yourself and me."* (Matthew 10:39 MSG)

Jeremiah 1:5

"Before I formed you in the womb, I knew you. Before you were born, I sanctified you. I have appointed you a prophet to the nations."

I'm not convinced that these people are lost or somehow misplaced themselves. If you look in the mirror, there you are...found. It's more likely that somewhere along the way they lost God, not because God left but because they left God out of their life. Stop looking for yourself and start looking for God and in your renewed relationship with Him, you will find what you have been seeking. God knows exactly who you are. All you have to do is remember who's you are.

- Day 156 -

I just watched a movie on Netflix about the coral reefs. I never knew they were the single largest structure built by a living thing on the planet. And that they are dying (called bleaching) at an alarming rate. Turns out that they're a lot like humans so far as temperature goes. Just a few degrees higher and they die. How long could you live at 101.6 degrees instead of 98.6? In fact, in the last year 29% of all coral died on the Great Barrier Reef alone due to the warming of the oceans. The bummer is that it is likely due to the increased CO_2 in the atmosphere…caused by humans…

Genesis 2:15

The Lord God took the man, and put him into the garden of Eden to cultivate and keep it.

1 Corinthians 4:2

Here, moreover, it is required of stewards, that they be found faithful.

Revelation 11:18

The nations were angry, and your wrath came, as did the time for the dead to be judged, and to give your bondservants the prophets, their reward, as well as to the saints, and those who fear your name, to the small and the great; and to destroy those who destroy the earth."

God trusted mankind with the care of this beautiful world He created. He requires us to be trustworthy in our stewardship of the resources He provided and scripture warns that those that destroy the Earth will themselves be destroyed. Kinda makes sense doesn't it. Check out the film, Chasing Coral. It's definitely worth the watch!
 https://youtu.be/b6fHA9R2cKI

- Day 157 -

Priority- the fact or condition of being regarded or treated as more important. Have you had to stop and consider what your priorities are lately? A good rule of thumb is to prioritize in this order: God first, family second, everything else third... or at least that's the way I do it.

Matthew 6:33

But seek first God's Kingdom, and his righteousness; and all these things will be given to you as well.

Romans 12:2

Don't be conformed to this world, but be transformed by the renewing of your mind, so that you may prove what is the good, well-pleasing, and perfect will of God.

Luke 12:34

For where your treasure is, there will your heart be also.

Often it will take a serious problem or a crisis to determine if you have your priorities in line. Biblically there are verses to support priorities that put God first, spouse second, children third, then parents, then extended family 'in Christ' and then the rest of the world. Just yesterday my son called to report he was in an automobile accident. He said he was fine (and thank God he was indeed just shaken up) but the car was a total loss. It didn't take more than a moment to put him first and cancel my day at the office to go check his spine and help him handle the details of the car and insurance. Get into the habit of putting first things first. Have you had your priorities tested lately?

- Day 158 -

Here's an interesting word for you... Soterilogy. It's the study of salvation. Salvation is the saving of the soul from the consequences of sin. Salvation can only be obtained and is only made possible by and through the life, death and resurrection of the Lord and Savior, Jesus Christ.

Romans 1:16
For I am not ashamed of the Good News of Christ, for it is the power of God for salvation for everyone who believes; for the Jew first, and also for the Greek.
Philippians 1:19
For I know that this will turn out to my salvation, through your supplication and the supply of the Spirit of Jesus Christ,
2 Timothy 3:15
From infancy, you have known the holy Scriptures which are able to make you wise for salvation through faith, which is in Christ Jesus.
Hebrews 9:28
so Christ also, having been offered once to bear the sins of many, will appear a second time, without sin, to those who are eagerly waiting for him for salvation.

The consequence of sin is death. Romans 6:23 is pretty clear. Here's the good news: The Lord Jesus Christ has already paid for our sins through His death on the cross. All we need to do to claim this salvation is to repent of our sins, ask Jesus into your heart and make him your Lord and Savior. Soteriology is pretty simple. Our salvation has already been worked out for us. It is as simple as making a decision to serve our Creator.

- Day 159 -

Making a difficult decision that will affect the rest of your life is one of the toughest things you will have to do. We need to pray for God's guidance before we make our decision and we need to ask for humble obedience to accept the answer He gives us. Too often our decisions are influenced by fear, greed, selfish desires for an easy way out, comfort, ambition or prestige. How do we choose not necessarily what we want but what God wants for us?

Proverbs 3:5-6
Trust in The Lord with all your heart, and don't lean on your own understanding. In all your ways acknowledge him, and he will make your paths straight.
James 1:5

But if any of you lacks wisdom, let him ask of God, who gives to all liberally and without reproach; and it will be given to him.

Isaiah 30:21

and when you turn to the right hand, and when you turn to the left, your ears will hear a voice behind you, saying, "This is the way. Walk in it."

Have the strength, wisdom and fortitude to pray, "Lord God, what will you have me do? Please Lord, help me choose rightly. Hear this prayer of mine and send me an answer so very clear that I cannot mistake it. I ask this in Jesus' holy name." Here's the catch… if the answer is not what you were hoping for or the answer will make you lose favor with your friends, or if you know the answer is the right thing to do but it's not going to be the easiest thing to do… be obedient and do it anyway.

- Day 160 -

Poverty- the state of being extremely poor. Most of us have been poor at one point in our lives and most of us have had more than we actually needed at some point in our lives. I have also noticed that most of us are more often than not, somewhere in the middle. But, we have all heard a terrible story about someone that felt they could go on no more just because they were in a place where they didn't have enough of something they desired or needed...

2 Corinthians 8:9
For you know the grace of our Lord Jesus Christ, that, though he was rich, yet for your sakes he became poor, that you through his poverty might become rich.
Mark 12:44
for they all gave out of their abundance, but she, out of her poverty, gave all that she had to live on."
Proverbs 30:8
Remove far from me falsehood and lies. Give me neither poverty nor riches. Feed me with the food that is needful for me;
Proverbs 24:34
so your poverty will come as a robber, and your want as an armed man.

To anyone who has had much in their lives, poverty and the fear of what life might be like without abundance is often too much to bear. The Bible teaches that there are seasons in our lives that will change over time. Wealth will come and go but those that study The Word understand that over time, God will always provide enough Manna for the day to those that are faithful. In a fascinating display of faith, out of her poverty, the widow gave all she had as an offering to God. Display your Faith and have no Fear for God is with you.

- Day 161 -

Doing the 'right thing' in this world can often mean doing the hard thing, not the easy thing. Unfortunately, being righteous in your actions can be quite a risk. We risk being mocked and ridiculed for deciding not to drink when we are out with friends, for choosing not to use profanity when everyone around us curses and takes The Lord's name in vain, for choosing to tell the truth and not joining in when others are gossiping. When we choose the righteous path, we are likely not to be accepted by the world but the risk/reward relationship makes it all worth it.

Proverbs 11:18 Wicked people earn deceitful wages, but one who sows righteousness reaps a sure reward.

Proverbs 12:14 A man shall be satisfied with good by the fruit of his mouth. The work of a man's hands shall be rewarded to him.

Matthew 6:2 Therefore when you do merciful deeds, don't sound a trumpet before yourself, as the hypocrites do in the synagogues and in the streets, that they may get glory from men. Most certainly I tell you, they have received their reward.

Colossians 3:8 but now you also put them all away: anger, wrath, malice, slander, and shameful speaking out of your mouth.

In the investment world there is risk-reward relationship and that principle can apply to how you live out your life in faith as well. Low levels of risk are associated with low potential returns, whereas high levels of risk are associated with high potential returns. According to the risk-return tradeoff, investing yourself in living a Godly, Biblically guided life can render higher profits only if you are willing to accept the possibility of losing worldly things including friendships, fame and fortune because you have done the 'right things' instead of the popular things. What have you risked for Jesus...Lately?

- Day 162 -

Bitterness... what feelings does that word bring up? When was the last time you were bitter about something? Can you remember the last person that was embittered by YOU? It's interesting what the definition of bitterness is. It's the sharpness of taste, lack of sweetness and anger or disappointment at being treated unfairly, resentment.

Genesis 27:34

When Esau heard the words of his father, he cried with an exceeding great and bitter cry, and said to his father, "Bless me, even me also, my father."

Matthew 26:75

Peter remembered the word which Jesus had said to him, "Before the rooster crows, you will deny me three times." He went out and wept bitterly"

Revelation 10:10 I took the little book out of the angel's hand, and ate it up. It was as sweet as honey in my mouth. When I had eaten it, my stomach was made bitter.

Can you relate with John, the author of Revelation? Have you ever seen something so sweet that it was irresistible and then once you had it, it actually turned your stomach? What looks so good for us can actually be awful for us. Can you relate with Peter? Have you ever made a promise and despite your best efforts you were unable to keep it and later regretted it bitterly? Can you relate to Essau having had something that was yours wrongfully taken away making you feel bitter? The Bible promises forgiveness to ALL who are saved. Both the ones that have made others bitter and those that have been embittered by someone else shall have their tears wiped away and they will be comforted.

- Day 163 -

Recently my friend Wheeler made an observation, ""Trust, as they say, is extremely (if not "impossible") difficult to restore once broken. I'm not certain in my heart of hearts that it is or can be restored to "like-new"..." I thought we would go to the Bible and see if God has a thing or two to say about that tough subject.

Proverbs 3:5-6

Trust in The Lord with all your heart, and don't lean on your own understanding. In all your ways acknowledge him, and he will make your paths straight.

Hebrews 13:7

Trust your leaders, men who spoke to you the word of God, and considering the results of their conduct, imitate their faith.

1 Peter 5:5

Likewise, you younger ones, be subject to the elder. Yes, all of you clothe yourselves with humility, to subject yourselves to one another; for "God resists the proud, but gives grace to the humble."

The Bible talks a lot about trust. We are encouraged to trust God, trust our spiritual leaders and to trust one another. But, when this trust is broken, is it possible to rebuild and restore? To restore trust, the offending person must take full responsibility for their actions, accept the consequences and be willing to wait because it may take time...perhaps more than you expected for healing to take place. Trusting again requires the restoration of the belief that faith can take the place of uncertainty, fear and doubt and that hope rules over despair. With God, anything is possible.

- Day 164 -

Have you washed anyone's feet lately? Why not? I mean, it's biblical. Jesus actually set up an ordinance to do it. What? You've never heard about this? Well, check this out...

John 13:3-5, 12-17

3 Jesus, knowing that the Father had given all things into his hands, and that he came from God, and was going to God, 4 arose from supper, and laid aside his outer garments. He took a towel, and wrapped a towel around his waist. 5 Then he poured water into the basin, and began to wash the disciples' feet, and to wipe them with the towel that was wrapped around him.

12 So when he had washed their feet, put his outer garment back on, and sat down again, he said to them, "Do you know what I have done to you? 13 You call me, 'Teacher' and 'Lord.' You say so correctly, for so I am. 14 If I then, the Lord and the Teacher, have washed your feet, you also ought to wash one another's feet. 15 For I have given you an example, that you also should do as I have done to you. 16 Most certainly I tell you, a servant is not greater than his lord, neither one who is sent greater than he who sent him. 17 If you know these things, blessed are you if you do them.

Footwashing was Jesus' way of teaching us humility and the importance of serving others. If we are to become great among people, we must willingly and obediently become servant to them all. So, I ask again, whose feet have you washed...Lately? (metaphorically or literally speaking...)

- Day 165 -

If we are going to talk about being saved, at some point we need to consider what it is to be LOST. How can we help those that are lost become found and how does God respond to those that are LOST?

Ezekiel 34:16

I will seek that which was lost, and will bring back that which was driven away, and will bind up that which was broken, and will strengthen that which was sick: but the fat and the strong I will destroy; I will feed them in justice.

Luke 15:7

I tell you that even so there will be more joy in heaven over one lost sinner who repents, than over ninety-nine righteous people who need no repentance.

There is nothing that gives God more joy than when one of His lost children is 'found' or SAVED. Conversely, I'm sure there is nothing more devastating for God than one of His children that could have been saved but died while they were still lost. Check out the stories in the Bible about the lost sheep, the lost coin and the lost son. You will find that there is nothing more pleasing to God than to have the lost become found. Are you doing your part to find the lost and show them the way to become saved?

- Day 166 -

When someone looks at us out in the world, how will they know we are Christians? Being a Christian is about our faith and strongly held beliefs but how about our works? What type of works, words and behavior do those around us see us display in our daily walk?

John 13:35 By this everyone will know that you are my disciples, if you have love for one another."

1 John 4:8 He who doesn't love doesn't know God, for God is love.

Ephesians 4:32 And be kind to one another, tender hearted, forgiving each other, just as God also in Christ forgave you.

Galatians 5:22 But the fruit of the Spirit is love, joy, peace, patience, kindness, goodness, faith,

Philippians 2:4 each of you not just looking to his own things, but each of you also to the things of others.

They will know us by our LOVE first and foremost. Respect, selflessness, purity, grace patience, sacrifice, commitment, overwhelming Joy, kindness, faith, prayer, gratefulness, goodness, peacemakers, tender hearted and forgiving are also kinda important but LOVE covers them all. What do onlookers gleen from your daily walk with God?

- Day 167 -

What would a success formula from the Bible look like? What advice does God give that can ensure that your life and your chosen vocation will be a success?

Be confident -   Philippians 1:6
being confident of this very thing, that he who began a good work in you will complete it until the day of Jesus Christ.
Give freely-   Matthew 10:8
Heal the sick, cleanse the lepers, and cast out demons. Freely you received, so freely give.
Love unconditionally-   1 Corinthians 13:13
But now faith, hope, and love remain—these three. The greatest of these is love.
Serve with humility-   Luke 1:48
for he has looked at the humble state of his servant. For behold, from now on, all generations will call me blessed.
Accept everyone-   Mark 2:17
When Jesus heard it, he said to them, "Those who are healthy have no need for a physician, but those who are sick. I came not to call the righteous, but sinners to repentance."

Want to be successful in life and business? Be confident in what you do knowing that God is working through you. Give for the sake of giving, Love for the sake of loving, Serve for the sake of serving so that others may live their lives more abundantly. And, Accept everyone regardless of the condition of their heart, position in society or ability to pay you back for what you willingly give or do for them. Not what you were taught in business school? Perhaps you were just listening to the wrong Teacher.

- Day 168 -

One of my favorite bands is Jars of Clay. I heard them play a song at Soulfest last night that I've heard many times but last night the true meaning really struck me for the first time. It's called Dead Man. Part of the lyrics say, "So carry me. I'm just a dead man lying on the carpet. Can't find a heartbeat. Make me breathe. I wanna be a new man Tired of the old one. Out with the old plan."

2 Corinthians 5:17 Therefore if anyone is in Christ, he is a new creation. The old things have passed away. Behold, all things have become new.

Ephesians 4:24 and put on the new man, who in the likeness of God has been created in righteousness and holiness of truth.

Colossians 3:10 and have put on the new man, who is being renewed in knowledge after the image of his Creator,

Ezekiel 11:19 I will give them one heart, and I will put a new spirit within you; and I will take the stony heart out of their flesh, and will give them a heart of flesh;

How many of us are walking around spiritually dead? Somehow the enemy was able to use someone, something or a situation to turn you away from your walk of faith. As a doctor I would be able to read your blood pressure but as a minister, I would find you have a weak spiritual pulse, perhaps you are spiritually dead. Here is the GOOD NEWS. It's not too late. God can give you a New Heart, a New Spirit, and a new LIFE. In effect you will become a new creation in Christ. Is it time for a new plan?

- Day 169 -

Tonight there was a talk about refugees from the stage of Soulfest by a well known singer. Did you know that the definition of a refugee is a person who has been forced to flee their country in order to escape war, persecution, or natural disaster. As a country we voiced our discontent with allowing refugees into our country for safety reasons, but did you know who else was a 'refugee'?

Matthew 2:13-14

Now when they had departed, behold, an angel of the Lord appeared to Joseph in a dream, saying, "Arise and take the young child and his mother, and flee into Egypt, and stay there until I tell you, for Herod will seek the young child to destroy him." He arose and took the young child and his mother by night, and departed into Egypt,

Mark 6:11

Whoever will not receive you nor hear you, as you depart from there, shake off the dust that is under your feet for a testimony against them. Assuredly, I tell you, it will be more tolerable for Sodom and Gomorrah in the day of judgment than for that city!"

That's right, Jesus was indeed a refugee by definition. When His family arrived in Egypt, His family would have had to rely on the kindness of strangers and the local synagogue. As a result part of His ministry focused on helping those that are less fortunate. In fact, He talks about the importance of feeding the hungry, taking in the homeless, and clothing the naked as well as the consequences of choosing not to... (Matthew 25:31-46). So, this question of taking in the refugees becomes a little more personal. If we say no to taking in refugees, are we in effect telling Jesus, "Sucks to be you. You're not welcome here."? And what is the consequence of that?

- Day 170 -

Most of us have eyes but many can not see. Most of us have ears but we can not hear. All of us have a heart but some of us have a hard time loving. The Bible actually has a lot to say about it...

Matthew 13:16-17 "But blessed are your eyes, for they see; and your ears, for they hear. For most certainly I tell you that many prophets and righteous men desired to see the things which you see, and didn't see them; and to hear the things which you hear, and didn't hear them.

Romans 10:17 So faith comes by hearing, and hearing by the word of God.

Mark 4:12 that 'seeing they may see, and not perceive; and hearing they may hear, and not understand; lest perhaps they should turn again, and their sins should be forgiven them.'"

Acts 28:26-27 'Go and say to this people: When you hear what I say, you will not understand. When you see what I do, you will not comprehend. For the hearts of these people are hardened, and their ears cannot hear, and they have closed their eyes— so their eyes cannot see, and their ears cannot hear,   and their hearts cannot understand, and they cannot turn to me and let me heal them.'

Acts 9:18 Instantly something like scales fell from Saul's eyes, and he regained his sight. Then he got up and was baptized.

May the scales fall from your eyes so that you can see the beauty of the glory of The Lord. May you hear the Word of God and thus by hearing, be filled with faith. May you invite the risen Savior into your heart and really feel it love and be loved as if for the very first time. The power of Christ is transforming. With it the blind will see, the deaf will hear and the lost will be saved.

- Day 171 -

I find it enlightening to look at the definition of words to clarify their meanings. Take the word RENEW for example. It means to resume (an activity) after an interruption or to re-establish (a relationship). REFRESH means to give new strength or energy to; reinvigorate. When was the last time you interrupted your routine and did something to RENEW and REFRESH your body, mind and spirit?

Exodus 31:17
It is a sign between me and the children of Israel forever; for in six days Yahweh made heaven and earth, and on the seventh day he rested, and was refreshed.'"
Isaiah 40:31
But those who wait for The Lord will renew their strength. They will mount up with wings like eagles. They will run, and not be weary. They will walk, and not faint.
Song of Solomon 2:5
Strengthen me with raisins, refresh me with apples; For I am faint with love.
2 Corinthians 7:13
Therefore we have been comforted. In our comfort we rejoiced the more exceedingly for the joy of Titus, because his spirit has been refreshed by you all.

The Bible admonishes us to take time to rest at least once a week for a day to refresh ourselves as even God Himself did when He created the world. Sometimes we need to refresh our body with good, healthy food and sometimes we need to have our mind and spirit refreshed and renewed by stopping to WAIT for The Lord. We are also reminded in scripture to comfort others and by doing so, refresh their spirit. How was your weekend? Are you refreshed and renewed?

- Day 172 -

I was talking to my friend Levi today about stress and its effect on the body. It's easy to give advice on how to manage stress but it's easier said than done. We've all been there. Job cried out, "My heart is troubled, and doesn't rest. Days of affliction have come on me."(Job 30:27) Do Job's words resonate with you? What advice does God give us in the Bible about stress management?

John 14:27 (AMP) Peace I leave with you; My [perfect] peace I give to you; not as the world gives do I give to you. Do not let your heart be troubled, nor let it be afraid. [Let My perfect peace calm you in every circumstance and give you courage and strength for every challenge.]

Luke 10:41-42 Jesus answered her, "Martha, Martha, you are anxious and troubled about many things, but one thing is needed. Mary has chosen the good part, which will not be taken away from her." (which is to say, "don't sweat the small stuff.")

Philippians 4:6-7 In nothing be anxious, but in everything, by prayer and petition with thanksgiving, let your requests be made known to God. And the peace of God, which surpasses all understanding, will guard your hearts and your thoughts in Christ Jesus.

Philippians 4:13 I can do all things through Christ, who strengthens me.

This is just the tip of the iceberg. God gives lots of other great advice too like in Matthew 11:28-30, Deuteronomy 31:6 and James 1:2-4 just to name a few. The common theme in all this advice is to pray to God. Know that in Christ, you are strengthened and can do all things including overcoming stress or depression. And, when your burden seems too heavy to carry any longer, hand it over to Jesus. He will not only carry it for you but He will trade your stress for a peace that surpasses all understanding. He will grant you beauty for your ashes and Joy for your sorrow.

- Day 173 -

I just heard about a friend that has what appears to be, in the natural, a pretty severe case of cancer. But here's the part that is most important. He knows that MIRACLES are REAL and that God has the power and authority to perform a miracle for him. He also knows that if God does not grant this miracle, he will be called home to be with Jesus. Both of these outcomes are acceptable to him. Some might ask, "How could someone have that kind of strong faith?" Here's how…

Hebrews 2:4 God also testifying with them, both by signs and wonders, by various works of power, miracles, and by gifts of the Holy Spirit, according to his own will?

Jeremiah 32:27 Behold, I am Yahweh, the God of all flesh: is there anything too hard for me?

Job 5:8-9 "But as for me, I would seek God. I would commit my cause to God, who does great things that can't be fathomed, marvelous things without number;

Romans 8:38-39 For I am persuaded, that neither death, nor life, nor angels, nor principalities, nor things present, nor things to come, nor powers, nor height, nor depth, nor any other created thing, will be able to separate us from the love of God, which is in Christ Jesus our Lord.

My friend has this kind of faith because he has preached the Word of God and accepts the scriptures in full faith. Make no mistake, he is OK with either of the two outcomes in this situation but as for me, selfishly or not, I'm praying for the miracle. In my own walk, I am encouraged that strong faith and strength in The Lord provides us peace, comfort and courage when we encounter the most difficult times in our life. So I ask for your prayers for my friend Rick's miracle and more importantly, I ask you to pray as he would have you pray that God's Will Be Done.

- Day 174 -

My friend Paul Chapman, pastor of the Curtis Corner Baptist Church, wrote an awesome blog entitled 4 Undeniable reasons to spread the gospel. In it, he explains what motivates people to go soulwinning at home and give to missions around the world.

Luke 6:46

"Why do you call me, 'Lord, Lord,' and don't do the things which I say?

Romans 4:20

Yet, looking to the promise of God, he didn't waver through unbelief, but grew strong through faith, giving glory to God,

2 Corinthians 5:14

For the love of Christ constrains us; because we judge thus, that one died for all, therefore all died.

1 Corinthians 10:31

Whether therefore you eat, or drink, or whatever you do, do all to the glory of God.

Why would people give their time to go find the lost and win back their soul to God? Why would people give to missions around the world? To be obedient to God, to prove that true faith moves us to action, to show Jesus we truly love Him and to give glory to God by sharing the gospel. Want to learn more through Pastor Chapman's teachings? Check out his blog at www.paulechapman.com.

- Day 175 -

What does it mean to be a blessing to others? It seems that in today's society that it's common for believers to say, "God bless you" and that's good onto itself but what does that really mean? It seems easy to say, "I'll keep you in prayer" but how many of us really continue to pray for that person? What does the Bible say about how we can BE a blessing to others?

1 Peter 3:9
not rendering evil for evil, or insult for insult; but instead blessing; knowing that to this were you called, that you may inherit a blessing.

Hebrews 13:16

But don't forget to be doing good and sharing, for with such sacrifices God is well pleased.

1 Timothy 2:1

I exhort therefore, first of all, that petitions, prayers, intercessions, and givings of thanks, be made for all men:

Proverbs 16:24

Pleasant words are a honeycomb, sweet to the soul, and health to the bones.

The Bible encourages us to give each other kind words so just the act of saying 'God Bless You' is a great thing to do but I think it may be done too lackadaisical these days kind of like a reflex after a sneeze without much thought. We are called to really Be a blessing to others with both our words and deeds. When we say 'God Bless You' next time, let's really mean it and take a moment to say a prayer to God, write the person's name down and keep them in prayer. Maybe we need instead to say, ' how can I be a blessing to you?'

- Day 176 -

I think Bible verses about fearing God are among the most misunderstood of all the verses in the Bible. I hear people say, "I don't fear God, I only love God." They say that as if fearing God was a bad thing. The fact is that Great Fear IS Great Love. In fact, Fear could give you instantaneous wisdom that could actually save your life.

Proverbs 9:10

The fear of The Lord is the beginning of wisdom. The knowledge of the Holy One is understanding.

Psalm 34:11
Come, you children, listen to me. I will teach you the fear of Yahweh.
Proverbs 10:27
The fear of The Lord prolongs days, but the years of the wicked shall be shortened.

For those of us that are parents, I'm sure you loved your child when they were very young and they loved you but it's the respect for you and a healthy fear of you that saved their lives at least once. I'm sure you remember a time when they got too close to the electrical outlet or near a pan of boiling hot oil on the stove. You screamed out "NO" at the top of your lungs so loud that it startled them and scared them into stopping dead in their tracks so you had enough time to run over and pull them away. Wasn't it that FEAR of your voice and respect that 'prolonged their days', not their love for you? It's great that you love God, but true wisdom comes from the fear of God and it will prolong your days.

- Day 177 -

I heard a good sermon about Faith versus Fear. Many people go around worried and in fear that bad things are going to happen to them and more often than not, they're right. Other people go around believing that good things will happen to them in FAITH that God is in control and that he will favor them, give them abundance and see to it that no weapon formed against them could ever prevail and more often than not, they're right.

Matthew 21:22

All things, whatever you ask in prayer, believing, you will receive."

Isaiah 54:17
No weapon that is formed against you will prevail; and you will condemn every tongue that rises against you in judgment. This is the heritage of Yahweh's servants, and their righteousness is of me," says Yahweh.
Philippians 4:8

Finally, brothers, whatever things are true, whatever things are honorable, whatever things are just, whatever things are pure, whatever things are lovely, whatever things are of good report; if there is any virtue, and if there is any praise, think about these things.

Proverbs 18:21 Death and life are in the power of the tongue; those who love it will eat its fruit.

Instead of going around in Fear thinking and talking negatively about what 'could' happen, walk around in FAITH thinking and speaking positive words of praise expecting blessings and favor. In a timeless book by Dr. Norman Vincent Peale called The Power Of Positive Thinking, he says, "Our happiness depends on the habit of mind we cultivate." It really is Fear versus FAITH, mind over matter and remember, if you don't mind, it doesn't matter. What you think about, you truly bring about.

- Day 178 -

Have you ever heard the phrase, 'youth is wasted on the young'? As we get older, many of us wish that we were younger. We wish that we could have the strong body and sharp mind that we had when we were young. What does the Bible say about getting old gracefully?

2 Corinthians 4:16 Therefore we don't faint, but though our outward man is decaying, yet our inward man is renewed day by day.

Proverbs 20:29 The glory of young men is their strength. The splendor of old men is their gray hair.

Psalm 37:25 I have been young, and now am old, yet I have not seen the righteous forsaken, nor his children begging for bread.

Genesis 6:3 The Lord said, "My Spirit will not strive with man forever, because he also is flesh; so his days will be one hundred twenty years."

Job 12:12 With aged men is wisdom, in length of days understanding.

There's one thing for sure, even if we get 120 years on this Earth, no one is getting out of this life alive. We will all spend some time here equivalent to a flash in the pan of eternity and then our mortal body will return to dust. But, while we are here, we can age gracefully by remaining righteous. Though our hair turns gray, over time we gain more wisdom. Our prize for having lived a righteous life will be trading our perishable bodies for imperishable bodies as we become part of the body of Christ and live forever with Him.

- Day 179 -

Seems as though I'm bumping into more and more people that claim to be very "spiritual" but they are not religious. I have to admit, I don't really understand what that means. Spiritual means: 1. relating to or affecting the human spirit or soul as opposed to material or physical things. 2. relating to religion or religious belief. Religious means: relating to or believing in a religion, forming part of someone's thought about or worship of a divine being, or belonging or relating to a monastic order or other group of people who are united by their practice of religion. This seems to be a topic that gets people hot under the collar but let's take a look at it.

James 1:26 If anyone among you thinks himself to be religious while he doesn't bridle his tongue, but deceives his heart, this man's religion is worthless.

Romans 12:1(AMP) Therefore I urge you, brothers and sisters, by the mercies of God, to present your bodies [dedicating all of yourselves, set apart] as a living sacrifice, holy and well-pleasing to God, *which is* your rational (logical, intelligent) act of worship.

Galatians 5:22-23 But the fruit of the Spirit is love, joy, peace, patience, kindness, goodness, faith, gentleness, and self-control. Against such things there is no law.

Both religion and spirituality can miss the mark on having a relationship with God. Religion might focus too much on rituals where spirituality might focus too much on the spiritual world. Religion is valuable in that it teaches us that we have fallen short and need a savior and spirituality is valuable in that it reminds us that there is more that exists beyond the physical world. True religion points to Jesus Christ and through Him we become spiritually fulfilled. When studying the Bible, it becomes obvious that God seeks to have relationship with us through both the church and the Holy Spirit. Both are important and inseparable.

- Day 180 -

As a rule, I don't watch the news on TV or listen to it on the radio. I just find it so negative except the last story at 6:56 PM on ABC World News Tonight which is the person of the day or person of the week. That's the only 3 minutes of news a day I will consent to watch. I mean, what can you personally do about all the negativity, violence and the political circus? Lately everyone is afraid of another war. The Bible gives some advice about this…

Matthew 24:6-7

You will hear of wars and rumors of wars. See that you aren't troubled, for all this must happen, but the end is not yet. For nation will rise against nation, and kingdom against kingdom; and there will be famines, plagues, and earthquakes in various places.

Matthew 28:20

teaching them to observe all things that I commanded you. Behold, I am with you always, even to the end of the age." Amen.

Stop watching the news for a week and see how you feel without the stress about things you have no direct power to change. The Bible already foretold what they're going to say anyway. There will be wars and rumors of war along with starvation, diseases and natural disasters. No surprise here nor will it be a surprise how the story of humankind ends…it too is in The Book. How about we do something more productive than watching the news? How about we focus on loving the person next to us? What if everyone did that instead?

- Day 181 -

What is Contentment and how do we acquire it? Contentment is defined as a state of happiness and satisfaction. Doesn't that sound good? As it turns out, contentment is a gift from God.

Philippians 4:11-13

Not that I speak in respect to lack, for I have learned in whatever state I am, to be content in it. I know how to be humbled, and I know also how to abound. In everything and in all things I have learned the secret to being content is all situations, both to be filled and to be hungry, both to abound and to be in need. I can do all things through Christ, who strengthens me.

Hebrews 13:5

Be free from the love of money, content with such things as you have, for he has said, "I will in no way leave you, neither will I in any way forsake you."

How cool is it that there are answers to 'secrets' in the Bible? Above is an answer to a secret that is worth more than gold or gems. It's the secret to becoming happy and satisfied. SPOILER ALERT--- faith in Jesus Christ as our savior IS the secret. No one can take away your happiness or your satisfaction or safety or comfort or peace or wisdom or love or blessed assurance so long as you have Jesus in your heart. That's the 'secret' to being joyful always and giving thanks for ALL THINGS. Jesus is the secret to contentment. Let's not keep it a secret.

- Day 182 -

Discernment is such a troubling thing for many Christians. We often wonder if we're hearing the word of God or are we being deceived by the enemy? How do we discern between the two before we take action? Well, as fortune has it, God has some advice on this matter for us in the Bible.

James 1:5 But if any of you lacks wisdom, let him ask of God, who gives to all liberally and without reproach; and it will be given to him.

Psalm 25:9 He will guide the humble in justice. He will teach the humble his way.

Hebrews 5:14 But solid food is for those who are full grown, who by reason of use have their senses exercised to discern good and evil.

1 John 4:1 Beloved, don't believe every spirit, but test the spirits, whether they are of God, because many false prophets have gone out into the world.

How will we discern good from evil? By testing it against the Truth found in God's Word recorded in the Bible. So next time you have to make an important decision, sit quietly in prayer, ask for the answer and when you receive it, test it against what the Bible says. Deception and chaos is the work of the enemy but take comfort in the fact that our God is not a God of confusion, He is a God of peace and He will grant you wisdom. When in doubt, choose the light over the darkness, good over evil, right over wrong, eternal reward over temporary gain, and serving over being served.

- Day 183 -

Have you ever been in a public place like a restaurant, the airport or the mall and observed someone with a short haircut, great posture, and in good shape, speaking respectfully to those he/she greets and whether or not they were wearing a uniform or carrying a rucksack, you knew they were in the military? There's just something about their presence that's different. We as Christians should stand out in a crowd as well…

Leviticus 20:26 You shall be holy to me; for I, The Lord, am holy, and have set you apart from the peoples, that you should be mine.

John 13:35 By this everyone will know that you are my disciples, if you have love for one another."

Matthew 7:16-20 By their fruits you will know them. Do you gather grapes from thorns, or figs from thistles? Even so, every good tree produces good fruit; but the corrupt tree produces evil fruit. A good tree can't produce evil fruit, neither can a corrupt tree produce good fruit. Every tree that doesn't grow good fruit is cut down, and thrown into the fire. Therefore by their fruits you will know them.

We as Christians should stand out in a crowd. We should stand out in our community as the ones that love unconditionally, pray continually, are grateful for all things and exude the abounding joy of The Lord. We should be known as those that live lives that are dedicated to God. We should rejoice in the fact that we are set apart from all other people because Jesus lives in our heart. What do people see in you when you're in a public place? More importantly, WHO do they see in YOU?

- Day 184 -

Listening to the messages of this world can be confusing at best and dangerous at its worst. One of the messages we hear often is 'Trust noone and be a leader not a follower if you want to get ahead in life." Perhaps it's true that trusting in people is getting tougher but there's most certainly someone you can put your full trust in...

Proverbs 3:5-6
Trust in The Lord with all your heart, and don't lean on your own understanding. In all your ways acknowledge him, and he will make your paths straight.
Psalm 22:5
They cried to you, and were delivered. They trusted in you, and were not disappointed.
Daniel 6:23
Then was the king exceeding glad, and commanded that they should take Daniel up out of the den. So Daniel was taken up out of the den, and no kind of harm was found on him, because he had trusted in his God.
John 12:26
If anyone serves me, let him follow me. Where I am, there will my servant also be. If anyone serves me, the Father will honor him.

Know this- no matter what this world may tell you, you can ALWAYS trust God... AND... If you are humble enough to follow Him as His servant instead of trying to be the leader, you will receive more riches than you could possible imagine. So are you strong enough to trust in the Lord? Do you desire to be first? Are you willing to do what it takes to become great? Here's a few hints- (Mark 10:44 & 9:35, Matthew 20:26).

- Day 185 -

There are lots of people that get pretty upset when the topics of predestination and 'the elect' come up. If there are people who were elect or 'chosen' from before the foundation of time, there must also be 'un-elect' or those that were not chosen. From a human perspective, why would God create someone that was not elect? Why would a loving God do that? Is the word "elect" even in the Bible and is there a reference to people being 'chosen before time' or 'predestined' to be with God in heaven after this life on Earth?

Romans 8:28-30
We know that all things work together for good for those who love God, to those who are called according to his purpose. For whom he foreknew, he also predestined to be conformed to the image of his Son, that he might be the firstborn among many brothers. Whom he predestined, those he also called. Whom he called, those he also justified. Whom he justified, those he also glorified.

Ephesians 1:4-6
even as he chose us in him before the foundation of the world, that we would be holy and without defect before him in love; having predestined us for adoption as children through Jesus Christ to himself, according to the good pleasure of his desire, to the praise of the glory of his grace, by which he freely gave us favor in the Beloved,

Matthew 20:16
So the last will be first, and the first last. For many are called, but few are chosen."

Trust me, I know this is some tough stuff. Romans 9 explains that God is not unjust in any way and is sovereign over His creation. We, as humans, want to be in control of our own salvation. We want our Free Will not only to choose ice cream over an apple for dessert even if the ice cream isn't the best choice but we want to be able to choose Jesus as our Savior and heaven over eternal separation from God. As it turns out, the most important choice may not be within our purview and may already have been made for us. Still, through faith, we are to continue to preach the gospel and witness His elect come to salvation through His grace so that He alone may receive all the glory. Do you trust fully in God's plan?

- Day 186 -

Have you ever gotten on your hands and knees and begged God to intervene on your behalf or for someone that you care about? Have you ever negotiated with God making promises to Him in exchange for your prayer to be answered? It's easy to live life after those prayers are answered but what happens when your prayers go unanswered? How are we to respond? Well, this actually happened to David…

2 Samuel 12:16-23
David therefore begged God for the child; and David fasted, and went in, and lay all night on the ground. The elders of his house arose beside him, to raise him up from the earth: but he would not, and he didn't eat bread with them. On the seventh day, the child died. David's servants were afraid to tell him that the child was dead, for they said, "Behold, while the child was yet alive, we spoke to him, and he didn't listen to our voice. How will he then harm himself, if we tell him that the child is dead?" But when David saw that his servants were whispering together, David perceived that the child was dead; and David said to his servants, "Is the child dead?" They said, "He is dead."
  Then David arose from the earth, and washed, and anointed himself, and changed his clothing; and he came into The Lord's house, and worshiped. Then he came to his own house; and when he requested, they set bread before him, and he ate. Then his servants said to him, "What is this that you have done? You fasted and wept for the child while he was alive, but when the child was dead, you rose up and ate bread." He said, "While the child was yet alive, I fasted and wept; for I said, 'Who knows whether The Lord will not be gracious to me, that the child may live?' But now he is dead, why should I fast? Can I bring him back again? I will go to him (when I die), but he will not return to me."

Do you have a faith great enough to shift gears from begging God for your will to be done to acknowledging that His will and plan is more important than your desires? Have you strengthened your faith to the point where you could Give Thanks that His will was done even if it wasn't your will? Perhaps you don't need to imagine how David felt when he begged for God to save his son. David's response demonstrated God's grace in his life through the peace he found knowing that this life is not our final destination and that he would see his son again in that day which there is no sunset and no dawning.

- Day 187 -

Have you considered that we as Christians are a lot like glow in the dark frisbees? Expose the frisbee to the light and it begins to glow. Expose a person to the love and grace of God and that person becomes radiant.

Exodus 34:29
When Moses came down from Mount Sinai with the two tablets of the testimony in Moses' hand, when he came down from the mountain, Moses didn't know that the skin of his face was radiant by reason of his speaking with God.
John 8:12
Again, therefore, Jesus spoke to them, saying, "I am the light of the world. He who follows me will not walk in the darkness, but will have the light of life."
Psalm 34:5
They looked to him, and were radiant. Their faces shall never be covered with shame.
Revelation 21:23
The city has no need for the sun, neither of the moon, to shine, for the very glory of God illuminated it, and its lamp is the Lamb.

Just as the frisbee has no choice but to glow when it's exposed to the sun, we have no choice but to become radiant when exposed to God's grace and love. Once we become radiant, our commission is to go out and share this light with others. We are admonished to spread the light and never hide it under a bushel basket. We are to let our light shine before men; that they may see our good works, and glorify our Father who is in heaven.

- Day 188 -

Faith is a strong belief in God or in the doctrines of a religion, based on spiritual apprehension rather than proof; complete trust or confidence in someone or something. Hope is a feeling of expectation and desire for a certain thing to happen. Recently a friend made an interesting comment about faith and hope. What he said was, "Where faith exists and hope ends in disappointment, faith persists."

Hebrews 11:1
Now faith is assurance of things hoped for, proof of things not seen.
Habakkuk 2:4
Behold, his soul is puffed up. It is not upright in him, but the righteous will live by his faith.
Hebrews 3:14
For if we are faithful to the end, trusting God just as firmly as when we first believed, we will share in all that belongs to Christ.
Jeremiah 29:11
For I know the thoughts that I think toward you, says Yahweh, thoughts of peace, and not of evil, to give you hope and a future.
Psalm 42:11
Why are you in despair, my soul? Why are you disturbed within me? Hope in God! For I shall still praise him, the saving help of my countenance, and my God.

Listen, not everything we hope for or desire or even pray for will come to pass. Inevitably there will come disappointment. But, here's the important thing to remember, the one thing that can't be taken from you is your faith. It is with that faith that we take consolation in the fact that even though we may have hopes that are dashed, doors that are unopened and prayers that are unanswered, we trust that God knows what is best for us. God's delays are not His necessarily denials.

- Day 189 -

The Kingdom of God is an interesting and important part of our faith. Did you know that right after John the Baptist was jailed, the first message Jesus preached was about The Kingdom of God and it was also nearly the last thing Jesus talked about on the cross? Check out these three passages in the Bible at the beginning of His ministry and at the very end...

Mark 1:14-15 Now after John was taken into custody, Jesus came into Galilee, preaching the Good News of God's Kingdom, and saying, "The time is fulfilled, and God's Kingdom is at hand! Repent, and believe in the Good News."

Luke 17:20-21 Being asked by the Pharisees when God's Kingdom would come, he answered them, "God's Kingdom doesn't come with observation; neither will they say, 'Look, here!' or, 'Look, there!' for behold, God's Kingdom is within you."

Luke 23:39-43 One of the criminals who was hanged insulted him, saying, "If you are the Christ, save yourself and us!" But the other answered, and rebuking him said, "Don't you even fear God, seeing you are under the same condemnation? And we indeed justly, for we receive the due reward for our deeds, but this man has done nothing wrong." He said to Jesus, "Lord, remember me when you come into your Kingdom." Jesus said to him, "Assuredly I tell you, today you will be with me in Paradise."

The Kingdom of God or the Kingdom of Heaven are synonymous in the Bible. There are also many meanings for it throughout the Bible but in general it refers to the eternal rule of our one sovereign God both here on Earth and throughout all creation. The kingdom was the first message Jesus preached about. To be a part of that eternal kingdom, we are taught it takes repentance and belief in the Good News. Even the criminal on the cross next to him knew about the kingdom to come, and was granted forgiveness and entrance into the Kingdom of Heaven... a true death bed conversion. So, If you stopped breathing right now, are you sure we would meet up again in the Kingdom of Heaven? If not, admit your sins against God's law, repent of those sins, ask Jesus into your heart and life and make Him your savior. If you did that, you were born again and I'll see you in the Kingdom.

- Day 190 -

LEGACY- something that is passed on to family, friends or to the world including reputation, a gift or property. Someday we'll all die and at our funeral there will be a moment in time where friends, family and most importantly your children will stand to say a word or two about you. And what they say will really matter. We are God's children. What we say about Him really matters.

Psalm 150 [Full Chapter]
Praise Yah! Praise God in his sanctuary! Praise him in his heavens for his acts of power! Praise him for his mighty acts! Praise him according to his excellent greatness! Praise him with the sounding of the trumpet! Praise him with harp and lyre! ...
Luke 19:37
As he was now getting near, at the descent of the Mount of Olives, the whole multitude of the disciples began to rejoice and praise God with a loud voice for all the mighty works which they had seen,

What people say about you is nothing compared to what you say about God. When you rise, praise Him. When you go about your daily business, praise Him. When you go to sleep at night, praise Him. Look at the legacy He has left you... a life of abundance, peace, calm, comfort and as the cherry on top He has given you access to eternal life with Him.

- Day 191 -

Here's a tough one to think about much less to sum up in two paragraphs and a few verses but let's give it a try. Is it true that we are made up of three separate and distinct parts? Body- Soul- and Spirit. Body is pretty easy to understand. That's the 'meat suit" we wear or the "temple of God". But what's the difference between the soul and the spirit?

Hebrews 4:12 For the word of God is living and active, and sharper than any two-edged sword, piercing even to the dividing of soul and spirit, of both joints and marrow, and is able to discern the thoughts and intentions of the heart.

Matthew 26:41 Watch and pray, that you don't enter into temptation. The spirit indeed is willing, but the flesh is weak."

Matthew 27:50 Jesus cried again with a loud voice, and yielded up his spirit.

Job 30:25 Didn't I weep for him who was in trouble? Wasn't my soul grieved for the needy?

Our body is our temporary home for our soul and our spirit. Soul literally means life. We have souls, our pets have souls and all living things have souls because they have "life". But, it is the Spirit within us that truly makes us human. It is our spirit that was made in the image of God. It is our spirit that makes us yearn for our connection to our Creator. It is like a bucket within our heart that seeks to be full of our God and when we do not have the connection to our God, it creates an emptiness within us, a thirst that can not be quenched. Our Spirit, when in relationship with God makes us whole and complete. The soul is the "life" that animates our "meat suit". The spirit is the immaterial part of us that connects us to God.

- Day 192 -

Fasting is an interesting concept. Our bodies need food to provide the basic building blocks to repair itself and the same food provides the fuel for us to sustain life in our physical body. Fasting is talked about in the Bible in more than 20 verses. Fasting can actually be beneficial to your physical health when done properly but the real benefit of fasting may be for your spiritual health.

Matthew 6:16-18 "Moreover when you fast, don't be like the hypocrites, with sad faces. For they disfigure their faces, that they may be seen by men to be fasting. Most certainly I tell you, they have received their reward. But you, when you fast, anoint your head, and wash your face; so that you are not seen by men to be fasting, but by your Father who is in secret, and your Father, who sees in secret, will reward you.

Mark 9:28-29 When he had come into the house, his disciples asked him privately, "Why couldn't we cast it out?" He said to them, "This kind can come out by nothing, except by prayer and fasting."

Daniel 6:18-19 Then the king went to his palace, and passed the night fasting; neither were instruments of music brought before him: and his sleep fled from him. Then the king arose very early in the morning, and went in haste to the den of lions.

When we're fasting from food or some other activity that we enjoy, we can feast on God's Word, praising Him and praying with less distractions. Listen carefully and prayerfully for God's guidance on when to fast and what specific need you are to fast for. There certainly is a right way and a wrong way to do a food fast so get credible information on how to do it properly. If you feel compelled to fast but are mentally or physically unable to do a food fast, what's something meaningful you could give up for a period of time to draw nearer to God?

- Day 193 -

Endurance- the fact or power of enduring an unpleasant or difficult process or situation without giving way. Are you going through a difficult situation? Do you feel as though you are being 'tested'? Do you feel as though you are running a marathon, you're tired and you can't quite see the finish line yet? You're not alone…

James 1:2-4 Count it all joy, my brothers, when you fall into various temptations, knowing that the testing of your faith produces endurance. Let endurance have its perfect work, that you may be perfect and complete, lacking in nothing.

Revelation 2:19 "I know your works, your love, faith, service, patient endurance, and that your last works are more than the first.

Hebrews 10:36 For you need endurance so that, having done the will of God, you may receive the promise.

Ecclesiastes 9:11 I returned, and saw under the sun, that the race is not to the swift, nor the battle to the strong, neither yet bread to the wise, nor yet riches to men of understanding, nor yet favor to men of skill; but time and chance happen to them all.

In the natural, running and winning a long race requires strong physical stamina. But, in the spiritual, winning our 'race' does not necessarily require strength, riches or some special skill. Winning at Life requires faith. With faith, you are never alone in your race. God is with you always. With God, you can not only endure the trial, He will propel you forward and help you win your race.

- Day 194 -

One of my young patients overheard me having a spiritual talk with his Mom. I asked her why she thought that we are brought closest to God in our lowest and darkest times. In other words, it seems that we are brought closest to God when we are brought to our knees. Phillip said something profound. He said it's like a trampoline... you have to go really far down into the trampoline if you want to be brought up really high into the air... WOW...

2 Corinthians 1:3-4

Blessed be the God and Father of our Lord Jesus Christ, the Father of mercies and God of all comfort; who comforts us in all our affliction, that we may be able to comfort those who are in any affliction, through the comfort with which we ourselves are comforted by God.

Ezra 9:5

At the evening offering I arose up from my fasting, even with my garment and my robe torn; and I fell on my knees, and spread out my hands to Yahweh my God;

Ruth 2:13
Then she said, "Let me find favor in your sight, my lord, because you have comforted me, and because you have spoken kindly to your servant, though I am not as one of your servants."

In our lowest and darkest times, when we are afflicted and brought to our knees, we draw near to God and we are comforted by Him. No person could ever stand as tall as when they are kneeling before God. The parable of the trampoline stands true. The lower we are thrust down by the enemy, the faster and higher we are drawn up to God where He provides peace and comfort that surpasses all understanding. When have you felt closest to God in your life?

- Day 195 -

In the Old Testament God's chosen people, the Jewish people, were admonished not to sin which amounted to not breaking the 10 commandments. Since they were human and it was nearly impossible not to break the commandments, nearly all the people (but one) sinned. In order to 'cover' their sins they were to make a sacrifice to God (Leviticus 4:20). Just one problem. They needed to make a perfect sacrifice to cover their sins perfectly. That turns out to be nearly impossible too (Hebrews 10:4)...

Leviticus 4:20

Thus shall he do with the bull; as he did with the bull of the sin offering, so shall he do with this; and the priest shall make atonement for them, and they shall be forgiven.

Hebrews 10:4

For it is impossible that the blood of bulls and goats should take away sins.

Hebrews 10:10-12

by which will we have been sanctified through the offering of the body of Jesus Christ once for all. Every priest indeed stands day by day serving and often offering the same sacrifices, which can never take away sins, but he, when he had offered one sacrifice for sins forever, sat down on the right hand of God;

Imperfect sacrifices cover sins imperfectly. The Perfect Sacrifice of Jesus Christ didn't just cover sins perfectly, it takes care of our sins For Good. Because of Jesus, there's no longer a need to offer sacrifices for our sins. Our slate is wiped clean and our path has been cleared all the way to heaven so that we may abide with God eternally.

- Day 196 -

The book of Job is an interesting read. Three of his buddies come to visit him when he is on his sick bed and after a long silence, they begin to accuse him of breaking God's law. It's obvious to them that there's no way God would allow him to be punished in body and spirit if he didn't do something that 'pissed off' God!

Galatians 6:1
Brothers, even if a man is caught in some fault, you who are spiritual must restore such a one in a spirit of gentleness; looking to yourself so that you also aren't tempted.
Luke 17:3
Be careful. If your brother sins against you, rebuke him. If he repents, forgive him.
James 5:19-20
Brothers, if any among you wanders from the truth and someone turns him back, let him know that he who turns a sinner from the error of his way will save a soul from death and will cover a multitude of sins.
1 Timothy 5:1-2
Don't rebuke an older man, but exhort him as a father; the younger men as brothers; the elder women as mothers; the younger as sisters, in all purity.

Well, as it turns out, Job's friends were wrong. His friends assumed he must've done something wrong but we all know what happens when you 'assume', right? Job happened to be God's most faithful servant at the time. His friends were trying to 'help' him in the only way they knew how. The above verses explain how we should effectively and biblically carry out the ministry of correction. Correction should be done tactfully, out of concern, with gentleness and love after having prayed good and long for guidance. You don't want to be caught having assumed anything do you?

- Day 197 -

Have you ever bought one of those single serving containers of ice cream? You know, the half gallon size. I don't know about you but when I start eating ice cream, there's no off button. There's the devil on one shoulder saying, "MMMmmm, look at that delicious ice cream. Keep eating it. Who knows the next time you'll get some?" On the other shoulder is my conscience saying, "Don't do it. Have some willpower. It's not good for you." It's the old story... Temptation versus Willpower, good vs. evil, God vs. the enemy.

1 Corinthians 10:13 No temptation has taken you except what is common to man. God is faithful, who will not allow you to be tempted above what you are able, but will with the temptation also make the way of escape, that you may be able to endure it.

Matthew 6:13 Bring us not into temptation, but deliver us from the evil one. For yours is the Kingdom, the power, and the glory forever. Amen. '

James 1:2-4 Count it all joy, my brothers, when you fall into various temptations, knowing that the testing of your faith produces endurance. Let endurance have its perfect work, that you may be perfect and complete, lacking in nothing.

Jesus himself was tempted in the desert after 40 days of fasting. He knows our pain. Willpower is just simply not enough to overcome temptation. It takes faith, endurance, prayer and an ability to find the 'way of escape' that God has provided for us. In most cases, it's just easier to remove the temptation than to rely on willpower. But, when the temptation is unavoidable, rely on the power of The Holy Spirit whom the Father will send to us in Jesus's name to guide our actions.

- Day 198 -

In a world that appears to be upside down, how about we keep today's Bible minute simple. Let's just talk about LOVE.

Mark 12:30-31
you shall love the Lord your God with all your heart, and with all your soul, and with all your mind, and with all your strength.' This is the first commandment. The second is like this, 'You shall love your neighbor as yourself.' There is no other commandment greater than these."
1 Corinthians 16:14
Let all that you do be done in love.
1 Peter 4:8
And above all things be earnest in your love among yourselves, for love covers a multitude of sins.
1 John 4:18-19
There is no fear in love; but perfect love casts out fear, because fear has punishment. He who fears is not made perfect in love. We love him, because he first loved us.
1 John 4:8
He who doesn't love doesn't know God, for God is love.
Song of Solomon 8:7
Many waters cannot quench love, neither can floods drown it. If a man would give all the wealth of his house for love, he would be utterly scorned.

Keep it simple. Want to change the world and turn it rightside up again? Just love God by unconditionally loving all the people you encounter each day. What would the world look like if everyone just loved God and all His children?

- Day 199 -

Have you been praying for something or someone and you don't see the results you've been asking for? Have you been faithful to God and waiting in expectancy but now you're beginning to get frustrated, discouraged, bitter or sour?

James 1:6-7
But let him ask in faith, without any doubting, for he who doubts is like a wave of the sea, driven by the wind and tossed. For let that man not think that he will receive anything from the Lord.
Matthew 8:8
The centurion answered, "Lord, I'm not worthy for you to come under my roof. Just say the word, and my servant will be healed.
Proverbs 15:29
The LORD is far from the wicked, But He hears the prayer of the righteous.
Mark 11:24
Therefore I tell you, all things whatever you pray and ask for, believe that you have received them, and you shall have them.
John 14:13-14
Whatever you will ask in my name, that will I do, that the Father may be glorified in the Son. If you will ask anything in my name, I will do it.

Take a deep breath, put those negative thoughts out of your mind and don't loose faith. Keep praying and thanking God that whatever you have been praying for WILL come to pass. Let's keep praying with the conviction of the Centurion, with complete faith in God, in the name of Jesus.

- Day 200 -

Many of us have watched a family pet get sick and begin to suffer in pain. We are left with an agonizing decision. Do we allow them to continue to suffer or do we do put them to sleep and end their suffering even if it means that we begin our own process of grieving their loss? The real question is at what point does our selfish desire end compassion begin?

Proverbs 18:1
An unfriendly man pursues selfishness, and defies all sound judgment.
Isaiah 49:13
Sing, heavens; and be joyful, earth; and break out into singing, mountains: for The Lord has comforted his people, and will have compassion on his afflicted.
Lamentations 3:32
For though he cause grief, yet he will have compassion according to the multitude of his loving kindnesses.
Luke 7:13
When the Lord saw her, he had compassion on her, and said to her, "Don't cry."

Once again, the Bible gives us sound advice we can use to guide us in our most difficult times. Through His Word, He warns us that our selfish desires will ruin our judgment. But, God also demonstrates through His Word how compassion can end suffering. In our compassion, demonstrated by our willingness to end suffering above our own desires, we get a glimpse into our Savior's mind as He demonstrated His willingness to make the ultimate sacrifice to prevent our suffering. I pray we all look for opportunities to show compassion and as a result ease or end someone's suffering.

- Day 201 -

I'm not sure this is going to be a Bible minute or a personal reflection but here goes. Have you ever had food poisoning or a really bad stomach virus? I did recently. I left work early and was in my bed by 11 AM. By 11 PM I was still in bed going back and forth with fevers, nausea, and the feeling an alien child was attempting to claw it's way out of my gut. At one point the pain was so intense that I literally told God that "I had a really good life so if he couldn't stop the pain, I was completely OK with Him taking me home instead".

Revelation 21:4
He will wipe away from them every tear from their eyes. Death will be no more; neither will there be mourning, nor crying, nor pain, any more. The first things have passed away."
Job 14:22
But his flesh on him has pain, and his soul within him mourns."
Psalm 69:29
But I am in pain and distress. Let your salvation, God, protect me.
1 Peter 3:18
Because Christ also suffered for sins once, the righteous for the unrighteous, that he might bring you to God; being put to death in the flesh, but made alive in the spirit;

193 passages about suffering in the Bible and 212 about pain. God doesn't take this topic lightly and He's no stranger to it. Jesus knows what you're experiencing first hand. Our affliction came unwelcomed by us. Jesus willingly allowed himself to be lead to the cross to suffer in pain and die for our sins. So when we're suffering in pain know that Jesus is right there comforting us and if the flesh does cease to take another breath, our soul will live with Him for eternity because of the salvation He offered and we accepted.

- Day 202 -

One of the true mentors of my faith, Dr. Robert H. Schuller once said this, "If you listen to your fears, you will die never knowing what a great person you might have been."

Deuteronomy 31:6
Be strong and courageous. Don't be afraid or scared of them; for The Lord your God himself is who goes with you. He will not fail you nor forsake you."
Hebrews 13:6
So that with good courage we say, "The Lord is my helper. I will not fear. What can man do to me?"
Isaiah 41:13
For I, The Lord your God, will hold your right hand, saying to you, 'Don't be afraid. I will help you.'
2 Timothy 1:7
For God didn't give us a spirit of fear, but of power, love, and self-control.

Repeat after me- "NO FEAR HERE! Jesus Christ is my Savior. There's NO FEAR HERE!" Cast out all fear! Evict it from your life so that you can live it more fully. No weapon formed against you will prosper. If God be for you, who can be against you? NO FEAR HERE! HALLELUJAH!!! AMEN!!!

- Day 203 -

Have you ever prayed fervently for something? I mean on your hands and knees kind of praying. Maybe you even began bargaining with God making promises that you'll keep contingent upon God 'making good' on your request? Maybe it was a prayer of desperation and 'desperate times called for desperate measures'. As it turns out, you're not alone.

1 Samuel 1:6-20
(read Hannah's story it's worth it but here's verse 11 and 20)
11 She vowed a vow, and said, "The Lord of Armies, if you will indeed look at the affliction of your servant, and remember me, and not forget your servant, but will give to your servant a boy, then I will give him to The Lord all the days of his life, and no razor shall come on his head."
20 When the time had come, Hannah conceived, and bore a son; and she named him Samuel, saying, "Because I have asked him of Yahweh."
Hebrews 5:7-8
Jesus, in the days of his flesh, having offered up prayers and petitions with strong crying and tears to him who was able to save him from death, and having been heard for his godly fear, though he was a Son, yet learned obedience by the things which he suffered.

The two things both Hannah and Jesus had in common were their strong faith and fervent prayers. Hannah begged and pleaded and even bargained with God and was granted the desires of her heart. Jesus cried to God until tears fell from His eyes asking that the cup be taken from Him but in the end His prayers were answered in a different way so that His Father's will could be done. Are you capable of praying fervently and being grateful for the outcome and still loving God even if your prayers aren't answered exactly they way you wanted them to be?

- Day 204 -

Showing kindness to someone is just good manners that your parents taught you. But, how about showing kindness to those that don't deserve it? THAT kind of kindness imitates the kind of kindness that God demonstrates towards us….

Luke 6:35
But love your enemies, and do good, and lend, expecting nothing back; and your reward will be great, and you will be children of the Most High; for he is kind toward the unthankful and evil.
Romans 12:14
Bless those who persecute you; bless, and don't curse.
Matthew 5:43-46
"You have heard that it was said, 'You shall love your neighbor and hate your enemy.' But I tell you, love your enemies, bless those who curse you, do good to those who hate you, and pray for those who mistreat you and persecute you, that you may be children of your Father who is in heaven. For he makes his sun to rise on the evil and the good, and sends rain on the just and the unjust. For if you love those who love you, what reward do you have? Don't even the tax collectors do the same?

Ohhhhh, I don't know about you, but this is going to be a tough one for me to live out! Love your enemies? Be kind to the people that you know are not being kind to you, your friends or family? And wait a minute…we're supposed to not just be nice to people that piss us off…we're called to pray for them? Yes, yes and yes. So who have you been upset with, even considered an enemy, that you can take time to genuinely pray for today?

- Day 205 -

What's the deal with praying to saints or Mary? It really is a Catholic thing and many of us go to Catholic church so what does the Bible have to say about that? Just so you know, the official Catholic position is that we don't pray TO saints, we merely ask the saints or Mary to pray on our behalf. But is a prayer from the saints on our behalf more powerful or effective than us going directly to God?

Hebrews 4:16
Let us therefore draw near with boldness to the throne of grace, that we may receive mercy, and may find grace for help in time of need.
Colossians 3:17
Whatever you do, in word or in deed, do all in the name of the Lord Jesus, giving thanks to God the Father, through him.
Romans 8:26-27
In the same way, the Spirit also helps our weaknesses, for we don't know how to pray as we ought. But the Spirit himself makes intercession for us with groanings which can't be uttered. He who searches the hearts knows what is on the Spirit's mind, because he makes intercession for the saints according to God.

The Bible lists at least three ways that you can get prayers to God. First is by boldly approaching the throne through prayer directly to God Himself. Second is by praying through Jesus and in His name. Lastly, the Holy Spirit can help us in our weakness and intercede with prayer for us. After long search in the Bible, I am unable to find a verse that suggests that we should ask people that have died to pray for us even if they have been "beatified" or "canonized" by the Pope. So, don't kill the messenger. I love the Catholic church however doctrine and the Bible should be congruent. How do you get your prayers through to God?

- Day 206 -

This world drains the positivity out of people. We are bombarded with negativity and stress from all angles. You don't even need to watch the nightly news anymore to hear about all the terrible things going on. Bad news travels at the speed of light (or at least the speed of the internet). What this world needs is more POSITIVITY. More hope, more faith, more love, more possibility thinking and positive thinkers. Even God encourages us to be positive thinkers in the Bible.

Philippians 4:8
Finally, brothers, whatever things are true, whatever things are honorable, whatever things are just, whatever things are pure, whatever things are lovely, whatever things are of good report; if there is any virtue, and if there is any praise, think about these things.
Proverbs 17:22
A cheerful heart makes good medicine, but a crushed spirit dries up the bones.
Ephesians 5:20
giving thanks always concerning all things in the name of our Lord Jesus Christ, to God, even the Father;
Philippians 4:13
I can do all things through Christ, who strengthens me.

"To become a happy person have a clean soul, eyes that see romance in the commonplace, a child's heart, and spiritual simplicity. Keep your heart free from hate, your mind from worry. Live simply, expect little, give much. Scatter sunshine, forget self, think of others. Try this for a week and you will be surprised."
― Norman Vincent Peale, The Power of Positive Thinking

- Day 207 -

Here's another tough topic to talk about. Violence and Murder. Violence is a behavior involving physical force intended to hurt, damage, or kill someone or something. Seems pretty clear cut that we as followers of Jesus should not commit an act of violence or murder another human being. So, what about wars? Some parts of the Bible seem to imply that it's OK to bear a sword against evildoers. But something doesn't feel quite right or congruent about being violent or even worse, committing murder.

Exodus 20:13
You shall not murder.
Matthew 5:21-22
"You have heard that it was said to the ancient ones, 'You shall not murder;' and 'Whoever murders will be in danger of the judgment.' But I tell you, that everyone who is angry with his brother without a cause will be in danger of the judgment; and whoever says to his brother, 'Raca!' will be in danger of the council; and whoever says, 'You fool!' will be in danger of the fire of Gehenna.
Proverbs 3:31
Don't envy the man of violence. Choose none of his ways.

Jesus instructed us not to murder and went a step further to say that we shouldn't even get angry without 'just cause'. Over and over He gives us the same instructions to 'turn the other cheek', 'repay no one evil for evil'. In the same breath, God seems to approve of David slaying the Giant and many others that took up the sword as God's instruments of righteousness. As for me, I'm going to error on the side of caution. Prayer and love beat violence and anger any day of the week. Let's pray that we'll have the wisdom to discern when violence in the name of self defense is warranted and that we will never have to put our wisdom to the test.

Gospel, from the Old English gōdspel, from gōd 'good' + spel 'news means the teaching or revelation of Christ and/or the record of Jesus' life and teaching in the first four books of the New Testament. The Bible instructs us to go forth and preach the Gospel. What exactly does that mean? Does that mean that we should be on the lookout for anyone that's doing something contrary to the commandments or teachings of Jesus and call them out on it and 'correct them' OR does it mean we should seek out opportunities to tell people about the saving grace of Jesus so that they will believe and be baptized?

Mark 16:15-16
He said to them, "Go into all the world, and preach the Good News to the whole creation. He who believes and is baptized will be saved; but he who disbelieves will be condemned.

Proverbs 15:1
A gentle answer turns away wrath, but a harsh word stirs up anger.

Perhaps the old adage, "You catch more flies with honey than with vinegar" might apply here. If we judge others by the Word, particularly those who are not yet saved, it's likely to offend them. Being offended, gives the devil a foothold on them. On the other hand, fear of offending is one of the primary ways the devil steals, kills and destroys a person's testimony. It's a balancing act. So where does that leave us? How about we focus on sharing, with love, just ONE MESSAGE- The Good News, The Gōdspel.

- Day 209 -

I heard a great sermon on the radio today from a pastor in Texas. He commented on hurricane Irma which hit Florida. One interesting part of that storm was that the ocean was pushed back away from the beaches exposing the sea floor. It looked like the beaches were forever changed. But, once the storm passed, the storm surge came in with great speed and force and not only brought the ocean water back but it overflowed onto the land. Sometimes in our lives, storms will push us back and it may seem that we will never recover...

Proverbs 24:16
for a righteous man falls seven times, and rises up again; but the wicked are overthrown by calamity.
Micah 7:8
Don't rejoice against me, my enemy. When I fall, I will arise. When I sit in darkness, The Lord will be a light to me.
Job 13:15
Behold, he will kill me. I have no hope. Nevertheless, I will maintain my ways before him.

The storms in our life are merely setbacks. They only last for a season. Setbacks are really just set-ups for success. Lots of people in the Bible had huge setbacks. Moses was a murderer and came back to deliver his people to the promised land. David was a murderer and adulterer but through confession and repentance he repaired his relationship with God and became an effective king. Joseph, through no fault of his own, was sold into slavery but was elevated by God to the second most powerful person in Egypt. Job lost everything but through faith and integrity, everything was restored to him double. Peter denied Jesus 3 times but went on to lead the church. If Moses, David, Joseph, Job and Peter could survive the storm and make their comeback, so can you. If you've been pushed out to sea by a storm in your life, remember that the storm surge is coming and it will bring you back into a place of overflow and abundance.

- Day 210 -

What could be more personal and private than your own thoughts? What could be more secure places than your own heart and mind? Ever have a conversation with someone and in your heart and mind you disagree with them but you say that you agree with them just to keep the peace? Well, when it comes to our own thoughts and what goes on in our heart and mind, it's not quite as private as you may think especially when it come to God.

Psalm 7:9
Oh let the wickedness of the wicked come to an end, but establish the righteous; their minds and hearts are searched by the righteous God.
Jeremiah 17:10
I, The Lord, search the mind, I try the heart, even to give every man according to his ways, according to the fruit of his doings.
Ezekiel 11:5
The Lord's Spirit fell on me, and he said to me, Speak, Yahweh says: Thus you have said, house of Israel; for I know the things that come into your mind.
1 Peter 4:7
But the end of all things is near. Therefore be of sound mind, self-controlled, and sober in prayer.

God's ability to see into our heart and our mind is a double edged sword for sure! On one hand, He is able to see into our mind to know our thoughts and prayers before we speak them and He knows the desires of our heart. On the other hand, He knows when we are thinking unholy, impure thoughts. We are living in the flesh so our thoughts are susceptible to the desires of the flesh. Our job is to try to live according to the Spirit within the flesh for the mind of the spirit is life and peace but the mind of the flesh leads to death. Easier said than done...

- Day 211 -

Courage is defined as mental or moral strength to venture, persevere, and withstand danger, fear, or difficulty. In this world and in this time courage is needed to survive, press forward and thrive. It takes courage to stand for the truth in a world full of lies. It takes courage to live a godly life in a godless culture. It takes courage to preach the gospel to those who would prefer not to hear it.

Deuteronomy 31:6
Be strong and courageous. Don't be afraid or scared of them; for The Lord your God himself is who goes with you. He will not fail you nor forsake you."
Psalm 31:24
Be strong, and let your heart take courage, all you who hope in The Lord.
2 Corinthians 5:8
We are courageous, I say, and are willing rather to be absent from the body, and to be at home with the Lord.
Hebrews 13:6
So that with good courage we say, "The Lord is my helper. I will not fear. What can man do to me?"

God grant me the serenity to accept the things I cannot change; courage to change the things I can; and wisdom to know the difference. Living one day at a time; enjoying one moment at a time; accepting hardships as the pathway to peace; taking, as He did, this sinful world as it is, not as I would have it; trusting that He will make all things right if I surrender to His Will; that I may be reasonably happy in this life and supremely happy with Him forever in the next. Amen. - Reinhold Niebuhr

- Day 212 -

I recently heard a great Bible teaching about making sure we don't keep bad company. The minister told a story about a person that goes out into their backyard after a heavy rain with beautiful white gloves on. The go right to the muddiest part of the yard and start rolling around in the mud and making mud pies…

1 Corinthians 15:33
Don't be deceived! "Evil companionships corrupt good morals."
Proverbs 13:20
One who walks with wise men grows wise, but a companion of fools suffers harm.
1 Corinthians 5:11
But as it is, I wrote to you not to associate with anyone who is called a brother who is a sexual sinner, or covetous, or an idolater, or a slanderer, or a drunkard, or an extortionist. Don't even eat with such a person.
Psalm 26:4-5
I do not sit with deceitful men, Nor will I go with pretenders. I hate the assembly of evildoers, And I will not sit with the wicked.

The result of the story above is that the beautiful white gloves always become muddy but the mud never becomes 'glovey'. The glove doesn't come off on the mud, the mud always comes off on the glove. Bad company is a lot like mud. Bad company always corrupts good people. Lord God, please surround us with good company and protect us from evil.

- Day 213 -

What is Sanctification? To sanctify is to literally "set apart for particular use in a special purpose or work and to make holy or sacred." Etymologically, "sanctify" derives from the Latin verb sanctificare which in turn derives from sanctus "holy" and facere "to make". What does the Bible say about sanctification?

John 17:16-18 (a quote from Jesus)
They are not of the world even as I am not of the world. Sanctify them in your truth. Your word is truth. As you sent me into the world, even so I have sent them into the world.
Romans 6:22
But now, being made free from sin, and having become servants of God, you have your fruit of sanctification, and the result of eternal life.
1 Corinthians 1:30
Because of him, you are in Christ Jesus, who was made to us wisdom from God, and righteousness and sanctification, and redemption:
Hebrews 10:10
by which will we have been sanctified through the offering of the body of Jesus Christ once for all.

Did you get that? We are made holy, we are sanctified because Jesus offered His own body for our sins. In the Old Testament every year the Jewish people had to make a sacrifice to 'cover' their sins. With Jesus a sacrifice was made once to remove sins for all and never needs to be done again. If we have accepted Jesus as our savior, we have been washed from sin and we willingly and lovingly serve God by serving man with our talents and gifts. Oh yeah, one other perk... eternal life with God. Have you been sanctified?

- Day 214 -

Have you ever sat expectantly, anxiously waiting for something to happen or for some decision to be made that will affect your life or for results of an important test to come back? How did you feel inside? Was there fear, worry or doubt in your mind? Those feelings are absolutely normal but as Christians we are given the power to cast fear, worry and doubt out of our lives...

1 Peter 5:7
casting all your worries on him, because he cares for you.
Revelation 2:10
Have no fear of the things which you are about to suffer. Behold, the devil is about to throw some of you into prison, that you may be tested; and you will have oppression for ten days. Be faithful to death, and I will give you the crown of life.
James 1:6
But let him ask in faith, without any doubting, for he who doubts is like a wave of the sea, driven by the wind and tossed.

As we sit and wait for decisions, results or outcomes, we can cast all our worries on Him. We can banish our fear knowing that our faith will get us through even the toughest of times. We can discard our doubt as we come boldly to the throne and ask for our prayers to be answered. We as Christians take comfort in knowing that whatever the outcome, He is with us and His right hand strengthens us.

- Day 215 -

I'm a big fan of respecting everyone's faith journey. Having said that, biblically, there are no atheists or agnostics in hell. The Bible clearly demonstrates that once they realize they're in hell... they believe (know) God. One account of a man in just that predicament begs Father Abraham to warn his 5 brothers in order that they may believe that there is only one true God and that heaven and hell are real places so that they would be saved from his predicament.

Luke 16:19-31 There was a certain rich man, which was clothed in purple and fine linen, and fared sumptuously every day: And there was a certain beggar named Lazarus, which was laid at his gate, full of sores, And desiring to be fed with the crumbs which fell from the rich man's table: moreover the dogs came and licked his sores. And it came to pass, that the beggar died, and was carried by the angels into Abraham's bosom: the rich man also died, and was buried; And in hell he lift up his eyes, being in torments, and seeth Abraham afar off, and Lazarus in his bosom. And he cried and said, Father Abraham, have mercy on me, and send Lazarus, that he may dip the tip of his finger in water, and cool my tongue; for I am tormented in this flame. But Abraham said, Son, remember that thou in thy lifetime receivedst thy good things, and likewise Lazarus evil things: but now he is comforted, and thou art tormented. And beside all this, between us and you there is a great gulf fixed: so that they which would pass from hence to you cannot; neither can they pass to us, that would come from thence. Then he said, I pray thee therefore, father, that thou wouldest send him to my father's house: For I have five brethren; that he may testify unto them, lest they also come into this place of torment. Abraham saith unto him, They have Moses and the prophets; let them hear them. And he said, Nay, father Abraham: but if one went unto them from the dead, they will repent. And he said unto him, If they hear not Moses and the prophets, neither will they be persuaded, though one rose from the dead.

I believe that the faith of an atheist and an agnostic is WAY GREATER than that of a Christian. As Christians, we need only repent and believe in Christ as our Savior to be saved from an eternity of torment separated from our Creator. Atheists and Agnostics have to believe that the oldest and most accurately kept text in the world and all the rest of us are wrong and they're betting their life on it.

- Day 216 -

God encourages us to ask questions about our faith. What a shallow faith it would be if we couldn't question it. In fact, it is in receiving answers to our most challenging questions that our faith is strengthened. In the Gospel of Luke, both Zacharias and Mary question the Angel Gabriel. What happened as a result of questioning the angel is recorded in the gospel and the outcomes are quite different for Zacharias and Mary. Why?

Luke 1:18-20
Zacharias said to the angel, "How can I be sure of this? For I am an old man, and my wife is well advanced in years." The angel answered him, "I am Gabriel, who stands in the presence of God. I was sent to speak to you, and to bring you this good news. Behold, you will be silent and not able to speak, until the day that these things will happen, because you didn't believe my words, which will be fulfilled in their proper time."

Luke 1:34-38
Mary said to the angel, "How can this be, seeing I am a virgin?" The angel answered her, "The Holy Spirit will come on you, and the power of the Most High will overshadow you. Therefore also the holy one who is born from you will be called the Son of God. Behold, Elizabeth, your relative, also has conceived a son in her old age; and this is the sixth month with her who was called barren. For nothing spoken by God is impossible." Mary said, "Behold, the servant of the Lord; let it be done to me according to your word."

So, what's the deal? Both were told they were having a child, both asked how it could possibly come to pass. Zacharias was very old, Mary was a virgin so you can understand both their questions but there were some important differences. Zacharias asks, "How can I be sure" in other words, 'How do I know I can trust you? Prove it.' Mary asks, "How can this be" in other words, she doesn't doubt that it's the truth and asks her question with a spirit of wonder and amazement. Listen, God welcomes all questions. In fact He knows your questions before you ask them. But, be careful you ask them respectfully in the right spirit or you may not like the answers.

- Day 217 -

I don't care who you are, everyone wants to live a happy, joyful life but there's no instruction book we're given when we're born on how to accomplish that. Or is there?

Psalm 100:2
Serve The Lord with gladness. Come before his presence with singing.
Psalm 51:12
Restore to me the joy of your salvation. Uphold me with a willing spirit.
Hebrews 6:10
For God is not unrighteous, so as to forget your work and the labor of love which you showed toward his name, in that you served his people, and still do serve them.

If you want to live a joyful life, live your life out in joyful service to others. It's really that simple. In fact a 2014 study by the Pew Research Center in Washington, DC confirmed that "Those who serve are more content and happy with their life than those who do not serve the Lord and others." It's not just biblical advice, it's a scientific and statistical fact. So, what are you waiting for? Go serve God by serving His children with the talents you were given and joy will fill your heart.

- Day 218 -

Fire is such an interesting thing. Nearly everyone loves to sit in front of the fireplace in the dark enjoying the warmth and the glow of the fire dancing on the logs. Interestingly, if we were to be awoken in the middle of the night to the smell of smoke and the sound of the fire alarm going off, the same fire would instill fear in our heart. So fire is something that we both love and are afraid of but we should always show it great respect.

Exodus 3:1-6
Now Moses was keeping the flock of Jethro, his father-in-law, the priest of Midian, and he led the flock to the back of the wilderness, and came to God's mountain, to Horeb. God's angel appeared to him in a flame of fire out of the middle of a bush. He looked, and behold, the bush burned with fire, and the bush was not consumed. Moses said, "I will turn aside now, and see this great sight, why the bush is not burnt." When The Lord saw that he turned aside to see, God called to him out of the middle of the bush, and said, "Moses! Moses!" He said, "Here I am." He said, "Don't come close. Take your sandals off of your feet, for the place you are standing on is holy ground." Moreover he said, "I am the God of your father, the God of Abraham, the God of Isaac, and the God of Jacob." Moses hid his face; for he was afraid to look at God.

Interesting that God chose fire as the way He appeared to Moses. I'm sure the warmth of God was felt by Moses atop the mountain which comforted him but the power and strength of the fire also caused him to be afraid. Fire is a great analogy for our God. Let's follow Moses' example and draw near to the warmth and comfort of The Lord while remembering to be respectful of His power and might.

- Day 219 -

Doing something new, especially something that you previously spoke out against can be a scary, uncomfortable thing. But, as we grow older, we gain new insights, new wisdom. Sometimes we come to a fork in the road of life and we are forced to rethink things and make a decision we previously wouldn't have considered. The road leading to belief and faith is often a long and winding road and other times it's an exit that comes upon us quickly.

Acts 9:1-22 But Saul, still breathing threats and slaughter against the disciples of the Lord, went to the high priest, and asked for letters from him to the synagogues of Damascus, that if he found any who were of the Way, whether men or women, he might bring them bound to Jerusalem. As he traveled, he got close to Damascus, and suddenly a light from the sky shone around him. He fell on the earth, and heard a voice saying to him, "Saul, Saul, why do you persecute me?" He said, "Who are you, Lord?" The Lord said, "I am Jesus, whom you are persecuting. But rise up, and enter into the city, and you will be told what you must do."... Saul arose from the ground, and when his eyes were opened, he saw no one. They led him by the hand, and brought him into Damascus. He was without sight for three days, and neither ate nor drank.   ...(Ananias was sent by The Lord to restore Saul's sight)... Immediately something like scales fell from his eyes, and he received his sight. He arose and was baptized... Immediately in the synagogues he proclaimed the Christ, that he is the Son of God. All who heard him were amazed, and said, "Isn't this he who in Jerusalem made havoc of those who called on this name? And he had come here intending to bring them bound before the chief priests!" But Saul increased more in strength, and confounded the Jews who lived at Damascus, proving that this is the Christ.

If you're absolutely sure that Jesus is not the Son of God and you think that you can get to heaven on your own, search your heart again reflecting on Saul's experience. When Saul's eyes were opened, he became Paul and went on to write the majority of the New Testament. Perhaps it's time to make a radical change by asking God for forgiveness and allowing Jesus to enter your heart. What would your future look like with Jesus, and unconditional love in your heart?

- Day 220 -

Making difficult decisions is one of the toughest things we have to do. Usually we make decisions based on our best guess at what the outcome of an event will be; however, Esther and her uncle Mordecai made their decisions on what was right and trusted God to work out the details.

Esther 4:8, 10-11, 15-17
8 He also gave him the copy of the writing of the decree that was given out in Shushan to destroy them, to show it to Esther, and to declare it to her, and to urge her to go in to the king, to make supplication to him, and to make request before him, for her people.

10 Then Esther spoke to Hathach, and gave him a message to Mordecai: 11 "All the king's servants, and the people of the king's provinces, know, that whoever, whether man or woman, comes to the king into the inner court without being called, there is one law for him, that he be put to death, except those to whom the king might hold out the golden scepter, that he may live. I have not been called to come in to the king these thirty days."... 15 Then Esther asked them to answer Mordecai, 16 "Go, gather together all the Jews who are present in Shushan, and fast for me, and neither eat nor drink three days, night or day. I and my maidens will also fast the same way. Then I will go in to the king, which is against the law; and if I perish, I perish." 17 So Mordecai went his way, and did according to all that Esther had commanded him.

So, you might have guessed how Esther's story ends... Esther made the difficult decision to speak to the king and she influenced him to save all the Jews from death. Next time you're confronted with a difficult decision, try not to take the easy way out. Instead, DO THE RIGHT THING and trust God to work out the details.

Everyone can use a little encouragement.

- Day 221 -

Here's an interesting thing to think about. God created time but He is not bound by time. That is, He exists outside the parameters of time and space yet He is with us in this very moment. He is the beginning and the end and He hears your prayers in real time, in our time.

2 Peter 3:8
But don't forget this one thing, beloved, that one day is with the Lord as a thousand years, and a thousand years as one day.

Psalm 102:24-27
I said, "My God, don't take me away in the middle of my days. Your years are throughout all generations. Of old, you laid the foundation of the earth. The heavens are the work of your hands. They will perish, but you will endure. Yes, all of them will wear out like a garment. You will change them like a cloak, and they will be changed. But you are the same. Your years will have no end.

1 John 5:13
These things I have written to you who believe in the name of the Son of God, that you may know that you have eternal life, and that you may continue to believe in the name of the Son of God.

Einstein studied time and space in his theory of relativity. Even he must have had trouble Imagining a time where time itself becomes infinite and unending. A time with no sickness, no pain, just unending joy. As believers, we don't have to imagine that for very long as our time fast approaches when we will stand before Jesus in that day that has no sunset and no dawning. Be confident in Jesus and you can be confident in the promise of eternity with God.

- Day 222 -

GLORY... Now that's a great word to describe our Lord God Almighty! Glory actually means magnificence or great beauty. There are over 360 verses in the Bible that talk about the magnificence and beauty of God and talk about God's Glory.

Psalm 3:3
But you, The Lord, are a shield around me, my Glory, and the one who lifts up my head.
Psalm 19:1
The heavens declare the glory of God. The expanse shows his handiwork.
Ezekiel 43:2
Behold, the glory of the God of Israel came from the way of the east: and his voice was like the sound of many waters; and the earth shined with his glory.
Matthew 6:13
Bring us not into temptation, but deliver us from the evil one. For yours is the Kingdom, the power, and the glory forever. Amen. '

Magnificent, splendid, spectacular, impressive, striking, glorious, superb, majestic, awesome, awe-inspiring, breathtaking. Beautiful, attractive, pretty, handsome, lovely, charming, delightful, appealing, engaging, stunning, graceful, exquisite. Magnificent and Beautiful, our God is truly Glorious. Amen.

- Day 223 -

Have you ever gotten so upset that you did something that you regretted? Maybe you said something that was hurtful. Maybe you became violent. Maybe you just thought something terrible and prayed for something bad to happen to the person that got you upset. Believe it or not, you're not alone. Even God has done that...

Genesis 6:5
The Lord saw that the wickedness of man was great in the earth, and that every imagination of the thoughts of man's heart was continually only evil.
Genesis 6:6
The Lord was sorry that he had made man on the earth, and it grieved him in his heart.
Genesis 6:7
The Lord said, "I will destroy man whom I have created from the surface of the ground—man, along with animals, creeping things, and birds of the sky—for I am sorry that I have made them."
Genesis 8:21
The Lord smelled the pleasant aroma. Yahweh said in his heart, "I will not again curse the ground any more for man's sake because the imagination of man's heart is evil from his youth. I will never again strike every living thing, as I have done.

Do you ever wonder if God is still upset with the evil in His creation? Look at how crazy, upside down, immoral and out of control our world is. It's full of sin no matter where you look. Let's take a moment to give thanks that God holds back His own wrath so that there's time for another person to come to Jesus.

- Day 224 -

It seems there's one thing people yearn for today, Peace of Mind. Peace of Mind, what does that really mean? It means being completely calm stress-free, worry free and anxiety free. Sounds good? If Peace of Mind sounds good, how about Perfect Peace of mind? Wanna know how to achieve that? I thought you did...

Isaiah 26:3
Thou will keep him in perfect peace, whose mind is stayed on thee: because he trusteth in thee.
Philippians 4:6-7
In nothing be anxious, but in everything, by prayer and petition with thanksgiving, let your requests be made known to God. And the peace of God, which surpasses all understanding, will guard your hearts and your thoughts in Christ Jesus.
2 Corinthians 9:15
Now thanks be to God for his unspeakable gift!

So, how do we acquire Perfect Peace of Mind? Instead of being distracted by the nonsense in the media about politics, violence, and immorality, focus your mind on God. Pray more, give thanks more and allow God to guard your heart and mind through Jesus. Talk about an unspeakably good gift! Perfect Peace of Mind can be ours and we have the instruction manual on how to obtain it. It's called the Bible. Check it out.

- Day 225 -

We need to acquire an abundance mentality. We were not created to be in a state of lack and want. Even in the face of our enemies, a table is prepared for us. Consider this: sickness is an enemy, lack is an enemy, depression is an enemy, fear is an enemy, sometimes even our own bad decisions are an enemy and can lead us into valleys of lack and want in our life...

Psalm 23: 1-6 (KJV)
The Lord is my shepherd; I shall not want. He maketh me to lie down in green pastures: he leadeth me beside the still waters. He restoreth my soul: he leadeth me in the paths of righteousness for his name's sake. Yea, though I walk through the valley of the shadow of death, I will fear no evil: for thou art with me; thy rod and thy staff they comfort me. Thou preparest a table before me in the presence of mine enemies: thou anointest my head with oil; my cup runneth over. Surely goodness and mercy shall follow me all the days of my life: and I will dwell in the house of the Lord for ever.

Did you get that rod and staff part? God uses His rod and staff to correct us and to guide us back to a better path which will lead us out of the valley to a place of comfort where He can console us. All those enemies listed above are no match for our God and even in their presence, our cup (which is our life) runs over with the abundance He pours into us. Feel like you're in a valley? Fear no evil and trust God to lead you to a green pasture.

- Day 226 -

We've all got a sickness, a terminal condition. Some try to medicate it but the pain won't go away. The cure… Everybody's searching for it, Everybody's reaching out, Trying to grab a hold of something real. Only one thing can satisfy us, fill up the void inside us, there's never been a heart it couldn't heal.

Mark 2:17
When Jesus heard it, he said to them, "Those who are healthy have no need for a physician, but those who are sick. I came not to call the righteous, but sinners to repentance."
Ephesians 3:17-19
that Christ may dwell in your hearts through faith; to the end that you, being rooted and grounded in love, may be strengthened to comprehend with all the saints what is the width and length and height and depth, and to know Christ's love which surpasses knowledge, that you may be filled with all the fullness of God.
Romans 15:13
Now may the God of hope fill you with all joy and peace in believing, that you may abound in hope, in the power of the Holy Spirit.

See the eyes of a million faces looking for it in a million places. Only one can save us… Jesus. You are the doctor, healer and father to the orphan without a home. We fell into darkness, lost till you found us. You are the remedy we're looking for. Jesus, you are the cure.
(inspired by the song The Cure by the band Unspoken)
http://bit.ly/2yvIhtY

- Day 227 -

Every time you're out for a walk and pass by a simple ROCK on the ground, does it remind you of anything? If not, perhaps the following verses will allow you have a simple ROCK remind you of our Lord God, your Rock and Redeemer, your Saviour and your Salvation.

1 Samuel 2:2
There is no one as holy as The Lord, For there is no one besides you, nor is there any rock like our God.
Deuteronomy 32:4
The Rock, his work is perfect, for all his ways are just. A God of faithfulness who does no wrong, just and right is he.
Luke 6:47-48
Everyone who comes to me, and hears my words, and does them, I will show you who he is like. He is like a man building a house, who dug and went deep, and laid a foundation on the rock. When a flood arose, the stream broke against that house, and could not shake it, because it was founded on the rock.
1 Corinthians 10:4
and all drank the same spiritual drink. For they drank of a spiritual rock that followed them, and the rock was Christ.

Jesus Christ is our Rock. The next time you see a big rock while outside, really study it. Notice that it was here long before we were. Consider that it will be here long after we are gone. Feel how strong and solid it is. Imagine how sturdy a house would be if it were built and secured to a rock. Now imagine how sturdy and secure your life would be if you secured yourself to Jesus.

- Day 228 -

Trust is a tough thing to give and usually it must be earned. Once trust is lost, it's exceedingly difficult to earn back. We've all heard that phrase, 'trust in The Lord'. What does it mean to really and truly Trust in The Lord?

Proverbs 3:5-6
Trust in The Lord with all your heart, and don't lean on your own understanding. In all your ways acknowledge him, and he will make your paths straight.
2 Kings 18:5
He trusted in The Lord, the God of Israel; so that after him was no one like him among all the kings of Judah, nor among them that were before him.
Psalm 56:4
In God, I praise his word. In God, I put my trust. I will not be afraid. What can flesh do to me?
2 Corinthians 1:9
Yes, we ourselves have had the sentence of death within ourselves, that we should not trust in ourselves, but in God who raises the dead,

Trusting in God is something more than just obeying His commandments. Trusting involves placing our belief and confidence in Him during every step of our journey, the good times and more importantly in the challenging times. Trusting God means trusting His Word, not our heart and that's not easy. What's the reward for freely giving your trust to The Lord? Straight paths, freedom from fear and life everlasting. In whom do you put YOUR trust?

- Day 229 -

Every once in awhile, we get to a bump in the road where things just seem as though they're not going our way. We can even feel as though we're being tested. If you're finding it hard to make sense of it all, God's Word provides the answers, the strength and the the comfort you seek.

James 1:12
Blessed is the man that endureth temptation: for when he is tried, he shall receive the crown of life, which the Lord hath promised to them that love him.
Jeremiah 29:11
For I know the thoughts that I think toward you, says The Lord, thoughts of peace, and not of evil, to give you hope and a future.
Habakkuk 3:17-18
For though the fig tree doesn't flourish, nor fruit be in the vines; the labor of the olive fails, the fields yield no food; the flocks are cut off from the fold, and there is no herd in the stalls: yet I will rejoice in The Lord. I will be joyful in the God of my salvation!
Hebrews 6:10
For God is not unrighteous (unfair), so as to forget your work and the labor of love which you showed toward his name, in that you served the saints (his people), and still do serve them.

I usually tie up the Bible minute in a nice bow in this third paragraph... not today. A new friend of mine suggested I leave that up to you. Take a moment to reflect on the idea that things don't always go our way or that we feel 'tested' from time to time, meditate on the verses above and maybe seek out others that apply and write your own 'third paragraph' below if you feel so moved...

- Day 230 -

Have you ever heard the phrase, 'What you think about, you bring about'? Truly what we focus on is what we get in life. What is the Bible's advice on what to focus on?

Colossians 3:2
Set your mind on the things that are above, not on the things that are on the earth.
Romans 8:5
For those who live according to the flesh set their minds on the things of the flesh, but those who live according to the Spirit, the things of the Spirit.
Philippians 4:8
Finally, brothers, whatever things are true, whatever things are honorable, whatever things are just, whatever things are pure, whatever things are lovely, whatever things are of good report; if there is any virtue, and if there is any praise, think about these things.
1 Peter 5:8
Be sober and self-controlled. Be watchful. Your adversary, the devil, walks around like a roaring lion, seeking whom he may devour.

If you're watching the news on TV, shut it off until they start sharing good news. If you see the glass half empty, take another look. You'll also notice that it's half full. Focusing on the darkness? Turn around and face the light. Want to occupy your mind with truth, honor, purity, beauty, goodness, virtue and praise? Take time to focus on God.

- Day 231 -

For King And Country have a song called God forgive us. Some of the powerful lyrics expose our angst that often our prayers go up with no reply, that our doubt is often greater than our faith and that has left us spiritually broke and often broken...

Isaiah 59:2
But your iniquities have separated you and your God, and your sins have hidden his face from you, so that he will not hear.
James 4:3
You ask, and don't receive, because you ask with wrong motives, so that you may spend it for your pleasures.
Psalm 13:2
How long shall my soul be in doubt, having sorrow in my heart every day? How long shall my enemy triumph over me?
Matthew 28:17
And when they saw him, they worshipped him: but some doubted.
Matt 21:21
Jesus answered and said unto them, Verily I say unto you, If ye have faith, and doubt not, ye shall not only do this which is done to the fig tree, but also if ye shall say unto this mountain, Be thou removed, and be thou cast into the sea; it shall be done.

"A slave to our uncertainty, Help us with our unbelief. Oh, oh God forgive us. Young and old, black and white, Rich and poor, there's no divide. Hear the mighty, hear the powerless, singing...Oh God forgive us. Oh God forgive us."- by For King And Country

- Day 232 -

It is so important to surround yourself with people with strong faith. Life is a marathon, not a sprint. Along the way, you will run on parts of the path that are flat, you will run on parts of the path that are downhill and feel like a breeze and there will be parts of your path that are nearly a vertical climb uphill. It is during those times that these friends of faith will be there to give you advice to look at scriptures like these...

Romans 5:3
Not only this, but we also rejoice in our sufferings, knowing that suffering produces perseverance;
Lamentations 3:21-24
This I recall to my mind; therefore have I hope. It is because of The Lord's loving kindnesses that we are not consumed, because his compassion doesn't fail. They are new every morning; great is your faithfulness. The Lord is my portion, says my soul; therefore will I hope in him.
Isaiah 41:10-13
Don't you be afraid, for I am with you. Don't be dismayed, for I am your God. I will strengthen you. Yes, I will help you. Yes, I will uphold you with the right hand of my righteousness. Behold, all those who are incensed against you will be disappointed and confounded. Those who strive with you will be like nothing, and shall perish. You will seek them, and won't find them, even those who contend with you. Those who war against you will be as nothing,as a non-existent thing. For I, Yahweh your God, will hold your right hand, saying to you, 'Don't be afraid. I will help you.'

Those are the scriptures my wife and two friends offered to me at a challenging time of my life. Countless friends messaged me to just say that they were praying for me. Are you surrounding yourself with people that cover you in prayer and surround you in the protection of the Word? Know that right now, even though I may not know you, I am praying for anyone that reads this after I write it... Yes, that means YOU.

- Day 233 -

Never underestimate the power of God. It is possible to go to bed in Fear, in frustration, defeated, in pain with little or no strength to even get fully through your prayers and wake up with renewed strength, Faith, optimism and health. Nothing is impossible with God.

Romans 8:28
We know that ALL THINGS work together for good for those who love God, to those who are called according to his purpose.

Genesis 24:1
Abraham was old, and well stricken in age. Yahweh had blessed Abraham in ALL THINGS.

1 Chronicles 29:14
But who am I, and what is my people, that we should be able to offer so willingly as this? For ALL THINGS come from you, and of your own have we given you.

Job 42:2
"I know that you can do ALL THINGS, and that no purpose of yours can be restrained.

Isaiah 44:24
The Lord, your Redeemer, and he who formed you from the womb says: "I am Yahweh, who makes ALL THINGS; who alone stretches out the heavens; who spreads out the earth by myself;

(Continued tomorrow...)

- Day 234 -

Matthew 19:26
Looking at them, Jesus said, "With men this is impossible, but with God ALL THINGS are possible."

Matthew 21:22
ALL THINGS, whatever you ask in prayer, believing, you will receive."

Mark 11:24
Therefore I tell you, ALL THINGS whatever you pray and ask for, believe that you have received them, and you shall have them.

John 3:35
The Father loves the Son, and has given ALL THINGS into his hand.

2 Corinthians 6:10
as sorrowful, yet always rejoicing; as poor, yet making many rich; as having nothing, and yet possessing ALL THINGS.

Ephesians 5:20
giving thanks always concerning ALL THINGS in the name of our Lord Jesus Christ, to God, even the Father;

Philippians 4:12-13
I know how to be humbled, and I know also how to abound. In everything and in ALL THINGS I have learned the secret both to be filled and to be hungry, both to abound and to be in need. I can do ALL THINGS through Christ, who strengthens me.

Remember this, ALL THINGS are possible with God through Jesus. Take a few minutes to write down ALL the THINGS that are causing you fear, anxiety, pain and frustration. When you're done and have the whole complete list, pray in faith, believing in Him with thanksgiving He has already at work answering your prayer. Lastly, destroy the list knowing that your mind, body and spirit are being strengthened at this very moment.

I heard a great quote from a friend of mine today. "The new is in the Old (Testament) concealed, the old is in the New (Testament) revealed." That's something you have to hear or read several times to wrap your head around. Let's see what the Bible has to say about that.

Matthew 5:17
"Don't think that I came to destroy the law or the prophets. I didn't come to destroy, but to fulfill.
John 1:17
For the law was given through Moses. Grace and truth were realized through Jesus Christ.
2 Timothy 1:9-10
who saved us and called us with a holy calling, not according to our works, but according to his own purpose and grace, which was given to us in Christ Jesus before times eternal,but has now been revealed by the appearing of our Savior, Christ Jesus, who abolished death, and brought life and immortality to light through the Good News.

Grace was partially concealed behind a veil in the Old Testament and was revealed through the death of Jesus which tore the veil wide open. No one is worthy of God's grace including David, Abraham, Joseph, Moses, Noah, or the Israelites or me or you for that matter. That's what makes it grace. But, all these Biblical figures received God's grace in the Old Testament none the less giving us a glimpse into what was in store for all of us when our Savior, Jesus the Christ, was born.

- Day 236 -

About 20 years ago, I made a vow not to watch the news until they start only showing good, positive, uplifting news and do away with the violence, disaster and political stories meant to divide the nation instead of unite it. But, you have to live under a rock not to know that racism and discrimination is still a huge issue in the United States. How are we as Christians supposed to respond to this crisis?

Romans 12:3
For I say, through the grace that was given me, to every man who is among you, not to think of himself more highly than he ought to think; but to think reasonably, as God has apportioned to each person a measure of faith.
Romans 12:21
Don't be overcome by evil, but overcome evil with good.
Galatians 2:12-13
For before some people came from James, he ate with the Gentiles. But when they came, he drew back and separated himself, fearing those who were of the circumcision. And the rest of the Jews joined him in his hypocrisy; so that even Barnabas was carried away with their hypocrisy.
Ephesians 2:11,16
Therefore remember that once you, the Gentiles in the flesh, who are called "uncircumcision" by that which is called "circumcision", (in the flesh, made by hands); ...and might reconcile them both in one body to God through the cross, having killed the hostility thereby.
Colossians 3:14-15
Above all these things, walk in love, which is the bond of perfection. And let the peace of God rule in your hearts, to which also you were called in one body; and be thankful.

Why can't we just bring it in and hug it out? That's what my Grandpa would have suggested but he also taught me not to talk too much about religion or politics with people you wanted to keep as friends. Too late for the religion part but as for politics, I'm going to take his advice. So, search your heart and the scriptures on this topic and see what YOU find and write it below if you are so moved.

- Day 237 -

So what's the deal with the ichthys or ichthus from the Greek ikhthýs ("fish")? Well, it's a symbol consisting of two intersecting arcs, the ends of the right side extending beyond the meeting point so as to resemble the profile of a fish. You've seen it before, the fish signs on the back of cars and on Christian religious items...

Matthew 4:19
He said to them, "Come after me, and I will make you fishers for men."
Luke 24:41-43
While they still didn't believe for joy, and wondered, he said to them, "Do you have anything here to eat?" They gave him a piece of a broiled fish and some honeycomb. He took them, and ate in front of them.
Mark 6:38-44
He said to them, "How many loaves do you have? Go see." When they knew, they said, "Five, and two fish." ...He took the five loaves and the two fish, and looking up to heaven, he blessed and broke the loaves, and he gave to his disciples to set before them, and he divided the two fish among them all. They all ate, and were filled. They took up twelve baskets full of broken pieces and also of the fish. Those who ate the loaves were five thousand men.
John 21:5-7
Jesus therefore said to them, "Children, have you anything to eat?" They answered him, "No." He said to them, "Cast the net on the right side of the boat, and you will find some." They cast it therefore, and now they weren't able to draw it in for the multitude of fish. That disciple therefore whom Jesus loved said to Peter, "It's the Lord!"

Many people identify the ichthys or fish symbol with being a Christian. Is that biblical? Kinda not really. Is it OK? That's up to you. Are there lots of connections between Jesus and fish in the Bible, sure there are and lots more than listed above. Find some more and post a verse below that speaks to you.

- Day 238 -

"A tree is known by its fruit; a man by his deeds. A good deed is never lost; he who sows courtesy reaps friendship; he who plants kindness gathers love." - Saint Basil What does the Bible say about friendship?

Ecclesiastes 4:9-10
Two are better than one, because they have a good reward for their labor. For if they fall, the one will lift up his fellow; but woe to him who is alone when he falls, and doesn't have another to lift him up.
Proverbs 12:26
A righteous person is cautious in friendship, but the way of the wicked leads them astray.
Proverbs 18:24
A man of many companions may be ruined, but there is a friend who sticks closer than a brother.
Proverbs 17:17
A friend loves at all times; and a brother is born for adversity.

Lately I've been in close contact with some very good friends. I find it interesting that tough times don't seem so tough when you've got good friends by your side and I'm grateful I have those people in my life. Did you know that you and I have a friend in common? His name is Jesus and if you haven't met Him yet, He wanted me to pass His "phone number" along. It's Jeremiah 33:3. Give Him a call.

- Day 239 -

Did you know that some people are hoping for a Eucatastrophe? Yup, that's a real word. It means a sudden and favorable resolution of events in a story; a happy ending.

2 Corinthians 5:17
Therefore if anyone is in Christ, he is a new creation. The old things have passed away. Behold, all things have become new.
Job 42:10, 12 (NKJV)
10 And the Lord restored Job's losses when he prayed for his friends. Indeed the Lord gave Job twice as much as he had before.
12 Now the Lord blessed the latter days of Job more than his beginning; for he had fourteen thousand sheep, six thousand camels, one thousand yoke of oxen, and one thousand female donkeys.
Revelation 21:3-4
And I heard a loud voice from heaven saying, "Behold, the tabernacle of God is with men, and He will dwell with them, and they shall be His people. God Himself will be with them and be their God. And God will wipe away every tear from their eyes; there shall be no more death, nor sorrow, nor crying. There shall be no more pain, for the former things have passed away."

Like I said, some people are hoping for a Eucatastrophe. The difference is that Christians aren't among them. We know there will be a Eucatastrophe because it's promised to us in God's Word, The Bible. Are you hoping or are you Confident that your life will end in Eucatastrophe?

- Day 240 -

Follow me on this one. It may not be theologically or doctrinally correct but I will leave that up to you to decide. This will be a little shorter than usual but may take more time to study.

1 Corinthians 6:17
But he who is joined to the Lord is one spirit.
1 Corinthians 12:27-28
Now you are the body of Christ, and members individually. God has set some in the assembly: first apostles, second prophets, third teachers, then miracle workers, then gifts of healings, helps, governments, and various kinds of languages.
John 8:12
Again, therefore, Jesus spoke to them, saying, "I am the light of the world. He who follows me will not walk in the darkness, but will have the light of life."
Mark 16:15
He said to them, "Go into all the world, and preach the Good News to the whole creation.

So, we are one with Christ, who is The Light of the world. He is in us and we are in Him... One Light. We are asked to go out and preach (share) this Light in the world. But how? The answer (as I interpret it) is through the gift of The Spirit we were given. It is through this gift that we shine the brightest and share the gospel with the world. What do you think?

Truly inexplicable. The message in the gospels is truly inexplicable. How can you explain the inexplicable to someone who is in this world? Many of the teachings we know to be true are paradoxical and counterintuitive. I mean how do you explain this?...

Matthew 16:25
For whoever desires to save his life will lose it, and whoever will lose his life for my sake will find it.
Matthew 5:11-12
"Blessed are you when people reproach you, persecute you, and say all kinds of evil against you falsely, for my sake. Rejoice, and be exceedingly glad, for great is your reward in heaven. For that is how they persecuted the prophets who were before you.
Matthew 5:38-39
"You have heard that it was said, 'An eye for an eye, and a tooth for a tooth.' But I tell you, don't resist him who is evil; but whoever strikes you on your right cheek, turn to him the other also.
As a matter of fact, check out nearly all of Matthew chapter 5...

When you think about it, nearly everything about Jesus' teachings was counterintuitive (contrary to expectations). He was born of a virgin. He was born into a poor family yet he was declared King. He waited for people to die before he saved them (Lazarus). I mean, inexplicable in the natural. How do you explain it? Through a faith that can only be understood when you are one in Spirit with Him.

- Day 242 -

How many people remember a popular TV show called Get Smart? When he made a huge mistake, he would sarcastically comment, "Missed it by THAT MUCH" showing a small space between his thumb and pointer finger. You've all heard the phrase, "Close but no cigar". In archery, the term is "missed the mark". Well, in Greek the word for "sin" is hamartia, an archery term for "missing the mark."

Romans 3:23
for all have sinned, and fall short of the glory of God;
Romans 3:9
What then? Are we better than they? No, in no way. For we previously warned both Jews and Greeks, that they are all under sin.
James 4:17
To him therefore who knows to do good, and doesn't do it, to him it is sin.
1 John 3:4
Everyone who sins also commits lawlessness. Sin is lawlessness.
Romans 14:23
But he who doubts is condemned if he eats, because it isn't of faith; and whatever is not of faith is sin.

How many times have we known the "right thing" to do but chose not to? Or worse yet, knew what the right thing was but chose to do the "wrong thing"? Fortunately for those of us that have sinned, God provided The Way, Jesus as an atonement for our sins. Nothing less could have rescued us from the penalty for our sins and at the same time satisfied an infinitely loving, holy and just God. Meditate on Sin and Grace and jot a few thoughts down.

- Day 243 -

Peace is often the last thing we expect to find in a horrific storm. Have you ever experienced waiting out a tropical storm or hurricane in your home? It can get pretty hairy to say the least. There is always the thought in the back of your head that the next strong wind could be the one that causes a tree to come through the roof or blows in a window. But, if you stop focusing on the storm and focus on God, you too can find peace in your storm.

John 14:27
Peace I leave with you. My peace I give to you; not as the world gives, give I to you. Don't let your heart be troubled, neither let it be fearful.
Philippians 4:6-7
In nothing be anxious, but in everything, by prayer and petition with thanksgiving, let your requests be made known to God. And the peace of God, which surpasses all understanding, will guard your hearts and your thoughts in Christ Jesus.
Ephesians 2:14
For he is our peace…

Have you found yourself in a "storm"? Which one are you focusing on… the storm or God? Find another verse in the Bible that fits with the theme "finding peace in a storm" and post it below.

- Day 244 -

TRUST is an interesting thing. It's defined as a firm belief in the reliability, truth, ability, or strength of someone or something. Trust can be a hard thing to give and once it's lost, it can be nearly impossible to regain. Many people have been hurt because they have trusted and have been betrayed. But there is one person in whom your trust is well deserved...

Proverbs 3:5-6
Trust in The Lord with all your heart, and don't lean on your own understanding. In all your ways acknowledge him, and he will make your paths straight.
2 Kings 18:5
He trusted in Yahweh, the God of Israel; so that after him was no one like him among all the kings of Judah, nor among them that were before him.
1 Timothy 4:10
For to this end we both labor and suffer reproach, because we have set our trust in the living God, who is the Savior of all men, especially of those who believe.
Joshua 24:15
And if it seem evil unto you to serve the Lord, choose you this day whom ye will serve; ...but as for me and my house, we will serve the Lord.

In whom do YOU trust? If you trust in The Lord God who created you from dust and clay, breathed life into you, sacrificed Himself on the cross for you, and promised to never leave you or forsake you (Deuteronomy 21:6), then your trust is well founded. Again I ask, In whom do you trust?

- Day 245 -

There aren't many things that are guaranteed in this world. There's birth, death, taxes, back pain and Really Really hard and trying times that will test your mental, physical and spiritual strength. In those times do you have a Bible verse you can stand on? Do you have a verse you can recall from memory that will comfort and strengthen you?

Philippians 4:13
I can do all things through Christ, who strengthens me.
Isaiah 40:29
He gives power to the weak. He increases the strength of him who has no might.
Psalm 119:28
My soul is weary with sorrow: strengthen me according to your word.
Isaiah 40:31
But those who wait for The Lord will renew their strength. They will mount up with wings like eagles. They will run, and not be weary. They will walk, and not faint.
Proverbs 18:10
The Lord's name is a strong tower: the righteous run to him, and are safe.

Choose one of these verses and memorize it. Say it over and over until you own it. And then, when troubles come, you can recite it over and over to gain strength when you are feeling weak. Do you have any other verses you 'stand on' in trying times?

- Day 246 -

Trying times are not the only reason we should have a few Bible verses in our 'back pocket', memorized and tucked away in our brain. Occasionally we slip and think that we can earn our way to God's heart by being "good enough" to "earn" His love. OR we listen to the whisper of the devil in our ear telling us that we made too many mistakes to deserve God's love...

Jeremiah 31:3
The Lord appeared of old to me, saying, Yes, I have loved you with an everlasting love: therefore with loving kindness have I drawn you.
John 3:16
For God so loved the world, that he gave his only Son, that whoever believes in him should not perish but have eternal life.
Romans 5:8
God shows his love for us in that while we were still sinners, Christ died for us.
1 John 4:7-8
Beloved, let us love one another, for love is of God; and everyone who loves has been born of God, and knows God. He who doesn't love doesn't know God, for God is love.

There's nothing we can do to earn God's love and there's nothing we can do that God didn't already forgive us for when we are in Christ and Christ is in us. Nonetheless, it's a good idea to have a verse about God's love for us at the ready to remind us just how much and for how long He will love us. Do you have a verse at the ready that reminds you of God's love for YOU when the devil whispers in your ear? If you don't, borrow one of mine from above until you find your own. If you do, share it below.

- Day 247 -

So many people are so stressed out these days about all the crud going on in the world. It begs a question. Could God have just created a sinless world, a world where no sin was possible? And, if it's not blasphemous to ask, Why didn't He? That would have saved a lot of heartache.

God did create a sinless world- Genesis 1:31
God saw everything that he had made, and, behold, it was very good. There was evening and there was morning, a sixth day.
This is what happened- Genesis 3:4-5
The serpent said to the woman, "You won't surely die, for God knows that in the day you eat it, your eyes will be opened, and you will be like God, knowing good and evil."

If He made us so we couldn't sin, we would have been like robots or puppets unable to choose to love Him or anyone else genuinely of our own choice. Because He understands love is only real when we can choose it, He gave us free will knowing we would sin...But, he also planned our salvation before creating the world...   Ephesians 1:4 (AMP)
just as [in His love] He chose us in Christ [actually selected us for Himself as His own] before the foundation of the world, so that we would be holy [that is, consecrated, set apart for Him, purpose-driven] and blameless in His sight. In love

- Day 248 -

Ever wish you could take 7 stupid decisions back that you've made over the course of your life? How would your life be different now had you not made those errors of judgment? Read about these 7 stupid decisions in the Bible...

Genesis 3:6
And when the woman saw that the tree was good for food, and that it was delightful to look at, and a tree to be desired in order to make one wise and insightful, she took some of its fruit and ate it; and she also gave some to her husband with her, and he ate.

Genesis 16:1-3 (Sarah and Abraham doubt God's promise)
Now Sarai, Abram's wife had borne him no children, and she had an Egyptian maid whose name was Hagar. So Sarai said to Abram, "Now behold, the LORD has prevented me from bearing children. Please go in to my maid; perhaps I will obtain children through her." And Abram listened to the voice of Sarai. After Abram had lived ten years in the land of Canaan, Abram's wife Sarai took Hagar the Egyptian, her maid, and gave her to her husband Abram as his wife.

2 Samuel 11:2-4 (David commits adultery and murder to cover it up)
Now when evening came David arose from his bed and walked around on the roof of the king's house, and from the roof he saw a woman bathing; and the woman was very beautiful in appearance. So David sent and inquired about the woman. And one said, "Is this not Bathsheba, the daughter of Eliam, the wife of Uriah the Hittite?" David sent messengers and took her, and when she came to him, he lay with her; and when she had purified herself from her uncleanness, she returned to her house.

(continued tomorrow...)

- Day 249 -

Mark 10:22
But at these words he was saddened, and he went away grieving, for he was one who owned much property.

Luke 15:13
"And not many days later, the younger son gathered everything together and went on a journey into a distant country, and there he squandered his estate with loose living.

Matthew 26:14-16
Then one of the twelve, named Judas Iscariot, went to the chief priests and said, "What are you willing to give me to betray Him to you?" And they weighed out thirty pieces of silver to him. From then on he began looking for a good opportunity to betray Jesus.

Matthew 27:1-2
Now when morning came, all the chief priests and the elders of the people conferred together against Jesus to put Him to death; and they bound Him, and led Him away and delivered Him to Pilate the governor.

There are 7 really bad mistakes by people in the Bible we know really well. Eve, Sarah and Abraham, David, the rich young man, the prodigal son, Judas, and the Jewish chief priests, elders and Pontius Pilate all wished they could take back a stupid decision. Looks like we're not alone! Going forward, consult the Bible and pray to God before making a decision and maybe we can avoid our NEXT stupid mistake.

- Day 250 -

A Denizen is an inhabitant or occupant of a particular place. What particular place do you associate yourself with? An American? A citizen of a particular place state? A resident of a particular city, either the one you were born in or currently live in? How about a human of this world?

John 17:14-16
I have given them your word. The world hated them, because they are not of the world, even as I am not of the world. I pray not that you would take them from the world, but that you would keep them from the evil one. They are not of the world even as I am not of the world.
Philippians 3:20
For our citizenship is in heaven, from where we also wait for a Savior, the Lord Jesus Christ;
Ephesians 2:18-19
For through him we both have our access in one Spirit to the Father. So then you are no longer strangers and foreigners, but you are fellow citizens with the saints, and of the household of God,

As it turns out, we are denizens of heaven, not this earth. We are in this world, not of this world. Our temporary physical address is only of fleeting importance. Make sure you've secured your new forwarding address: Heaven.

- Day 251 -

This morning in church, Father Jared gave another great sermon. He pointed out the two main things that Martin Luther called the Roman Catholic Church out for in 1517 which became known as the Protestant Reformation. One was the sale of indulgences (buying your way into heaven). Luther also took issue with the church pardoning people for their sins, pointing out that only faith in Jesus, and not good works, is the only way to obtain God's pardon for sin.

Ephesians 2:8-9
for by grace you have been saved through faith, and that not of yourselves; it is the gift of God, not of works, that no one would boast.
Romans 5:17
For if by the trespass of the one, death reigned through the one; so much more will those who receive the abundance of grace and of the gift of righteousness reign in life through the one, Jesus Christ.
Titus 3:5
not by works of righteousness, which we did ourselves, but according to his mercy, he saved us, through the washing of regeneration and renewing by the Holy Spirit,
Isaiah 45:22
"Look to me, and be saved, all the ends of the earth; for I am God, and there is no other.

The worst part of any church is that it's made up of people that are imperfect and sinful by nature. But to our church's credit we learned from Luther and now the sale of indulgences is considered an abomination. We teach that we are saved by grace but because of this grace we are encouraged to do good works. I think if you look at an article called "The 18 Most Surprising Things The Pope Has Done!", you will see that Pope Francis is doing his part to ensure that Love is the central theme not only of the Bible but of the Catholic Church and our lives as Christians.

- Day 252 -

While speaking to a good friend today, the topic of 'luck' came up. He told me he would take a blessing over luck any day. He noted that blessings last forever but luck is fleeting.

Proverbs 16:33
The lot is cast into the lap, but its every decision is from The Lord.
Proverbs 16:9
A man's heart plans his course, but Yahweh directs his steps.
Romans 15:29
I know that, when I come to you, I will come in the fullness of the blessing of the Good News of Christ.
Deuteronomy 28:1-6
And it shall come to pass, if thou shalt hearken diligently unto the voice of the Lord thy God, to observe and to do all his commandments which I command thee this day, that the Lord thy God will set thee on high above all nations of the earth: And all these blessings shall come on thee, and overtake thee, if thou shalt hearken unto the voice of the Lord thy God. Blessed shalt thou be in the city, and blessed shalt thou be in the field. Blessed shall be the fruit of thy body, and the fruit of thy ground, and the fruit of thy cattle, the increase of thy kine, and the flocks of thy sheep. Blessed shall be thy basket and thy store.Blessed shalt thou be when thou comest in, and blessed shalt thou be when thou goest out.

Another friend of mine used to own the Stardust Casino in Las Vegas. He explained to me that 'Luck' eventually runs out... every time, which is why the casino business is such a big money maker. So, when it comes to luck or a blessing, I'll take a blessing over luck any day.

- Day 253 -

Have you ever been in a funk and something or someone causes you to look at your circumstances and make you realize that things are actually much better than you thought they were? My friend Steve is working on a project called Wake Up Humans and is in the process of writing a book by the same name. It's the kind of book that causes you to realize how much we have to be grateful for.

Psalm 138:8
The Lord will fulfill His purpose for me; your loving kindness, Yahweh, endures forever. Don't forsake the works of your own hands.
Ephesians 1:6
to the praise of the glory of his grace, by which he freely gave us favor in the Beloved,
Philippians 1:6
being confident of this very thing, that he who began a good work in you will complete it until the day of Jesus Christ.
1 Peter 2:9
But you are a chosen race, a royal priesthood, a holy nation, a people for God's own possession, that you may proclaim the excellence of him who called you out of darkness into his marvelous light:
Ephesians 2:10
For we are his workmanship, created in Christ Jesus for good works, which God prepared before that we would walk in them.

Do you get that? When you feel you're not 'good enough', or 'things are not going that great'... WAKE UP HUMANS! YOU were created and chosen by God, called into the light by Him and He began a good work in you that He WILL finish in and through you. Things may not look good right now but not only will God provide everything you need in abundance, but He will see to it that you always have everything you need and plenty left over to share with others. (2 Cor. 9:8)

- Day 254 -

There's an Irish proverb I read about recently. It says, "A good laugh and a long sleep are the two best cures for anything." Interesting what the Bible has to say about that.

Proverbs 17:22
A merry heart doeth good like a medicine: but a broken spirit drieth the bones.
Psalm 126:2
Then our mouth was filled with laughter, And our tongue with singing. Then they said among the nations, "The Lord has done great things for them."
Proverbs 3:24
When you lie down, you will not be afraid; Yes, you will lie down and your sleep will be sweet.
Jeremiah 31:26
After this I awoke and looked around, and my sleep was sweet to me.
Matthew 11:28
"Come to me, all you who labor and are heavily burdened, and I will give you rest.

A good laugh and a long sleep may indeed be a good solution to whatever is ailing you. A joyful heart, a hearty laugh and singing a song of praise are all in God's plan for your life and health. Likewise, we need to heed God's commandment to rest once a week, and get some deep, sweet, restorative sleep. We are admonished to go to Jesus when we are heavily burdened and He will give us the rest we need. When's the last time you went to Jesus and asked for a deep restorative rest?

- Day 255 -

The author of the Harry Potter series, J.K. Rowling, wrote this: "It is our choices that show what we truly are, far more than our abilities." So, what does the Bible have to say about that?

1 Samuel 17:4-7, 32-33, 48-49

4-7 A champion out of the camp of the Philistines named Goliath, of Gath, whose height was six cubits and a span went out. He had a helmet of brass on his head, and he wore a coat of mail; and the weight of the coat was five thousand shekels of brass. He had brass shin armor on his legs, and a brass javelin between his shoulders. The staff of his spear was like a weaver's beam; and his spear's head weighed six hundred shekels of iron.

32-33 David said to Saul, "Let no man's heart fail because of him. Your servant will go and fight with this Philistine." Saul said to David, "You are not able to go against this Philistine to fight with him; for you are but a youth, and he a man of war from his youth."

48-49 When the Philistine arose, and walked and came near to meet David, David hurried, and ran toward the army to meet the Philistine. David put his hand in his bag, took a stone, and slung it, and struck the Philistine in his forehead.

David was just a young man, a shepherd, the smallest of 4 brothers. He could easily have said to himself, "Woah, this giant is way bigger than I am. I'll just stay out in the field with the sheep where I'm safe." But that's not what he chose to do. He made a choice to step up and defend his nation with a small smooth stone and a slingshot. He made the choice to TRUST The Lord to deliver Goliath into his hand (verse 46). What God given abilities do you have that you have not yet made the choice to use for His Glory?

- Day 256 -

Hey, listen, you're not alone. We all have bad habits. The real secret to being able to break a bad habit is to find something you love even more than that habit. I have a suggestion...

Matthew 22:37
Jesus said to him, "'You shall love the Lord your God with all your heart, with all your soul, and with all your mind.'
Mark 12:30
you shall love the Lord your God with all your heart, and with all your soul, and with all your mind, and with all your strength.' This is the first commandment.
Luke 10:27
He answered, "You shall love the Lord your God with all your heart, with all your soul, with all your strength, and with all your mind; and your neighbor as yourself."
1 John 1:9
If we confess our sins, he is faithful and righteous to forgive us the sins, and to cleanse us from all unrighteousness.

When you love God with all your heart, all your mind, all your strength, all your soul and your neighbor as yourself, seemingly alluring bad habits become unimportant and even repulsive. Habits that break a commandment or destroy the temple of God (our body) result in sins which separate us from God. (Isaiah 59:2 But your iniquities have separated you and your God, and your sins have hidden his face from you, so that he will not hear.) If that doesn't sicken you and make you break your bad habit, refer back to the verses above. Let's pray about our bad habits and ask God to help us with them.

- Day 257 -

Have you ever heard the quote, "Some cause happiness wherever they go; others whenever they go." We all know someone that lights up the room when they arrive and we also know someone that seems to drain the room of energy when they are present. We need to attract more people into our lives that cause happiness when they arrive...

Matthew 5:14-16
You are the light of the world. A city located on a hill can't be hidden. Neither do you light a lamp, and put it under a measuring basket, but on a stand; and it shines to all who are in the house. Even so, let your light shine before men; that they may see your good works, and glorify your Father who is in heaven.
Ephesians 5:7-8
Therefore don't be partakers with them. 8 For you were once darkness, but are now light in the Lord. Walk as children of light,
John 8:12
Again, therefore, Jesus spoke to them, saying, "I am the light of the world. He who follows me will not walk in the darkness, but will have the light of life."

Jesus really knows how to light up a room. The very power of His presence prevailed and people chose to follow Him. It is our job now to go into the darkness and shine His light through us. As we share the Light of Christ, hopefully we will bring happiness and joy to a world filled with sorrow. How have you shared the light of Christ today?

- Day 258 -

Today I was meditating on God's Word and really thought about the thief on the cross next to Jesus. Scripture doesn't tell us a lot about this dude. All we know is that he was a criminal, was hung on the cross next to Jesus and was guaranteed a spot in paradise with Jesus hours before his death...

Luke 23:32, 39-43
32 There were also others, two criminals, led with him to be put to death. 33 When they came to the place that is called The Skull, they crucified him there with the criminals, one on the right and the other on the left.

39 One of the criminals who was hanged insulted him, saying, "If you are the Christ, save yourself and us!" 40 But the other answered, and rebuking him said, "Don't you even fear God, seeing you are under the same condemnation? 41 And we indeed justly, for we receive the due reward for our deeds, but this man has done nothing wrong." 42 He said to Jesus, "Lord, remember me when you come into your Kingdom."

43 Jesus said to him, "Assuredly I tell you, today you will be with me in Paradise."

There's so much going on here. The innocent Savior is hanging from a cross between two criminals. One criminal mocks Him, the other humbly defends Him. And what is the response from Jesus? He assures the man that asks for mercy that he will receive it. This is blessed assurance to us that a humble heart that cries out to God through Jesus for salvation will be heard. Even in the last moments of life, Romans 10:13 stands true. Don't wait until moments before your death to call out to Him. Do it now and see what you've been missing. What exactly do you have to lose?

- Day 259 -

My friend Jason shared a quote today: "He who believes is strong; he who doubts is weak. Strong convictions precede great actions." —Louisa May Alcott. He then commented, "When you find something worth living for, something that you believe in with all your heart- act on it and spread it!" What does the Bible say about a strong belief and doubt?

Mark 9:23-24
Jesus said to him, "If you can believe, all things are possible to him who believes."
Immediately the father of the child cried out with tears, "I believe. Help my unbelief!"
Mark 11:23
For most certainly I tell you, whoever may tell this mountain, 'Be taken up and cast into the sea,' and doesn't doubt in his heart, but believes that what he says is happening; he shall have whatever he says.
James 1:6
But let him ask in faith, without any doubting, for he who doubts is like a wave of the sea, driven by the wind and tossed.

The power of belief is the power to move mountains. Doubt is the wedge that is driven between us and the power of our Creator and separates us from Him. Doubt weakens us and steals our strength and conviction. Jesus is someone worth living for and His message is something that we believe in that empowers us to fulfill the great command- to go out and preach the Good News to all creation. Have you acted on your belief and spread the Good News today? Given the opportunity, will you tomorrow?

- Day 260 -

There are a boatload of promises that God makes in the Bible. One estimate is over 3000, another is over 5000. There is a hymn I loved the first time I heard it at the Curtis Corner Baptist Church called standing on the promises of God and starts off- "Standing on the promises of Christ my King, Through eternal ages let his praises ring; Glory in the highest, I will shout and sing, Standing on the promises of God...

2 Peter 1:4
by which he has granted to us his precious and exceedingly great promises; that through these you may become partakers of the divine nature, having escaped from the corruption that is in the world by lust.
Jeremiah 29:11
For I know the plans I have for you," says the Lord. "They are plans for good and not for disaster, to give you a future and a hope.
John 14:13-16
Whatever you will ask in my name, that will I do, that the Father may be glorified in the Son. If you will ask anything in my name, I will do it. If you love me, keep my commandments. I will pray to the Father, and he will give you another Counselor, that he may be with you forever,—
Proverbs 1:33
But all who listen to me will live in peace, untroubled by fear of harm."

...Standing, standing, Standing on the promises of God my Savior; Standing, standing, I'm standing on the promises of God. Standing on the promises I cannot fall, Listening every moment to the Spirit's call, Resting in my Savior as my all in all, Standing on the promises of God." Which of God's promises to you cherish and stand on?

- Day 261 -

After listening to the Mormon Tabernacle Choir sing Standing on the Promises of God, I went on and listened to them sing another favorite, It Is Well With my Soul. Here are some of the lyrics, "Though Satan should buffet, though trials should come, Let this blest assurance control, That Christ has regarded my helpless estate,
And hath shed His own blood for my soul. It is well, it is well with my soul…

John 14:27
Peace I leave with you. My peace I give to you; not as the world gives, give I to you. Don't let your heart be troubled, neither let it be fearful.
John 3:16
For God so loved the world, that he gave his one and only Son, that whoever believes in him should not perish, but have eternal life.
1 Corinthians 11:24
And when he had given thanks, he brake it, and said, Take, eat: this is my body, which is broken for you: this do in remembrance of me.
1 John 4:10
In this is love, not that we loved God, but that he loved us, and sent his Son as the atoning sacrifice for our sins.

…My sin, oh, the bliss of this glorious thought; My sin, not in part but the whole, Is nailed to the cross, and I bear it no more, Praise the Lord, praise the Lord, o my soul. It is well (it is well), With my soul (with my soul), It is well, it is well with my soul." Is it well with your soul?

- Day 262 -

What's the scoop with angels? Who and what are they? Do they have spiritual or physical bodies? Do they have unlimited intelligence like God? Do we become an angel after we die? Do they have Free will? Are they subject to the will of God?

Matthew 28:2-3
Behold, there was a great earthquake, for an angel of the Lord descended from the sky, and came and rolled away the stone from the door, and sat on it. His appearance was like lightning, and his clothing white as snow.
Hebrews 13:2
Don't forget to show hospitality to strangers, for in doing so, some have entertained angels without knowing it.
Matthew 24:36
But no one knows of that day and hour, not even the angels of heaven, but my Father only.
Hebrews 12:22-23
But you have come to Mount Zion, and to the city of the living God, the heavenly Jerusalem, and to innumerable multitudes of angels, ... to the spirits of just men made perfect,
Revelation 12:9
And the great dragon was cast out, that old serpent, called the Devil, and Satan, which deceiveth the whole world: he was cast out into the earth, and his angels were cast out with him.
2 Peter 2:4
For if God spared not the angels that sinned, but cast [them] down to hell, and delivered [them] into chains of darkness, to be reserved unto judgment;

Angels are ministering spirits that don't have physical bodies but can take on physical appearances when the situation requires it. They may have more knowledge than humans but they don't have all the knowledge of God. Angels and humans are different and we don't become angels when we die. They have free will and can be tempted but like all creatures, they are subject to the will of God and the good ones are sent to help believers. Does that about cover it? Nope, there's still lots more to learn.

- Day 263 -

What if all the people in the world that said they were a Christian actually acted like one in thought and deed?

John 13:34-35
A new commandment I give to you, that you love one another. Just as I have loved you, you also love one another. By this everyone will know that you are my disciples, if you have love for one another."
Matthew 16:24
Then Jesus said to his disciples, "If anyone desires to come after me, let him deny himself, and take up his cross, and follow me.
1 Peter 3:1 & 7
In the same way, wives, be in subjection to your own husbands; so that, even if any don't obey the Word, they may be won by the behavior of their wives without a word; & You husbands, in the same way, live with your wives according to knowledge, giving honor to the woman, as to the weaker vessel, as being also joint heirs of the grace of life; that your prayers may not be hindered.
Luke 14:13-14
But when you make a feast, ask the poor, the maimed, the lame, or the blind; and you will be blessed, because they don't have the resources to repay you. For you will be repaid in the resurrection of the righteous."

Really, I could have stopped after the first verse. Love One Another, Just as Jesus Loves Us. You know how we can make this world a better place? Just love the people around you and pray for the rest of humanity. So simple. Don't complicate it.

- Day 264 -

At Bible study this week, my friend Paul told a story about one of the most memorable times he had in church as a young man. A homeless person walked into church who obviously hadn't showered in a very long time smelling of cigarettes and booze and the odor could be smelled from across the room. The man took a seat in the back of the church by himself. A church elder who typically sat up front, took a Bible out of the pew, walked to the back and sat next to the visitor. He handed the man his own well worn Bible, opened the pew Bible for himself and made the visitor feel welcomed.

James 2:1-5
My brothers, don't hold the faith of our Lord Jesus Christ of glory with partiality. For if a man with a gold ring, in fine clothing, comes into your synagogue, and a poor man in filthy clothing also comes in; and you pay special attention to him who wears the fine clothing, and say, "Sit here in a good place"; and you tell the poor man, "Stand there," or "Sit by my footstool"; haven't you shown partiality among yourselves, and become judges with evil thoughts? Listen, my beloved brothers. Didn't God choose those who are poor in this world to be rich in faith, and heirs of the Kingdom which he promised to those who love him?

How would that visitor have been greeted in YOUR church? Would YOU have been the one to walk to the back and take the seat next to him? Tonight, as we search our souls, I pray we find the person that we ought to be in Christ and have the strength to demonstrate that we are that person when given the opportunity to choose between sitting comfortably in our seat and getting up to sit next to one of God's children to comfort them in their time of need.

- Day 265 -

I recently read a quote by Khurshed Batliwala- "We are made by love, we are made of love, and we are made for love." That's worth looking at the Bible to explore a little further.

1 John 4:7-21
Beloved, let us love one another, for love is of God; and everyone who loves has been born of God, and knows God. He who doesn't love doesn't know God, for God is love. By this God's love was revealed in us, that God has sent his one and only Son into the world that we might live through him. In this is love, not that we loved God, but that he loved us, and sent his Son as the atoning sacrifice for our sins. Beloved, if God loved us in this way, we also ought to love one another. No one has seen God at any time. If we love one another, God remains in us, and his love has been perfected in us.

By this we know that we remain in him and he in us, because he has given us of his Spirit. We have seen and testify that the Father has sent the Son as the Savior of the world. Whoever confesses that Jesus is the Son of God, God remains in him, and he in God. We know and have believed the love which God has for us. God is love, and he who remains in love remains in God, and God remains in him. In this love has been made perfect among us, that we may have boldness in the day of judgment, because as he is, even so are we in this world. There is no fear in love; but perfect love casts out fear, because fear has punishment. He who fears is not made perfect in love. We love him, because he first loved us. If a man says, "I love God," and hates his brother, he is a liar; for he who doesn't love his brother whom he has seen, how can he love God whom he has not seen? This commandment we have from him, that he who loves God should also love his brother.

Have you been searching for love in 'all the wrong places'? If you want to find love, find God. Want to find God? Begin by realizing that HE is not lost, WE ARE. Want to be found? Simply ask Jesus into your heart through prayer and make Him your Lord and Savior. God made you and loves you and our job is go and love others.

- Day 266 -

To begin with, all I have to say is that if you don't go to church at least once a week, man, you're missing out! Not only did Father Matt give an awesome homily worth waking up early and traveling 40 minutes to St. Rose and Clements Church on Thursday morning before Bible study, but Father Jared inspired everyone here at Christ The King Church in South Kingston this morning. Though they preached on completely different verses, the message was the same. Make your relationship with God and Jesus personal. Really take what God said to you and me in the Bible to heart.

2 Corinthians 6:18 I will be to you a Father. You will be to me sons and daughters,' says the Lord Almighty."
1 John 3:1 See how great a love the Father has given to us, that we should be called children of God! For this cause the world doesn't know us, because it didn't know him.
Galatians 3:26 For you are all children of God, through faith in Christ Jesus.
John 17:21 that they may all be one; even as you, Father, are in me, and I in you, that they also may be one in us; that the world may believe that you sent me.

I've heard that it's hard for many people to completely and fully love God because they had a poor relationship with their earthly parents. We got our earthly body (our meat suit) from our earthly parents who were bound by their own earthly body and as such were subject to sin just like us. As a result, it's impossible to have a perfect relationship with our earthly parents who are imperfect. However, try not to hold that against God. God gave us our spiritual body, created in His image, and The Way for us, His children to stay in relationship with Him forever. He has always and will always love us with Agape (unconditional) love. How much do you (or would you if you don't have any) love your children? God loves YOU even more than that! WOW! Hallelujah! AMEN.

Here's a great quote to meditate on: "Humility does not mean that you think less of yourself. It means that you think of yourself less." - Ken Blanchard. Humility is a quality that can be seen throughout the Bible...

James 4:10
Humble yourselves in the sight of the Lord, and he will exalt you.
1 Peter 5:5-6
Likewise, you younger ones, be subject to the elder. Yes, all of you clothe yourselves with humility, to subject yourselves to one another; for "God resists the proud, but gives grace to the humble." Humble yourselves therefore under the mighty hand of God, that he may exalt you in due time;
Luke 14:11
For everyone who exalts himself will be humbled, and whoever humbles himself will be exalted."
Philippians 2:5-8
Have this in your mind, which was also in Christ Jesus, who, existing in the form of God, didn't consider equality with God a thing to be grasped, but emptied himself, taking the form of a servant, being made in the likeness of men. And being found in human form, he humbled himself, becoming obedient to death, yes, the death of the cross.

In a world where false idols of money and material wealth are put on a pedestal, where pride and ego are rewarded by society, humility is a rare characteristic. But, do you know what 'exalt' means? It means to hold in a very high regard, to be in an extreme state of happiness. When you are humble, as Jesus was, God promises that YOU will be exalted. How will you show your humility before man and God today?

At Bible study we discussed the only human feeling that Jesus never experienced. He never experienced the feelings associated with sin. Although he never sinned, that doesn't mean that he can't comfort us when we sin…

Hebrews 4:15
For we don't have a high priest who can't be touched with the feeling of our infirmities, but one who has been in all points tempted like we are, yet without sin.
2 Corinthians 5:21
For him who knew no sin he made to be sin on our behalf; so that in him we might become the righteousness of God.
2 Corinthians 1:3-7
Blessed be the God and Father of our Lord Jesus Christ, the Father of mercies and God of all comfort; who comforts us in all our affliction, that we may be able to comfort those who are in any affliction, through the comfort with which we ourselves are comforted by God. For as the sufferings of Christ abound to us, even so our comfort also abounds through Christ. But if we are afflicted, it is for your comfort and salvation. If we are comforted, it is for your comfort, which produces in you the patient enduring of the same sufferings which we also suffer. Our hope for you is steadfast, knowing that, since you are partakers of the sufferings, so also are you of the comfort.

Jesus was no stranger to temptation. He knows how hard it is for us to resist the temptations of the flesh. He knows that we live in a world where satan desperately wants to steer us astray from doing the will of God. And our promise, from Him, is that when we fall, He will be there to pick us up and comfort us. Jesus is our comforter and our savior. Amen.

- Day 269 -

We've all been there. You're laying in bed on a Sunday morning thinking, "Oh, this bed is so warm and I'm still so tired. God won't mind if I don't get up and go to church. In fact, I'll just say a few prayers right here and then watch some 'church' on TV. That's kinda the same thing. Right?"

Hebrews 10:25
not neglecting to meet together, as the custom of some is, but exhorting one another; and so much the more, as you see the Day approaching.
Matthew 18:20
For where two or three are gathered together in my name, there I am in the middle of them."
Luke 4:16
He came to Nazareth, where he had been brought up. He entered, as was his custom, into the synagogue on the Sabbath day, and stood up to read.
Romans 12:5
so we, who are many, are one body in Christ, and individually members one of another.
Proverbs 25:28
A man without self discipline is like a city that is broken down and without walls

Hey, listen, I get it. You work hard all week long and Sunday seems like the perfect day to sleep in. But at what cost? Why do you think Jesus went to church (synagogue)? Jesus made it his regular "custom" or "practice" to observe the Sabbath in temple. He made it a priority to meet with other believers on the Sabbath. Shouldn't we follow His example as Christians?

- Day 270 -

Have you ever 'rescued' someone that was in a tight spot? How did that feel? Now a more important question. Have you ever been 'rescued' from a situation or circumstance? Maybe it was of no fault of your own or maybe you got yourself into a tight spot because of your own poor judgement and yet someone came to help you whether you deserved it or not. How did that make you feel?

Romans 5:7-8
For one will hardly die for a righteous man. Yet perhaps for a righteous person someone would even dare to die. But God commends his own love toward us, in that while we were yet sinners, Christ died for us.

Yes, I know, you're used to seeing more scriptures but today Romans 5:7-8 is profound. We were sinners, going against God's will and heading for an eternity in a really bad place separated from our Creator, separated forever from The Light, separated from Agape (unconditional) Love. Talk about a situation we needed rescuing from! And, despite our disobedience, our sin, he chose to rescue us by making the ultimate sacrifice. He loved us so much that He gave His life so that we may live for eternity with God. Do you know someone that needs rescuing?

- Day 271 -

One of the biggest influencers of my faith as I grew up was Dr. Robert H Schuller through his television program The Hour Of Power, now lead by his grandson Bobby. When I was going through tough times in high school, Dr. Schuller gave a sermon on Proverbs 23:7. He summed his understanding of that proverb up in this easy to remember phrase: "The me I see is the me I'll be." His friend Mary Kay had a similar view of Proverbs 23:7 and she began sharing the 10 most important 2 letter words she knew: "If it is to be, it is up to me."

Proverbs 23:7 (NKJV)
For as he thinks in his heart, so is he. …

How do you see yourself? As valuable or worthless? Dr. Schuller joked that "No man is worthless! He can always serve as a bad example." He noted that even back then in 1982, there was a "widespread negativity in our country." So what was his suggestion? "The solution is not to look at the problem, but to look at the possibilities." I believe that to be sound advice even today. I leave you with one last piece of advice from Dr. Schuller for these tough times. "Tough Times Never Last But Tough People Do." Because of Dr. Schuller, the me I saw was the me I became. I will be eternally grateful for his encouragement. Who can YOU encourage today? Take a moment and send an encouraging text to someone right now.

- Day 272 -

Never let your problems become an Excuse for quitting, or giving up or running away. Play down your problems and pray them up to God.

Exodus 4:10-14
Moses said to The Lord, "O Lord, I am not eloquent, neither before now, nor since you have spoken to your servant; for I am slow of speech, and of a slow tongue." The Lord said to him, "Who made man's mouth? Or who makes one mute, or deaf, or seeing, or blind? Isn't it I, Yahweh? Now therefore go, and I will be with your mouth, and teach you what you shall speak." He said, "Oh, Lord, please send someone else." The Lord's anger burned against Moses, and he said, "What about Aaron, your brother, the Levite? I know that he can speak well. Also, behold, he comes out to meet you. When he sees you, he will be glad in his heart.
Luke 9:59-62
He said to another, "Follow me!" But he said, "Lord, allow me first to go and bury my father." But Jesus said to him, "Leave the dead to bury their own dead, but you go and announce God's Kingdom." Another also said, "I want to follow you, Lord, but first allow me to say good-bye to those who are at my house." But Jesus said to him, "No one, having put his hand to the plow, and looking back, is fit for God's Kingdom."

Based on scripture, it doesn't look like God or Jesus are too big on excuses. You have talents and abilities that God has given you which are sufficient to overcome any problem that comes your way. "Throw away your wishbone, straighten up your backbone, stick out your jawbone and go to it."- BJ Palmer. Throw away your excuses and tell your problem how big your God is. Let the God that sent His son to die for you, believes in you and loves you help you eliminate your excuses and overcome your problems.

- Day 273 -

Proseuchomai from the Greek Word: προσεύχομαι, meaning To Pray, To offer prayers, or literally, "to exchange wishes" or "to interact with the Lord by switching human wishes (ideas) for His wishes as He imparts faith ("divine persuasion")." Wow, to exchange wishes with God. That's Big.

Luke 22:42
saying, "Father, if you are willing, remove this cup from me. Nevertheless, not my will, but yours, be done."
John 5:30
I can of myself do nothing. As I hear, I judge, and my judgment is righteous; because I don't seek my own will, but the will of my Father who sent me.
John 4:34
Jesus said to them, "My food is to do the will of him who sent me, and to accomplish his work.
Matthew 6:9-13
Pray like this: 'Our Father in heaven, may your name be kept holy. Let your Kingdom come. Let your will be done, as in heaven, so on earth. Give us today our daily bread. Forgive us our debts, as we also forgive our debtors. Bring us not into temptation, but deliver us from the evil one. For yours is the Kingdom, the power, and the glory forever. Amen.'

So intimate and so loving is our God that He exchanges His wishes with us through prayer. We come to the throne to Proseuchomai, to share our wishes for our daily bread, for our debts to be forgiven, for protection from satan while acknowledging that in the end, we only desire that His will be done. Thanks to my friend Heather for sharing this magnificent word with me.

- Day 274 -

"To Rebuke- express sharp disapproval or criticism of (someone) because of their behavior or actions." Jesus did some pretty amazing things when He rebuked in the Bible.

Psalm 57:3
He will send from heaven, and save me, he rebukes the one who is pursuing me. Selah. God will send out his loving kindness and his truth.
Mark 4:39
He awoke, and rebuked the wind, and said to the sea, "Peace! Be still!" The wind ceased, and there was a great calm.
Matthew 17:18
Jesus rebuked him, the demon went out of him, and the boy was cured from that hour.
Luke 9:42
While he was still coming, the demon threw him down and convulsed him violently. But Jesus rebuked the unclean spirit, and healed the boy, and gave him back to his father.

From scripture, we know that Jesus rebuked evil spirits and by the power of God through the Holy Spirit, we are empowered to do the same. The cool part is that we really don't need to do the rebuking though. We're able to call on Jesus himself to protect us and God Himself gave us the full armor to withstand any attack. Who do you know that's currently under attack? Step up to the plate for them. Rebuke the enemy and call on Jesus for help.

Day 275

A good friend asked what the word Selah (Hebrew: סֶלָה) meant in the Bible. The truth is that although that word appears seventy-one times in the Psalms and three times in Habakkuk, no one really knows for sure what it truly means. Some say that it means 'exclamation'. The Amplified Bible translates selah as "pause, and think of that." Still other meanings are 'Amen', 'forever' and 'always'. Here are a few scriptures. Which of these meanings resonates with you in these verses?

Psalm 3:8
Salvation belongs to The Lord. Your blessing be on your people. Selah.
Psalm 21:2
You have given him his heart's desire, and have not withheld the request of his lips. Selah.
Psalm 32:7
You are my hiding place. You will preserve me from trouble. You will surround me with songs of deliverance. Selah.
Habakkuk 3:13
You went out for the salvation of your people, for the salvation of your anointed. You crushed the head of the land of wickedness. You stripped them head to foot. Selah.

So, what do you think? Which meaning of Selah speaks to you though God's Word? Share it below.

- Day 276 -

We would be remiss not to do a Bible minute on Thanksgiving and Gratitude each year. We set aside one day every year in America to give thanks. This holiday actually started by decree on November 25th, 1623 by Governor William Bradford where he set aside a day " For rendering thanksgiving to the Almighty God for all His blessings."

Psalm 100:4
Enter into his gates with thanksgiving, into his courts with praise. Give thanks to him, and bless his name.
Leviticus 7:15
The flesh of the sacrifice of his peace offerings for thanksgiving shall be eaten on the day of his offering. He shall not leave any of it until the morning.
Philippians 4:6
In nothing be anxious, but in everything, by prayer and petition with thanksgiving, let your requests be made known to God.
Revelation 7:12
saying, "Amen! Blessing, glory, wisdom, thanksgiving, honor, power, and might, be to our God forever and ever! Amen."

Did you catch that in Leviticus 7:15? Apparently we're supposed to eat the entire Turkey on Thanksgiving and not have any leftovers for the next day. Who would-a thunk it? But seriously folks, this Thanksgiving, let's give thanks where thanks are due. Let's give thanks to God from whom all our blessings flow. God bless you all and Happy Thanksgiving.

- Day 277 -

I always tell people that I'd like to live to 120 years old. I don't quite remember why or when I began to tell people this but I know it's an interesting part of the Bible that declares that it's possible. Truth be told, I'm not at all afraid of death because I know my destination after I'm done with this 'meat suit' but I am indeed concerned about dying.

Genesis 6:3
The Lord said, "My Spirit will not strive with man forever, because he also is flesh; so his days will be one hundred twenty years."

There are 2 men in the Bible who never died but were instead caught up into Heaven are Enoch, from Genesis, and Elijah:
Genesis 5:22-24
After Methuselah's birth, Enoch walked with God for three hundred years, and became the father of more sons and daughters. All the days of Enoch were three hundred sixty-five years. Enoch walked with God, and he was not found, for God took him.
2 Kings 2:11
As they continued on and talked, behold, a chariot of fire and horses of fire separated them, and Elijah went up by a whirlwind into heaven.

Instead of dying in a long, drawn out and uncomfortable way, wouldn't it be great to go sit down somewhere after a good long prayer and just give up the spirit? Getting caught up in a whirlwind into heaven wouldn't be too bad either…

There is a Dutch word called Voorpret. The word means, "The sense of enjoyment felt before a party or event takes place." Let me tell you, there is a huge party planned and you're invited. All you have to do is RSVP...

Romans 10:9-10
that if you will confess with your mouth that Jesus is Lord, and believe in your heart that God raised him from the dead, you will be saved. For with the heart, one believes unto righteousness; and with the mouth confession is made unto salvation.
Ephesians 2:8-9
for by grace you have been saved through faith, and that not of yourselves; it is the gift of God, not of works, that no one would boast.
John 14:2-4
In my Father's house are many homes. If it weren't so, I would have told you. I am going to prepare a place for you. If I go and prepare a place for you, I will come again, and will receive you to myself; that where I am, you may be there also.Where I go, you know, and you know the way."

Let me tell you, I feel Voorpret about what's to come in heaven! I can't wait to hear the heavenly host singing praises to God. I can't wait to see the light of Christ. I'm looking forward to being part of the body of Christ and dwelling among those who love peace and tranquility. I'm really looking forward to a place where there is no sunset and we enjoy a perfect, eternally healthy, imperishable body. How are you feeling about that? Voorpret?

- Day 279 -

My friend Drew is an amazing Chiropractor but what sets him apart is that he's an amazing person. He truly embodies the Christian values and walks his talk. A man came into his office once covered in feces. Instead of ushering him out, he chose to show the man love and acceptance and gave him the care he needed. After the man was adjusted, he cleaned him up and got him back to where he was staying. It didn't end there. Drew even went to adjust the man where he was staying instead of making him walk to his office.

John 12:26
If anyone serves me, let him follow me. Where I am, there will my servant also be. If anyone serves me, the Father will honor him.
Galatians 5:13
For you, brothers, were called for freedom. Only don't use your freedom for gain to the flesh, but through love be servants to one another.
Luke 10:30-37
Jesus answered, "A certain man was going down from Jerusalem to Jericho, and he fell among robbers, who both stripped him and beat him, and departed, leaving him half dead... But a certain Samaritan, as he traveled, came where he was. When he saw him, he was moved with compassion, came to him, and bound up his wounds, pouring on oil and wine. He set him on his own animal, and brought him to an inn, and took care of him... Then Jesus said to him, "Go and do likewise."

There are too many Christians that would walk around the man that needs help instead of stopping to lend a hand. There are too many of us that can write or read a Bible minute like this one and when push comes to shove, we take the easy way out instead of helping a brother or sister in need. We need more Drew Hendersons in this world.

- Day 280 -

Too many Christians have Bibles in their homes that have never been cracked open. Did you know that there's a Japanese word for that? Tsundoku. It means the act of buying a book and leaving it unread.

2 Timothy 3:16-17
Every Scripture is God-breathed and profitable for teaching, for reproof, for correction, and for instruction in righteousness, that the man of God may be complete, thoroughly equipped for every good work.
Psalm 119:105
Your word is a lamp to my feet, and a light for my path.
Matthew 4:4
But he answered, "It is written, 'Man shall not live by bread alone, but by every word that proceeds out of the mouth of God.'"
Romans 15:4
For whatever things were written before were written for our learning, that through patience and through encouragement of the Scriptures we might have hope.

Imagine having a treasure chest in the house with untold fortune inside. Imagine that it was sitting on the coffee table for decades, just because it "looked good" there. Perhaps this treasure chest was handed down for generations to you but you just never had the time to open it up and find out what was inside it. Your Ancestors wanted you to have it's contents and for you to benefit by its treasures but you just never had the time to 'get around to opening it up'. Yeah, your Bible is a treasure chest. Open it up and find out what treasures are found within it.

- Day 281 -

Do you know what the word sweven means? It means a vision that is seen in your sleep or in a dream. There's a lot of that going on in the Bible...

Genesis 15:1
After these things Yahweh's word came to Abram in a vision, saying, "Don't be afraid, Abram. I am your shield, your exceedingly great reward."
Genesis 28:10-17
Jacob went out from Beersheba, and went toward Haran. He came to a certain place, and stayed there all night, because the sun had set. He took one of the stones of the place, and put it under his head, and lay down in that place to sleep. He dreamed. Behold, a stairway set upon the earth, and its top reached to heaven. Behold, the angels of God ascending and descending on it. Behold, Yahweh stood above it, and said, "I am Yahweh, the God of Abraham your father, and the God of Isaac. The land whereon you lie, to you will I give it, and to your offspring... Jacob awakened out of his sleep, and he said, "Surely Yahweh is in this place, and I didn't know it."...
Matthew 1:20
But when he thought about these things, behold, an angel of the Lord appeared to him in a dream, saying, "Joseph, son of David, don't be afraid to take to yourself Mary, your wife, for that which is conceived in her is of the Holy Spirit.

Joseph, Pharaoh, Samuel, Solomon, Daniel, Zacharias, Pilot's wife, Ananias, Cornelius, Peter, Paul, John and on and on ALL had visions in dreams from God. Today that doesn't happen so much because we have God's written Word to guide us. But, it's cool to know that if need be, God can communicate with us through our dreams in the form of a vision. Sleep well!

- Day 282 -

I've found a word that comes close to describing how I feel about God! "Numinous: describing an experience that makes you fearful yet fascinated, awed yet attracted -- the powerful, personal feeling of being overwhelmed or inspired." How cool is that word?

Proverbs 15:33
The fear of The Lord teaches wisdom. Before honor is humility.
Acts 12:14
When she recognized Peter's voice, she didn't open the gate for joy, but ran in, and reported that Peter was standing in front of the gate.
1 Samuel 2:1
Hannah prayed, and said: "My heart exults in Yahweh! My horn is exalted in Yahweh. My mouth shouts over my enemies, because I rejoice in your salvation.
Acts 8:8
There was great joy in that city.
John 15:11
I have spoken these things to you, that my joy may remain in you, and that your joy may be made full.

I am Numinous over Jesus Christ and God! I fear God, yet I am fascinated by Him. I am in awe yet I am attracted to Him. I am overwhelmed by His willingness to offer me grace and I am inspired to tell others about him. Pretty cool, huh?

- Day 283 -

Have you ever been to a really, really cold, and overcast place and had the sun come out from behind the cloud? The freezing cold gets a little less cold when the sun is beating down on your face. The winds try to steal your body heat but the sun provides warmth that comforts you.

Psalm 84:11
For The Lord God is a sun and a shield. Yahweh will give grace and glory. He withholds no good thing from those who walk blamelessly.

Exodus 34:29
When Moses came down from Mount Sinai with the two tablets of the testimony in Moses' hand, when he came down from the mountain, Moses didn't know that the skin of his face was radiant by reason of his speaking with The Lord.

Deuteronomy 5:24
and you said, "Behold, Yahweh our God has shown us his glory and his greatness, and we have heard his voice out of the middle of the fire. We have seen today that God does speak with man, and he lives.

Revelation 21:23
The city has no need for the sun, neither of the moon, to shine, for the very glory of God illuminated it, and its lamp is the Lamb.

Imagine how warm and comforting the light of God will be on our faces when we come to be with Him forever. Moses' face was illuminated just by being in the presence of God. Though it may feel like a cold day today, close your eyes and imagine the warmth that is to come when we stand in God's presence.

I recently heard a really good prayer. "Lord, if it's not your will, let it slip through my grasp and give me the peace not to worry about it." WOW! Talk about true faith. Now, that's a prayer worth remembering.

Isaiah 41:13
For I, The Lord your God, will hold your right hand, saying to you, 'Don't be afraid. I will help you.'
Philippians 4:6
In nothing be anxious, but in everything, by prayer and petition with thanksgiving, let your requests be made known to God.
Proverbs 3:5-6
Trust in Yahweh with all your heart, and don't lean on your own understanding. In all your ways acknowledge him, and he will make your paths straight.
Romans 12:2
Don't be conformed to this world, but be transformed by the renewing of your mind, so that you may prove what is the good, well-pleasing, and perfect will of God.

Most of my life I was trying to make things happen under my own strength. That didn't always turn out so well. Now that I am older and a bit wiser, I take time to pause before making a decision. I take time to pray and listen for the will of God. Funny how much better the outcomes are. Have you made poor decisions because you were trying to get things done under your own power instead of following the will of God?

- Day 285 -

Romans 8:28
We know that all things work together for good for those who love God, to those who are called according to his purpose.

I asked for strength and God gave me difficulties to make me strong.
I asked for wisdom and God gave me problems to solve.
I asked for prosperity and God gave me brawn and brains to work.
I asked for courage and God gave me dangers to overcome.
I asked for patience and God placed me in situations where I was forced to wait.
I asked for love and God gave me troubled people to help.
I asked for favors and God gave me opportunities.
I asked for everything so I could enjoy life.
Instead, He gave me life so I could enjoy everything.
I received nothing I wanted, I received everything I needed.
- Unknown

Have I mentioned Romans 8:28? All things work together for good for those who love God, to those who are called according to his purpose! No matter what we ask for, we are always given what we need. God is good all the time!

- Day 286 -

"Watch your thoughts; for they become words. Watch your words; for they become actions. Watch your actions; for they become habits. Watch your habits; for they become character. Watch your character for it will become your destiny." -Frank Outlaw

Proverbs 23:7
For as he thinketh in his heart, so is he: Eat and drink, saith he to thee; but his heart is not with thee.
John 1:1
In the beginning was the Word, and the Word was with God, and the Word was God.
James 2:18
Yea, a man may say, Thou hast faith, and I have works: shew me thy faith without thy works, and I will shew thee my faith by my works.
Luke 4:16
And he came to Nazareth, where he had been brought up: and, as his custom (His habit) was, he went into the synagogue on the sabbath day, and stood up for to read.
Romans 5:4
and perseverance, proven character; and proven character, hope:
Jeremiah 29:11
For I know the thoughts that I think toward you, says The Lord, thoughts of peace, and not of evil, to give you hope and a future.

I guess Frank Outlaw knew a little about scripture. His quote above appears to have it's roots in the Bible. Be careful about your thoughts. Eventually they become your destiny. What are you thinking about lately?

- Day 287 -

Have you ever heard the low rumble of thunder in the distance? It's a signal to make sure the windows are closed and prepare for the storm that's approaching. There's actually a name for it. It's called a brontide. The Bible has several brontides in it warning of approaching storms...

Acts 20:31
Therefore watch, remembering that for a period of three years I didn't cease to warning everyone night and day with tears.
Luke 12:40
Therefore be ready also, for the Son of Man is coming in an hour that you don't expect him."
Ezekiel 3:17
Son of man, I have made you a watchman to the house of Israel: therefore hear the word from my mouth, and give them warning from me.
Hebrews 11:7
By faith, Noah, being warned about things not yet seen, moved with godly fear, prepared a ship for the saving of his house, through which he condemned the world, and became heir of the righteousness which is according to faith.

Brontides abound in the Bible. We are warned what the penalty for sin is. We are warned about the end of times. We are warned about false prophets. We are warned about coveting. We are warned about a lot of things in the Bible. The question is will we heed the warnings and take action like Noah did or will we ignore them and be unprepared for what's to come? What are some other Brontides found in the Bible?

Ever heard the phrase, "Some things are better left unsaid"? When it comes to family and friends, often with age comes the wisdom to 'pick our battles'. Often we choose to bite our tongue instead of causing a fight. But some things are just too important to be left unsaid.

Proverbs 15:2
The tongue of the wise commends knowledge, but the mouth of fools gush out folly.
Proverbs 18:21
Death and life are in the power of the tongue; those who love it will eat its fruit.
Proverbs 21:23
Whoever guards his mouth and his tongue keeps his soul from troubles.
Matthew 10:27
What I tell you in the darkness, speak in the light; and what you hear whispered in the ear, proclaim on the housetops.
Mark 16:15-16
He said to them, "Go into all the world, and preach the Good News to the whole creation. He who believes and is baptized will be saved; but he who disbelieves will be condemned.

When it comes to unimportant things that don't affect eternity, do the wise thing and hold your tongue. When it comes to things that affect life and death and eternity, speak up! Shout the Good News from the rooftops to anyone who will listen. To those that hear you and believe, the power of your tongue will have provided life. Continue to pray for those that hear and do not believe because it ain't over until it's over and it ain't over yet.

There are so many books out there. There are more books than any one person can read. Sometimes we read books to be entertained. Sometimes we read books to be informed. But, there is only one book that has the power to Transform us…

Romans 12:2
Don't be conformed to this world, but be transformed by the renewing of your mind, so that you may prove what is the good, well-pleasing, and perfect will of God.
2 Corinthians 3:18
But we all, with unveiled face seeing the glory of the Lord as in a mirror, are transformed into the same image from glory to glory, even as from the Lord, the Spirit.
1 Corinthians 15:51-52
Behold, I tell you a mystery. We will not all sleep, but we will all be changed, in a moment, in the twinkling of an eye, at the last trumpet. For the trumpet will sound, and the dead will be raised incorruptible, and we will be changed.
Hebrews 4:12
For the word of God is living and active, and sharper than any two-edged sword, piercing even to the dividing of soul and spirit, of both joints and marrow, and is able to discern the thoughts and intentions of the heart.
Matthew 4:4
But he answered, "It is written, 'Man shall not live by bread alone, but by every word that proceeds out of the mouth of God.'"

The Bible is God's written Word to us. It has the power to transform us. It literally feeds our soul. When we read and believe the message contained in the Word, we become changed, in a moment, in the twinkling of an eye. Be transformed. Read the Bible. You won't regret it.

- Day 290 -

There's an Inuit word called Iktsuarpok. It translates as the feeling of anticipation that leads you to keep checking outside to see if anyone is coming yet. Have you ever had that feeling? Maybe you were throwing a party or having a little get together, all the preparation is done and the time for the guests to arrive is drawing near. You think you hear a little sound outside so you go check the door. Maybe you do this 5 or 6 times because you're looking forward to their arrival so much...

Matthew 24:42
Watch therefore, for you don't know in what hour your Lord comes.
Matthew 25:13
Watch therefore, for you don't know the day nor the hour in which the Son of Man is coming.
Revelation 16:15
"Behold, I come like a thief. Blessed is he who watches, and keeps his clothes, so that he doesn't walk naked, and they see his shame."
Matthew 26:40-41
He came to the disciples, and found them sleeping, and said to Peter, "What, couldn't you watch with me for one hour? Watch and pray, that you don't enter into temptation. The spirit indeed is willing, but the flesh is weak."

Kind of exciting, don't you think? I mean, Jesus can show up at any moment. It may be in a minute or two, it may be in a year or two, it may be in a decade or a few but for sure, it's going to be sometime soon. All He requires of us is to watch for Him and pray with expectancy. In Revelation above, in essence, He's saying, "Alright already. I'm coming. Keep your shirt on." Are you ready for His arrival?

- Day 291 -

I recently read a review of a video and one word that the reviewer used to describe it was "Quintessential". The definition is: of the pure and essential essence of something or relating to the most perfect embodiment of something. I guess that explains why both Jesus and the Bible are called 'The Word'...

John 1
In the beginning was the Word, and the Word was with God, and the Word was God. The same was in the beginning with God. All things were made through him. Without him was not anything made that has been made.

1 Thessalonians 2:13
For this cause we also thank God without ceasing, that, when you received from us the word of the message of God, you accepted it not as the word of men, but, as it is in truth, the word of God, which also works in you who believe.

Colossians 1:19
For all the fullness was pleased to dwell in him;

2 Timothy 3:16-17
Every Scripture is God-breathed and profitable for teaching, for reproof, for correction, and for instruction in righteousness, that the man of God may be complete, thoroughly equipped for every good work.

Both Jesus and The Word of God known as The Bible are quintessential. They are both the pure essential essence of God. Both Jesus and The Bible are an outpouring of God's love for us and contain His Word so it's perfectly understandable why we refer to both Jesus and The Bible as His Word. Have you listened to The Word recently? Both are alive and active this very moment waiting for you (Hebrews 4:12).

- Day 292 -

Life is filled with new opportunities. Maybe it's an opportunity for a new job, maybe an opportunity to move to a new home or a completely new state or country, it could be an opportunity to do something you have always wanted to do but didn't think it was the right time or maybe you just didn't have the time to take advantage of an opportunity in the past. Maybe it's an opportunity to begin a new relationship…

Romans 14:22-23 (MSG)
Cultivate your own relationship with God, but don't impose it on others. You're fortunate if your behavior and your belief are coherent. But if you're not sure, if you notice that you are acting in ways inconsistent with what you believe—some days trying to impose your opinions on others, other days just trying to please them—then you know that you're out of line. If the way you live isn't consistent with what you believe, then it's wrong.
Luke 14:16-24
But he said to him, "A man once gave a great banquet and invited many. And at the time for the banquet he sent his servant to say to those who had been invited, 'Come, for everything is now ready.' But they all alike began to make excuses. The first said to him, 'I have bought a field, and I must go out and see it. Please have me excused.' And another said, 'I have bought five yoke of oxen, and I go to examine them. Please have me excused.' And another said, 'I have married a wife, and therefore I cannot come.' So the servant came and reported these things to his master. Then the master of the house became angry and said to his servant, 'Go out quickly to the streets and lanes of the city, and bring in the poor and crippled and blind and lame.' And the servant said, 'Sir, what you commanded has been done, and still there is room.' And the master said to the servant, 'Go out to the highways and hedges and compel people to come in, that my house may be filled. For I tell you, none of those men who were invited shall taste my banquet.'"

You'll have lots of opportunities to do some great things but only one will truly affect every aspect of your life now and forever. God has set the table and has invited you to the banquet. All you have to do is accept the invitation. How will you RSVP? As for the rest of the opportunities that present themselves, pause, take time to pray and make sure your decisions are such that you'd be happy to announce them at the banquet table before The Host.

- Day 293 -

Never underestimate the power of prayer. I've heard people say that the time of miracles has passed. They say, "that stuff happened thousands of years ago but not today." I say, "BUNK!" I see miracles all the time and they come as answers to prayer. Sometimes the answer is NO and it still produces a miracle.

1 Thessalonians 5:17
Pray without ceasing.

Jeremiah 32:27
Behold, I am The Lord, the God of all flesh: is there anything too hard for me?

Exodus 15:26
"If you will diligently listen to Yahweh your God's voice… I am Yahweh who heals you."

Job 5:9
"He performs wonders that cannot be fathomed, miracles that cannot be counted".

Ephesians 3:20-21
Now to him who is able to do exceedingly abundantly above all that we ask or think, according to the power that works in us, to him be the glory in the assembly and in Christ Jesus to all generations forever and ever. Amen.

Pray with expectancy to see a miracle. Pray knowing that God is listening and knows the desires of your heart. Pray continually… unceasingly. Pray knowing that miracles happen all the time. Have you taken the time to pray today?

- Day 294 -

What is it that causes us to cry tears of joy? We've all cried tears of pain and sorrow but the same wet tears stream from our eyes when we are moved beyond words by a kind gesture, a heartwarming story or a work of art. We may be brought to tears out of relief that a potentially bad situation had a good outcome. Sometimes tears of joy fall out of overwhelming jubilation or in response to a gratifying event that gives meaning to our lives or when we share in the happiness of someone else's life.

2 Kings 20:5
"Turn back, and tell Hezekiah the prince of my people, 'The Lord, the God of David your father, says, "I have heard your prayer. I have seen your tears. Behold, I will heal you. On the third day, you will go up to The Lord's house.
Psalm 126:5
Those who sow in tears will reap in joy.
Mark 9:24
Immediately the father of the child cried out with tears, "I believe. Help my unbelief!"
Jeremiah 31:9 (NLT)
Tears of joy will stream down their faces, and I will lead them home with great care. They will walk beside quiet streams and on smooth paths where they will not stumble. For I am Israel's father, and Ephraim is my oldest child.
Revelation 21:4
He will wipe away from them every tear from their eyes. Death will be no more; neither will there be mourning, nor crying, nor pain, any more. The first things have passed away."

"There is sacredness in tears. They are not the mark of weakness, but of power. They speak more eloquently than ten thousand tongues. They are messengers of overwhelming grief, of deep contrition, and of unspeakable love." - Washington Irving. Whom have you shed a tear for recently?

- Day 295 -

Everyone's so enthusiastic about working out at one point in their life or another. Look how packed the gyms are in January when everyone's trying to make good on their New Year's resolution. Physical training improves what's on the outside, but what are we doing for what's on the inside? What are we doing to train up our faith?

1 Timothy 4:7-8 (NLT)
Do not waste time arguing over godless ideas and old wives' tales. Instead, train yourself to be godly. "Physical training is good, but training for godliness is much better, promising benefits in this life and in the life to come."
Proverbs 22:6
Train up a child in the way he should go, and when he is old he will not depart from it.
Luke 6:40
A disciple is not above his teacher, but everyone when he is fully trained will be like his teacher.
2 Timothy 3:16
Every Scripture is God-breathed and profitable for teaching, for reproof, for correction, and for instruction in righteousness,
1 Samuel 16:7
...for I don't see as man sees. For man looks at the outward appearance, but The Lord looks at the heart."

While it's not entirely bad to work out and make the temple of God stronger, true strength requires a strong faith. We're given the Bible by God Himself to use to strengthen our faith so take it out and read it regularly. Big muscles or a lean body might impress other people but God looks at your heart and He's only impressed by the strength of your faith. So, when you're planning out your schedule, where will you spend the majority of your time? Training your physical body or training up your faith? Who are YOU trying to impress?

- Day 296 -

It has been said that adversity is like a strong wind. It tears away from us all but the things that can not be torn, so that we see ourselves as we really are. -Arthur Golden. Isn't that true? Often when we go through a time of adversity, we are stripped down to the most basic parts of ourselves. What we are left with is the very essence of ourselves as we stand humbly before God.

Proverbs 17:17
A friend loves at all times; and a brother is born for adversity.
Philippians 4:12-13
I know how to be humbled, and I know also how to abound. In everything and in all things I have learned the secret both to be filled and to be hungry, both to abound and to be in need. I can do all things through Christ, who strengthens me.
Job 36:15
"He delivers the afflicted by their affliction and opens their ear by adversity."
Ecclesiastes 7:14
In the day of prosperity be joyful, and in the day of adversity consider; yes, God has made the one side by side with the other, to the end that man should not find out anything after him.

We all encounter adversity at one point in our lives or another. It can either bring us to our knees and cause us to rely on God's love, mercy and grace or it can cause us to turn away from Him. That choice will be yours when adversity comes knocking at your door. If you're going through adversity right now, consider that God might be attempting to draw you closer to Him so that you trust in Jesus and by doing so be saved not only from adversity but from your ego and pride.

- Day 297 -

I volunteer each year to be a guide for a Christmas Tableaux. There are 9 scenes with actors that depict the life of Jesus from conception to the cross. One of the scenes is of the three wise guys (I mean magi or wisemen). Interestingly, they don't belong in the nativity scene because they came between a year and two years after Jesus' birth. They brought 3 gifts. Do you know the meaning of each gift?

Gold- a gift for royalty, in this case a gift for the King of Kings and Lord of Lords. Revelation 19:16
He has on his garment and on his thigh a name written, "KING OF KINGS, AND LORD OF LORDS."

Frankincense- an incense used by priests especially during temple sacrifices which was a foreshadowing that Jesus would be the high priest and would sacrifice Himself to pay the penalty of sin for all people who believe. 1 Peter 1:18-19 knowing that you were redeemed, not with corruptible things, with silver or gold, from the useless way of life handed down from your fathers, but with precious blood, as of a faultless and pure lamb, the blood of Christ;

Myrrh- a perfume that was put on the dead to cover up the stench of death in a mortal. John 19:39-40 Nicodemus, who at first came to Jesus by night, also came bringing a mixture of myrrh and aloes, about a hundred Roman pounds. So they took Jesus' body, and bound it in linen cloths with the spices, as the custom of the Jews is to bury.

Gold for a king, Frankincense for God, and Myrrh for a mortal man who would die for our sins. I guess the three wise guys were pretty wise after all. Their gifts foretold who people thought Jesus was, who He really was and what His mission here on earth was all about.

- Day 298 -

Death is not a topic I'm very good with. I don't think anyone is. This week two patients whom I considered friends will be laid to rest. Just today, I received a message from someone that expressed a concern... "I'm really having trouble with the fact that my husband has died and I'm so sad all of the time. I'm glad he is with Jesus and no longer suffers. I work, go out with friends to church and church related functions and I pray a lot but I'm worried that I'm depressed and will never feel better....

Psalm 34:18
The Lord is near to those who have a broken heart, and saves those who have a crushed spirit.
Matthew 5:4
Blessed are those who mourn, for they shall be comforted.
Romans 8:38-39
For I am persuaded, that neither death, nor life, nor angels, nor principalities, nor things present, nor things to come, nor powers, nor height, nor depth, nor any other created thing, will be able to separate us from the love of God, which is in Christ Jesus our Lord.
Proverbs 12:25
Anxiety in a man's heart weighs it down, but a kind word makes it glad.
Isaiah 41:10
Don't you be afraid, for I am with you. Don't be dismayed, for I am your God. I will strengthen you. Yes, I will help you. Yes, I will uphold you with the right hand of my righteousness.

Although death is painful for those of us that are left behind and mourn, as Christians we know it is not a good-bye, it is just an 'until we meet again'. Love and the love of Christ conquer all including grief.   I leave you today with this poem by Henry Van Dyke entitled For Katrina's sun dial... Time is too slow for those who wait, Too swift for those who fear, Too long for those who grieve, Too short for those who rejoice, But for those who love, time is Eternity.

- Day 299 -

Isn't it interesting that perhaps the best way to find ourselves is to get lost in service to others. Indeed, the best way to help ourselves is to help others. Whatever we want more of, the Bible encourages us to give that thing away…

Mark 10:21
Jesus looking at him loved him, and said to him, "One thing you lack. Go, sell whatever you have, and give to the poor, and you will have treasure in heaven; and come, follow me, taking up the cross."
Matthew 10:8
Heal the sick, cleanse the lepers, and cast out demons. Freely you received, so freely give.
1 Peter 4:10
As each has received a gift, employ it in serving one another, as good managers of the grace of God in its various forms.
Galatians 5:13
For you, brothers, were called for freedom. Only don't use your freedom for gain to the flesh, but through love be servants to one another.

When you truly find the gift that was given to you by God, use that gift to serve others. When you truly serve for the sake of serving, love for the sake of loving and give for the sake of giving, the Bible says you will store up treasure in heaven. If you haven't found that special gift that you were given to serve with, start by just loving those around you by sharing the Good News or by committing random acts of kindness. For it is in those acts of kindness that we find what we have been looking for within ourselves.

- Day 300 -

There's a story of Satan testing 3 of his demons for their final exam. The question he asked them was what deceitful lie they would tell to stop people from being saved. The first said he would tell them there's no God. Satan told this demon it would never work because all they had to do was look around at the perfection of creation and they would realize, without a doubt that there is a Creator. You Fail! The second said he would just tell people there is no evil or Hell and they can do as they wish. Satan got upset at this one as well and told the demon that the world is full of pain, suffering, cruelty and injustice and people realize that hell exists as a place of punishment for those that break God's laws and do not repent... You Fail too! And then the third demon spoke up...

Matthew 24:42-43
Watch therefore, for you don't know in what hour your Lord comes. But know this, that if the master of the house had known in what watch of the night the thief was coming, he would have watched, and would not have allowed his house to be broken into.
Romans 13:11
Do this, knowing the time, that it is already time for you to awaken out of sleep, for salvation is now nearer to us than when we first believed.
1 Peter 4:7
But the end of all things is near. Therefore be of sound mind, self-controlled, and sober in prayer.

The third demon said, "I will tell them there's no hurry." "EXCELLENT!", Satan shouted. "People will be fooled into believing that there's plenty of time to change and be saved. Hell will overflow with lost souls! You Pass!" Are you ready if Jesus comes back today or have you been lied to and believe there's plenty of time to change? You never know when we'll take our last breath. Take a moment right now to thank God for your salvation or ask Him to be your Lord and Savior if you haven't yet.

- Day 301 -

Do you know what Jesus' first miracle was? Turning water into wine. What an interesting story that is. Of all things…water into wine. Well, there's a little more to the story. Some traditions suggest that the groom's mother was Mary's sister. In their culture, the wedding celebration goes on for a week or two at the groom's home. At some point the wine runs out which is a huge embarrassment to the family and even punishable by a lawsuit from the bride's family. Mary, knowing who Jesus is as told to her by the Angel, asks her son to perform a miracle to spare her sister's family the shame and embarrassment of not having enough money to buy enough wine for the festivities…

John 2:1-11
The third day, there was a marriage in Cana of Galilee. Jesus' mother was there. Jesus also was invited, with his disciples, to the marriage. When the wine ran out, Jesus' mother said to him, "They have no wine."

Jesus said to her, "Woman, what does that have to do with you and me? My hour has not yet come."

His mother said to the servants, "Whatever he says to you, do it." Now there were six water pots of stone set there after the Jews' way of purifying, containing two or three metretes apiece (20-30 gallons each). Jesus said to them, "Fill the water pots with water." They filled them up to the brim. He said to them, "Now draw some out, and take it to the ruler of the feast." So they took it. When the ruler of the feast tasted the water now become wine, and didn't know where it came from (but the servants who had drawn the water knew), the ruler of the feast called the bridegroom, and said to him, "Everyone serves the good wine first, and when the guests have drunk freely, then that which is worse. You have kept the good wine until now!" This beginning of his signs Jesus did in Cana of Galilee, and revealed his glory; and his disciples believed in him.

WOW, there's a lot going on there! The time comes to all of us where we run out of wine. But, like Mary, we must not run away from our problems. Instead with confidence and assurance we must turn to the one that can turn our bitterness, anger and hatred into peace, love and joy once again. We must turn to Jesus. Only He can fill our emptiness by changing our judgment into grace, our water into wine. Have you been praying for a miracle in your life? All you need to do is obediently fill your empty jars with water and He will turn them into wine in due season.

- Day 302 -

Sometimes we do good deeds to serve God by serving His children with really pure intent but when we wind up getting accolades from man for having done these good deeds, if we're not careful, it creates pride and leads us into sin. Oftentimes, pride can be sinful especially if we take the credit for what we've done instead of giving all honor and glory to God. Pride is truly at the root of nearly every one of our sins.

Matthew 6:1-6 and 16-18
"Be careful that you don't do your charitable giving before men, to be seen by them, or else you have no reward from your Father who is in heaven. Therefore when you do merciful deeds, don't sound a trumpet before yourself, as the hypocrites do in the synagogues and in the streets, that they may get glory from men. Most certainly I tell you, they have received their reward. But when you do merciful deeds, don't let your left hand know what your right hand does, so that your merciful deeds may be in secret, then your Father who sees in secret will reward you openly. "When you pray, you shall not be as the hypocrites, for they love to stand and pray in the synagogues and in the corners of the streets, that they may be seen by men. Most certainly, I tell you, they have received their reward. But you, when you pray, enter into your inner room, and having shut your door, pray to your Father who is in secret, and your Father who sees in secret will reward you openly.

"Moreover when you fast, don't be like the hypocrites, with sad faces. For they disfigure their faces, that they may be seen by men to be fasting. Most certainly I tell you, they have received their reward. But you, when you fast, anoint your head, and wash your face; so that you are not seen by men to be fasting, but by your Father who is in secret, and your Father, who sees in secret, will reward you.

If you want to avoid Pride and really serve God merely for the sake of serving, not for the accolades, you need to enlist in The Secret Service! Be charitable, be merciful, pray and fast In Secret. Listen, I get it. It's nice to be recognized with a plaque, a reward, a party or even a pat on the back but the real reward, the one that matters most is the reward given to you from your Father in heaven when He sees your good deeds and says, "Well done, my good and faithful servant. Enter thou into the joy of thy Lord."

- Day 303 -

Do you remember gym class when we were young? Remember when the class had to be divided into two teams? Typically the two best athletes of the class were made 'captain' and they began alternately picking people one by one. Each captain would pick their favorite people first and then continue picking, alternating turns, until the two "least favorite" people were left. How humiliating it was to be picked last because it not only meant that you were not the "favorite", but it meant that you were the "least favorite"...

James 2:1-4
My brothers, don't hold the faith of our Lord Jesus Christ of glory with partiality. For if a man with a gold ring, in fine clothing, comes into your synagogue, and a poor man in filthy clothing also comes in; and you pay special attention to him who wears the fine clothing, and say, "Sit here in a good place"; and you tell the poor man, "Stand there," or "Sit by my footstool"; haven't you shown partiality among yourselves, and become judges with evil thoughts?

And yet, even today, our sinful human nature still picks favorites among our business associates, our friends and even amongst our family. How can we possibly claim to have faith in Jesus Christ if we favor one person over another? Let's strive to love all of God's people with the unconditional love He has shown to us. After all, when He died on the cross, didn't He do so because He picked YOU first even forsaking himself to do it? Of all God's creation, He picked YOU first. How does that make you feel in contrast to where you were picked in gym class?

- Day 304 -

Have you heard the story about the Salvation Army finding a gold coin worth thousands of dollars in the bucket? I was discussing that coin with some good friends of mine. At first glance, it's a great story of charity. And then, when you have a chance to think it over a little, a question arises. Is it possible that the coin was planted there by someone at Salvation Army and reported on the news just so they could get air time and encourage others to be similarly generous? Hmmm... Do we choose to be optimistic or pessimistic?

Philippians 4:19
My God will supply every need of yours according to his riches in glory in Christ Jesus.
Luke 12:30-31
For the nations of the world seek after all of these things, but your Father knows that you need these things. But seek God's Kingdom, and all these things will be added to you.
Romans 15:13
Now may the God of hope fill you with all joy and peace in believing, that you may abound in hope, in the power of the Holy Spirit.
Proverbs 14:15
A simple man believes everything, but the prudent man carefully considers his ways.

We are pessimistic by nature, optimistic by faith. Optimism in the Bible is the result of having faith in God and is referred to as hope. The Bible warns us, in the verse above, not to believe everything but don't let that destroy your faith or hope. When given the choice to be optimistic or pessimistic... be optimistic! We serve a mighty God. May He fill you with hope, joy and peace.

- Day 305 -

One of my patients came in today and made an interesting observation. He said he noticed that excuses and garbage cans had something in common. Everyone's got one and they all stink...

Genesis 3:12-13
The man said, "The woman whom you gave to be with me, she gave me fruit from the tree, and I ate it." The Lord God said to the woman, "What have you done?" The woman said, "The serpent deceived me, and I ate."
Exodus 4:10
Moses said to Yahweh, "O Lord, I am not eloquent, neither before now, nor since you have spoken to your servant; for I am slow of speech, and of a slow tongue."
Romans 1:20
For the invisible things of him since the creation of the world are clearly seen, being perceived through the things that are made, even his everlasting power and divinity; that they may be without excuse.
Luke 14:17-20
He sent out his servant at supper time to tell those who were invited, 'Come, for everything is ready now.' They all as one began to make excuses. "The first said to him, 'I have bought a field, and I must go and see it. Please have me excused.' "Another said, 'I have bought five yoke of oxen, and I must go try them out. Please have me excused.' "Another said, 'I have married a wife, and therefore I can't come.'

Excuses go all the way back to Adam and Eve! Adam blames Eve so Eve blames the serpent. God tells Moses he's chosen to free an entire nation and Moses says, "(TO GOD) ya know, maybe you picked the wrong guy. I don't 'talk so good.'" Really??? Is that the best excuse he could come up with on short notice while talking to GOD??!! I think my friend Andy is right. Seems everyone does have an Excuse and a garbage can and they both stink. What excuses have you been using lately to get out of doing something for God that you know you should be doing?

- Day 306 -

Isn't it interesting that some people would do anything for God and others would do anything for Money. Yes, capital 'M' in Money because it almost seems that they are more likely to serve Money than they are to serve God. The Bible has a little to say about that...

Matthew 6:24
"No one can serve two masters, for either he will hate the one and love the other; or else he will be devoted to one and despise the other. You can't serve both God and Mammon.
Luke 16:13
No servant can serve two masters, for either he will hate the one, and love the other; or else he will hold to one, and despise the other. You aren't able to serve God and Mammon."
1 Timothy 6:9-10
But those who are determined to be rich fall into a temptation and a snare and many foolish and harmful lusts, such as drown men in ruin and destruction. For the love of money is a root of all kinds of evil. Some have been led astray from the faith in their greed, and have pierced themselves through with many sorrows.
Hebrews 13:5
Be free from the love of money, content with such things as you have, for he has said, "I will in no way leave you, neither will I in any way forsake you."

Some people work hard all their lives at the expense of everything else to amass a fortune all for naught. But, have you ever seen a hearse being followed by a Brinks truck (armored car)? I haven't. When you die and people are called up to talk about you, what will your kids or close family say about you. Will they recall how much you worked and loved money or will they talk about the quality and quantity time you spent with them and how much you loved God? Truly you cannot serve two masters. You cannot serve God and money. What or Whom would you do anything for?

- Day 307 -

Some churches are what I would call 'vanilla' churches. They're often more like country clubs than a house of God. Sure, there's a steeple and even the token cross hanging somewhere in the building but the message is watered down so that it doesn't 'offend' anyone. Often they deny things like hell or sin to make the message more 'acceptable'. The problem is that if the Holy Spirit were to pull out of those churches, they wouldn't even know it...

Romans 8:11
But if the Spirit of him who raised up Jesus from the dead dwells in you, he who raised up Christ Jesus from the dead will also give life to your mortal bodies through his Spirit who dwells in you.
Acts 6:10
They weren't able to withstand the wisdom and the Spirit by which he spoke.
Acts 10:44
While Peter was still speaking these words, the Holy Spirit fell on all those who heard the word.
2 Timothy 4:3-4
For the time will come when they will not listen to the sound doctrine, but, having itching ears, will heap up for themselves teachers after their own lusts; and will turn away their ears from the truth, and turn aside to fables.

Many people today would rather go somewhere to hear an 'I'm OK, you're OK' message and sing the secular campfire version of 'Kumbaya' instead of digging into the tough topics in the Bible. Vanilla churches teach their children that the Bible is just a nice book instead of the incorruptible, indestructible, everlasting, literal Word of God. Vanilla churches hope for a short, non-offensive sermon so they can get to the coffee and doughnuts "part of the show" and catch up on all the latest gossip instead of dwelling with the Holy Spirit and being taught The Word. If the Holy Spirit pulled out of your church, would anyone notice?

- Day 308 -

There's a great quote attributed to Buddha, "Holding onto anger is like drinking poison expecting the other person to die." How true it is. What does the Bible teach us about anger?

Proverbs 19:11
The discretion of a man makes him slow to anger. It is his glory to overlook an offense.
Proverbs 22:24
Don't befriend a hot-tempered man, and don't associate with one who harbors anger:
Ephesians 4:31
Let all bitterness, wrath, anger, outcry, and slander, be put away from you, with all malice.
James 1:20
for the anger of man doesn't produce the righteousness of God.

Anger gets the best of all of us at one time or another. Have you ever been tailgated and become extremely angry at the driver behind you? That used to really upset me. Now I pull over, allow them to pass and say a prayer for them instead of hitting my brakes and allowing my blood to boil. How freeing! What if we just paused to say a prayer for anyone that upsets us instead of getting angry and cursing at them? How would that change our lives... and theirs?

- Day 309 -

The subject of holiness came up in church during the homily today. What exactly does it mean to be 'holy'? Well, it can mean being devoted to God, being morally and spiritually excellent or being sacred. Think consecrated, hallowed, sanctified, sacrosanct, venerated, revered, divine, religious, blessed, saintly, godly, saintlike, pious, pietistic, religious, devout, God-fearing and spiritual…

1 Thessalonians 3:13
to the end he may establish your hearts blameless in holiness before our God and Father, at the coming of our Lord Jesus with all his saints.
Ephesians 4:24
and put on the new man, who in the likeness of God has been created in righteousness and holiness of truth.
Matthew 6:9
Pray like this: 'Our Father in heaven, may your name be kept holy.
Isaiah 6:3
One called to another, and said, "Holy, holy, holy, is The Lord of Hosts! The whole earth is full of his glory!"

Holy, holy, holy indeed is the Lord God Almighty. In church we pray, "Holy, holy, holy Lord, God of power and might, heaven and earth are full of your glory. Hosanna in the highest. Blessed is he who comes in the name of the Lord. Hosanna in the highest." It is through this prayer that we praise God and ask His blessing on our bread and wine and by doing so, bless us, sanctify us and make us more holy through communion with Him.

- Day 310 -

My friend Martha had a great question yesterday. She asked, "I've always wondered about the expression 'God fearing' and have always wondered why on earth I would need to fear love. I can't understand it." I bet we've all wondered the same thing...

1 John 4:18
There is no fear in love; but perfect love casts out fear, because fear has punishment. He who fears is not made perfect in love.
2 Corinthians 7:1
Having therefore these promises, beloved, let us cleanse ourselves from all defilement of flesh and spirit, perfecting holiness in the fear of God.
Hebrews 12:28-29
Therefore, receiving a Kingdom that can't be shaken, let us have grace, through which we serve God acceptably, with reverence and awe, for our God is a consuming fire.
Deuteronomy 10:12
Now, Israel, what does the Lord your God require of you, but to fear the Lord your God, to walk in all his ways, and to love him, and to serve the Lord your God with all your heart and with all your soul,

Though we're admonished to 'fear God', it's a reverential fear that's being referred to. We, as believers have no reason to fear or be afraid of God because even though we deserve judgment for our sins, we are promised grace. So, to fear God is to revere Him, obey Him, serve Him and worship Him. In the end, like any parent, God wants us, His children, to respect Him, have a healthy fear of Him and love Him with the unconditional love with which He loves us.

- Day 311 -

I had a friend talk to me today about how difficult it is to wait patiently for something that we've been praying for with all our might. We're told to pray hard, pray often, without ceasing and with our whole heart. We know that there are 3 possible answers to our prayers... YES, NO and WAIT. WAITING is perhaps the hardest of all three answers.

Psalm 27:14
Wait for the Lord. Be strong, and let your heart take courage. Yes, wait for the Lord.
Genesis 8:10
He waited yet another seven days; and again he sent the dove out of the ship.
Job 6:11
What is my strength, that I should wait? What is my end, that I should be patient?
Psalm 130:5
I wait for Yahweh. My soul waits. I hope in his word.
Romans 8:23-24
Not only so, but ourselves also, who have the first fruits of the Spirit, even we ourselves groan within ourselves, waiting for adoption, the redemption of our body. For we were saved in hope, but hope that is seen is not hope. For who hopes for that which he sees?

Have you ever heard the phrase, "The best things in life are worth waiting for."? That may be so but it still doesn't make the waiting easier. So, until we're granted our prayers, we will patiently wait on the Lord with the hope that our answer will be YES. What have you been patiently waiting for?

Have you ever noticed that you always get more of whatever you give away? Give away love and you receive more love. Tithe away more money and you somehow have more money in your account. But, if you spread hate and fear, ultimately you will be hated and overcome with fear.

2 Timothy 2:11-13
This saying is trustworthy: "For if we died with him, we will also live with him. If we endure, we will also reign with him. If we deny him, he also will deny us. If we are faithless, he remains faithful. He can't deny himself."
Luke 6:38
"Give, and it will be given to you: good measure, pressed down, shaken together, and running over, will be given to you. For with the same measure you measure it will be measured back to you."
Proverbs 11:24-25 ESV
One gives freely, yet grows all the richer; another withholds what he should give, and only suffers want. Whoever brings blessing will be enriched, and one who waters will himself be watered.
2 Corinthians 9:6-7
Remember this: he who sows sparingly will also reap sparingly. He who sows bountifully will also reap bountifully. Let each man give according as he has determined in his heart; not grudgingly, or under compulsion; for God loves a cheerful giver.

Once again we see the great reversal at work in God's Word and plan for our future. If we give our lives for Christ, we gain life eternal. If we give of our money freely, we grow all the richer. But, if we deny Him, He will also deny us. Whatever you want more of, try giving more of whatever it is away. What is it that you've been yearning for? Have you given any of it away lately?

- Day 313 -

I think that sometimes religion gets in the way of the message of the gospel. Ritual and tradition often divide us rather than unite us in Christ. John Wesley tells of a dream he had. In the dream, he was ushered to the gates of Hell. There he asked, "Are there any Presbyterians here?" "Yes!", came the answer. Then he asked, "Are there any Baptists? Any Episcopalians? Any Methodists?" The answer was Yes! each time...

1 Corinthians 1:10-15
Now I beg you, brothers, through the name of our Lord, Jesus Christ, that you all speak the same thing and that there be no divisions among you, but that you be perfected together in the same mind and in the same judgment. For it has been reported to me concerning you, my brothers, by those who are from Chloe's household, that there are contentions among you. Now I mean this, that each one of you says, "I follow Paul," "I follow Apollos," "I follow Cephas," and, "I follow Christ." Is Christ divided? Was Paul crucified for you? Or were you baptized into the name of Paul? I thank God that I baptized none of you, except Crispus and Gaius, so that no one should say that I had baptized you into my own name.

Much distressed, Wesley was then ushered to the gates of Heaven. There he asked the same questions, and the answer was No! "No?" To this, Wesley asked, "Who then is inside?" The answer came back, "There are only Christians here." We need to be aware that denominational differences are the devil's tools. After all, aren't all of us Christians praying for the same team?

- Day 314 -

I've heard the phrase, "Holidays bring out the worst in people." But, yesterday our office had a patient appreciation day where we offered our services in exchange for non-perishable food to be donated to the food bank and/or a donation to one of two local charities. The event was on a walk in basis. Nobody was 'scheduled' to arrive so we didn't know how many people to plan for. WOW! People turned out in droves and we saw, first hand, how the "Holidays bring out the BEST in people".

Proverbs 11:17(AMP)
The merciful and generous man benefits his soul [for his behavior returns to bless him], But the cruel and uncharitable man does himself harm.
Matthew 2:10-11
When they saw the star, they rejoiced with exceedingly great joy. They came into the house and saw the young child with Mary, his mother, and they fell down and worshiped him. Opening their treasures, they offered to him gifts: gold, frankincense, and myrrh.

It is in mirroring Jesus, especially at this time of year, through merciful acts and generosity that we come to appreciate what His birth and ministry were all about. It is through these acts of kindness, charity and mercy that we more fully live out the gospel and prove to the world that being a Christian brings out the 'BEST' in us, particularly during the holidays but more importantly, throughout the entire year.

- Day 315 -

Come they told me parum pum pum pum A new born King to see parum pum pum pum Our finest gifts we bring parum pum pum pum To lay before the King parum pum pum pum rum pum pum pum rum pum pum pum So to honor Him Parum pum pum pum When we come. Baby Jesus parum pum pum pum I am a poor boy too parum pum pum pum I have no gift to bring parum pum pum pum That's fit to give a King parum pum pum pum Rum pum pum pum rum pum pum pum. Shall I play for you parum pum pum pum on my drum?

Luke 21:3-4
He said, "Truly I tell you, this poor widow put in more than all of them, for all these put in gifts for God from their abundance, but she, out of her poverty, put in all that she had to live on."

(Mary nodded parum pum pum pum The ox and lamb kept time parum pum pum pum) I played my drum for Him parum pum pum pum I played my best for Him parum pum pum pum Rum pum pum pum rum pum pum pum Then He smiled at me parum pum pum pum Me and my drum Me and my drum... God doesn't care that you have lots of wealth, fame or talent. God Only cares that you do your best with what you have to honor and glorify Him. Don't we all desire the same thing this Christmas? The smile from the baby Jesus confirming that He is well pleased with us?

- Day 316 -

We hear a lot about the people referred to as the Philistines. I don't know why but until tonight I never paid much attention to why they were called the Philistines or what the word meant or came to mean today. When you look Philistine up in the dictionary is means: a person who is hostile or indifferent to culture and the arts, or who has no understanding of them. In short, it means someone that's uncultured.

Zephaniah 2:5
Woe to the inhabitants of the sea coast, the nation of the Cherethites! Yahweh's word is against you, Canaan, the land of the Philistines. I will destroy you, that there will be no inhabitant.
Amos 1:8
I will cut off the inhabitant from Ashdod, and him who holds the scepter from Ashkelon; and I will turn my hand against Ekron; and the remnant of the Philistines will perish," says the Lord Yahweh.
Ezekiel 25:15
Thus says the Lord Yahweh: Because the Philistines have dealt by revenge, and have taken vengeance with despite of soul to destroy with perpetual hostility;
1 Chronicles 10:1-2
Now the Philistines fought against Israel, and the men of Israel fled from before the Philistines, and fell down slain on Mount Gilboa. The Philistines followed hard after Saul and after his sons; and the Philistines killed Jonathan, Abinadab, and Malchishua, the sons of Saul.

From biblical accounts, it appears as though the nation of Israel has been at odds with the Philistines for centuries before the birth of Christ. It seems that these 'uncultured' people of long ago thought the Jewish people might be an easy target. But they thought wrong. It really never ends well for anyone that goes against Yahweh's (The Lord God Almighty) people. Even to this day Israel is being threatened and attacked by 'philistines'. We all know that's not going to end well for the Philistines.

- Day 317 -

Hey, imagine you're just about to bake an important cake that calls for all the EVOO (that's extra virgin olive oil for those of you that aren't Rachael Ray fans) and flour you have. It's a really important cake. In fact, it's the dying wish of a close friend to have one last bite of your cake before she goes to be with the Lord. A stranger shows up at the door, tells you he's hungry. He wants a glass of water and the cake you just baked. You have no other food in the house to offer and he is clearly starving. What would you do?

1 Kings 17:7-16
After a while, the brook dried up, because there was no rain in the land. The Lord's word came to him, saying, "Arise, go to Zarephath, which belongs to Sidon, and stay there. Behold, I have commanded a widow there to sustain you." So he arose and went to Zarephath; and when he came to the gate of the city, behold, a widow was there gathering sticks. He called to her, and said, "Please get me a little water in a jar, that I may drink."

As she was going to get it, he called to her, and said, "Please bring me a morsel of bread in your hand." She said, "As the Lord your God lives, I don't have a cake, but a handful of meal in a jar, and a little oil in a jar. Behold, I am gathering two sticks, that I may go in and bake it for me and my son, that we may eat it, and die."

Elijah said to her, "Don't be afraid. Go and do as you have said; but make me a little cake from it first, and bring it out to me, and afterward make some for you and for your son. For Yahweh, the God of Israel says, 'The jar of meal will not run out, and the jar of oil will not fail, until the day that Yahweh sends rain on the earth.'" She went and did according to the saying of Elijah; and she, and he, and her house, ate many days. The jar of meal didn't run out, and the jar of oil did not fail, according to Yahweh's word, which he spoke by Elijah.

Now, it's true, we're no widow from the Old Testament, there's no drought and the stranger that knocks on our door is most likely not Elijah. But, we may be in another kind of drought... a financial drought or an emotional drought or maybe even a health drought. The stranger that knocks on our door may not ask for our last drop of water, EVOO or bread but he or she may ask for our spare change, a shoulder to cry on or perhaps a ride to the chiropractor for an adjustment. Remember, the stranger may not be Elijah, but it may be Jesus (Matthew 25:35-40). Will you give away your water to one who is thirsty during your drought when you need the water the most?

- Day 318 -

Have you ever stumbled upon the interesting word, lachesism? Lachesism is a secret desire to be struck by disaster. It's watching the news with the secret desire to hear that the apocalypse has started, it's waiting for the mega-storm to come secretly hoping it will wipe out all the power and destroy all of civilization as we know it. A part of us is waiting, often secretly, wondering when this life will end and praying for what comes next.

John 11:25
Jesus said to her, "I am the resurrection and the life. He who believes in me will still live, even if he dies.
Daniel 12:2
Many of those who sleep in the dust of the earth shall awake, some to everlasting life, and some to shame and everlasting contempt.
Philippians 1:21-23
For to me to live is Christ, and to die is gain. But if I live on in the flesh, this will bring fruit from my work; yet I don't know what I will choose. But I am in a dilemma between the two, having the desire to depart and be with Christ, which is far better.

I'm sure that we have all wondered what it'll be like after we shed this 'meat suit' we call our physical body. We've all read the Bible passage that claims the end of times is near and Jesus is coming to judge the living and the dead VERY SOON. Secretly we want to be back in the arms of Jesus and standing in the presence of our Father in Heaven. But, it's not our time or we would have been called home already. So until then, let's do our best to do our best to please, honor and glorify God.

- Day 319 -

Effervescent is a pretty cool word and it's fun to say. It's more common definition is 'giving off bubbles; fizzy' but it is also defined as vivacious and enthusiastic. By the latter definition, I'd say the better part of the Bible can be described as effervescent.

Romans 12:11 AMP
never lagging behind in diligence; aglow in the Spirit, enthusiastically serving the Lord;
Titus 2:14
who [willingly] gave Himself [to be crucified] on our behalf to redeem us and purchase our freedom from all wickedness, and to purify for Himself a chosen and very special people to be His own possession, who are enthusiastic for doing what is good.
1 Peter 3:13
Now who is there to hurt you if you become enthusiastic for what is good?
Revelation 3:19
Those whom I [dearly and tenderly] love, I rebuke and discipline [showing them their faults and instructing them]; so be enthusiastic and repent [change your inner self—your old way of thinking, your sinful behavior—seek God's will].

Shouldn't we all be more effervescent when it comes to praising and glorifying God? Shouldn't we all be more enthusiastic about what is good and right and perfect in our life through Jesus Christ? Shouldn't the Gospel just bubble up within us as we go forth into the world and preach it to every creature who will listen? Of course it should! Let's get more effervescent when it comes to God. How will you demonstrate your effervescence today?

- Day 320 -

Auld Lang Syne means "old long since" or "days gone by". The song Auld Lang Syne is really a song about a rhetorical question. It asks, "Is it right that old times be forgotten?" The answer is generally interpreted as a call to remember long-standing friendships.

Proverbs 17:17
A friend loves at all times; and a brother is born for adversity.
Exodus 33:11
The Lord spoke to Moses face to face, as a man speaks to his friend…
Proverbs 18:24
A man of many companions may be ruined, but there is a friend who sticks closer than a brother.
Proverbs 27:17
Iron sharpens iron; so a man sharpens his friend's countenance.
John 15:13
Greater love has no one than this, that someone lay down his life for his friends.
James 2:23
and the Scripture was fulfilled which says, "Abraham believed God, and it was accounted to him as righteousness"; and he was called the friend of God.

Should Old Acquaintance be forgot, and never thought upon? Let's not forget old times or old friends this year. Let's continue to learn from our experiences of Auld Lang Syne and from our friends who share this wonderful journey called life. Though it's true that friends may come and go in different seasons of our lives, we have one Friend who will never leave us, never fail us and never forsake us.

- Day 321 -

I was with a friend this afternoon and she had a pair of sneakers on with a small hole in one of the shoes. Jokingly I told her that I loved her 'religious' shoes. She looked at me inquisitively and asked what I meant. I told her they were 'Hole-y' shoes. To which she replied, "Yes, but they're only HALF holy." Isn't that just like it is in our lives? No matter how much we try to be completely holy, we end up only 'half holy".

Romans 3:23-25
for all have sinned, and fall short of the glory of God; being justified freely by his grace through the redemption that is in Christ Jesus; whom God sent to be an atoning sacrifice, through faith in his blood, for a demonstration of his righteousness through the passing over of prior sins, in God's forbearance;
1 John 1:
If we say that we have no sin, we deceive ourselves, and the truth is not in us.
1 Peter 1:15-16
but just as he who called you is holy, you yourselves also be holy in all of your behavior; because it is written, "You shall be holy; for I am holy.

We are admonished to be holy by God through His Word. We all want to please our Father in heaven but we have all sinned and fallen short of His Glory. In essence, we have good intentions but pretty bad follow-through. So, that makes us "Half- Holy" just like my friend's shoes. Luckily, being 'fully holy' is not a requirement for admission into heaven. A guy named Jesus was fully holy and it is through Him that we are granted eternity with God and all that's required is asking Him into your heart and making Him your Lord and Savior.

- Day 322 -

I read an extraordinary testimony from my friend Heather in which she described her trials of last year. She was diagnosed with cancer and has now completely and totally recovered (PRAISE GOD). She describes where her peace and calm came from during this 'storm' in her life. She recounts having heard the word of God, in her heart, clearly telling her "This is MY daughter. SHE IS MINE."

Isaiah 43:1
But now The Lord who created you, Jacob, and he who formed you, Israel says: "Don't be afraid, for I have redeemed you. I have called you by your name. You are mine.
Psalm 100:3
Know that The Lord, he is God. It is he who has made us, and we are his. We are his people, and the sheep of his pasture.
Ephesians 2:10
For we are his workmanship, created in Christ Jesus for good works, which God prepared before that we would walk in them.
Isaiah 41:13
For I, The Lord your God, will hold your right hand, saying to you, 'Don't be afraid. I will help you.'

I too heard God speak to my heart this past year. I broke 3 ribs and what was supposed to take 10 weeks, took 10 days to heal. I tore a disc in my lower back in half and what should have required a surgery and 5 months to repair took only 2 weeks before I returned to the office to serve God by serving His children through Chiropractic. I suspect Heather and I were not alone in witnessing God's miracles and blessings in our lives. Let us take a moment right now to thank God for both the answered and unanswered prayers acknowledging that although we may not understand why things happened the way they did, we believe that ALL THINGS work together for good for those that love the Lord and are called according to His purpose.

- Day 323 -

During a bad storm, one of our biggest concerns is that we might lose power. Without power we lose our sense of connectedness. Without being connected to the power, we lose our light. All we seek is to be reconnected to the power...

1 John 1:5-7
This is the message which we have heard from him and announce to you, that God is light, and in him is no darkness at all. If we say that we have fellowship with him and walk in the darkness, we lie, and don't tell the truth. But if we walk in the light, as he is in the light, we have fellowship with one another, and the blood of Jesus Christ, his Son, cleanses us from all sin.
Psalm 27:1
The LORD is my light and my salvation; Whom shall I fear? The LORD is the defense of my life; Whom shall I fear?
Micah 7:8
Do not rejoice over me, O my enemy Though I fall I will rise; Though I dwell in darkness, the LORD is a light for me.
Revelation 22:5
And there will no longer be any night; and they will not have need of the light of a lamp nor the light of the sun, because the Lord God will illumine them; and they will reign forever and ever.

There will come a day for all those that believe and are baptized where there will never again be the fear that the power will go out. There will come a day where we will be in the light and the light will be in us and the fear of darkness will be no more. There will come a day, very soon, when we will not have to call the power company to be reconnected during or after a storm because we will walk in the light of Christ forever more. Make sure you are firmly connected to The Source of Light and Life today. Are you ready for any storm that may come your way?

- Day 324 -

I recently watched an episode of The Crown on Netflix where the queen struggled with the concept of forgiveness. She was informed of her uncle's collusion with Hitler and the Nazis just before and after he abdicated the throne. In light of this revelation, she found herself in a position where she knew forgiveness was the Christian thing to do but as a human, a mortal and monarch she was unable to grant that forgiveness...

Matthew 6:14
"For if you forgive men their trespasses, your heavenly Father will also forgive you.
Ephesians 4:32
And be kind to one another, tender hearted, forgiving each other, just as God also in Christ forgave you.
Matthew 5:44
But I tell you, love your enemies, bless those who curse you, do good to those who hate you, and pray for those who mistreat you and persecute you,
1 Peter 4:8
And above all things be earnest in your love among yourselves, for love covers a multitude of sins.

The queen sat down with Billy Graham who was visiting England at the time and asked for advice. Billy advised her that the Bible is clear on this issue and we are admonished to forgive as Christ forgave us. Seeing her angst he offers one more piece of advice. If you find yourself unable to forgive, ask God for forgiveness yourself and pray for those you are unable to forgive. Sound Biblical advice. Is there someone you find yourself unable to forgive? Let's take a moment now to ask God for forgiveness and to pray for that person or persons that we find ourselves unable to forgive.

- Day 325 -

We are asked to pray often in the Bible. The Bible even goes so far as to say that we should pray without ceasing. As a result, prayer is a big part of many of our lives. When asked if we pray, we may even tell others that we pray "all the time" when, in fact, we really only pray regularly when we go to sleep at night or wake in the morning or are confronted with a tough situation during the day.

Psalm 32:6
For this, let everyone who is godly pray to you in a time when you may be found.
Psalm 69:13
But as for me, my prayer is to you, The Lord, in an acceptable time. God, in the abundance of your loving kindness, answer me in the truth of your salvation.
Ephesians 6:18
with all prayer and requests, praying at all times in the Spirit, and being watchful to this end in all perseverance and requests for all the saints:
1 Thessalonians 5:17
Pray without ceasing.

Maybe we ought to put aside time each day, perhaps during lunch or at another designated time to meditate (sit quietly) and pray. Maybe it's time to take your prayer life to a whole new level by dedicating a special time each day to sit in silence and listen to God while simultaneously allowing God to sit silently and listen to you. Would your relationship with God deepen if you made this a new practice?

Atelophobia is also called the fear of imperfection. This is a fear that whatever we do will not be good enough. Deeper still is the fear that we can never be good enough. That makes one wonder. Perhaps the real fear is the realization that we all fall short of perfection and without Jesus the outcome is pretty bleak.

Romans 3:23
for all have sinned, and fall short of the glory of God;
Hebrews 12:15
looking carefully lest there be any man who falls short of the grace of God; lest any root of bitterness springing up trouble you, and many be defiled by it;
Matthew 8:8
The centurion answered, "Lord, I'm not worthy for you to come under my roof. Just say the word, and my servant will be healed.
Colossians 3:14
Above all these things, walk in love, which is the bond of perfection.

There's a big difference between being saved and not accepting Jesus as your personal Lord and Savior. We all know that we are not perfect. We all know that according to Levitical law, we have all sinned and thus fallen short of the glory of God. The difference is that those of us that are saved are saved not only from eternal separation from God (Hell), we are also saved from atelophobia because we know that with Him, we are made perfect in our imperfection.

- Day 327 -

Today I had a great experience at a local repair shop. I went in thinking I wanted one thing to be done and the owner suggested something that was even better than what I wanted. Often in life, we think we want something. We are absolutely sure we want that thing but God has something even better waiting for us.

Jeremiah 29:11
For I know the plans that I have for you, says The lord, plans of peace, and not of evil, to give you hope and a future.
1 Timothy 2:3-4
For this is good and acceptable in the sight of God our Savior; who desires all people to be saved and come to full knowledge of the truth.
Proverbs 16:9
A man's heart plans his course, but the Lord directs his steps.
Psalm 37:23
A man's steps are established by The Lord. He delights in his way.

I've heard it said that "man makes plans and God laughs". Even when we think we know what's best for us, God has something even better in store for us. Just as I went into the repair shop today hoping for an ordinary fix for my problem and came away with an extraordinary solution, God doesn't want us to hope for an ordinary life; He has an extraordinary life planned for us. Have you been settling for 'ordinary' when God has been trying to provide 'extraordinary' for you?

- Day 328 -

When we are in a dark place in our lives or going through a valley, it's perfectly normal to be afraid. In fact it's totally OK to feel overwhelmed and frustrated. But, can you think of any time in your life when you were in a bad situation and God abandoned you there?

Psalm 27:2
When evildoers came at me to eat up my flesh, even my adversaries and my foes, they stumbled and fell.
Deuteronomy 31:8
Yahweh himself is who goes before you. He will be with you. He will not fail you nor forsake you. Don't be afraid. Don't be discouraged."
Isaiah 41:10-13
Don't you be afraid, for I am with you. Don't be dismayed, for I am your God. I will strengthen you. Yes, I will help you. Yes, I will uphold you with the right hand of my righteousness. Behold, all those who are incensed against you will be disappointed and confounded. Those who strive with you will be like nothing, and shall perish. You will seek them, and won't find them, even those who contend with you. Those who war against you will be as nothing, as a non-existent thing. For I, Yahweh your God, will hold your right hand, saying to you, 'Don't be afraid. I will help you.'

When you're going through a valley in your life and it seems that darkness has surrounded you, realize THAT IS IMPOSSIBLE! God promised never to leave you nor forsake you. It only looks dark because you are facing away from the light which is Him. Turn and face the light and feel the warmth of His love. Remember that He has never forsaken you in the past, why would you believe the lie that He would do that now? Can you see the light and feel the warmth? If not, turn and face Him by picking up the Bible and reading The Word He wrote for you.

- Day 329 -

How is it possible that we experience Confidence and Exuberance in The Lord and in nearly the same moment we feel apprehension and discouragement? Somehow we feel 'less than' and guilty because of our insufficiency when we know that God wants us to be resolute in our faith that with Him we are Victors not victims. It's almost as though we are double-minded.

James 4:8
Draw near to God, and he will draw near to you. Cleanse your hands, you sinners; and purify your hearts, you double-minded.
1 John 5:4
For whatever is born of God overcomes the world. This is the victory that has overcome the world: your faith.
Romans 8:37
No, in all these things, we are more than conquerors through him who loved us.
Deuteronomy 31:8
The Lord himself is who goes before you. He will be with you. He will not fail you nor forsake you. Don't be afraid. Don't be discouraged."

You are not alone. Even though spiritually we are victors, overcomers and conquerors, our flesh is weak and we all have thoughts of being insufficient, unworthy and discouraged. There is a constant battle within us between the flesh and the spirit. Know that as you draw nearer to God, the spirit wins over the flesh and you will overcome all doubt. Have you drawn near to God or have you drifted away?

Day 330

I don't know about you but I take objection to the use of so many adjectives placed in front of the noun Christian. Whether the adjective is inherently good or bad, sinful or moral makes no difference, I still object. I also take objection to adjectives placed in front of the noun Church. Evangelical, Baptist, Catholic, Lutheran, White, Black, traditional, Contemporary, etc...

Acts 11:26
When he had found him, he brought him to Antioch. For a whole year they were gathered together with the assembly, and taught many people. The disciples were first called Christians in Antioch.
1 Peter 4:16
But if one of you suffers for being a Christian, let him not be ashamed; but let him glorify God in this matter.
1 Corinthians 12:25, 26
that there should be no division in the body, but that the members should have the same care for one another... Now you are the body of Christ, and members individually.
Romans 12:16
Live in peace with one another. Don't set your mind on high things, but associate with the humble. Don't be wise in your own conceits.

Adjectives only serve to divide the body and the message contained in the ONE WORD given to us by ONE GOD through the ONE AND ONLY SAVIOR, JESUS CHRIST. Let's focus less on adjectives for Christ's church and His followers and focus more on verbs like Giving, Loving, Serving and Doing.

- Day 331 -

At Bible study last week, an interesting question came up. What is the most valuable thing you possess or can give away. At first, TIME came to mind. Time, I thought, was something I highly value and once you give it away, you can never get it back. But, there is indeed something way more important than time and it is the most valuable thing you can give away.

Psalm 19:7
The Lord's law is perfect, restoring the soul. The Lord's testimony is sure, making wise the simple.
Joshua 1:8
This book of the law shall not depart from your mouth, but you shall meditate on it day and night, that you may observe to do according to all that is written in it; for then you shall make your way prosperous, and then you shall have good success.
Romans 10:17
So faith comes by hearing, and hearing by the word of God.
2 Timothy 3:16-17
Every Scripture is God-breathed and profitable for teaching, for reproof, for correction, and for instruction in righteousness, that the man of God may be complete, thoroughly equipped for every good work.

I remember my son and I were having a heart to heart talk when he was younger. I told him that if I died and there were only one thing I could leave for him, it would be my faith in God. The same would apply for my daughter. The thing I value most is my faith. Since faith is not something you can just simply give away, I believe, now that I have had a chance to think about it, the most valuable thing I possess or could give away would be my Bible. How valuable is YOUR Bible?

The Bible is a vehicle for us to speak to God and for God to communicate with us. When the Bible is viewed that way, the slight differences between different translations become unimportant. His words, written for us, are always there to give us answers to the most difficult questions in our lives.

Hebrews 4:12
For the word of God is living and active, and sharper than any two-edged sword, piercing even to the dividing of soul and spirit, of both joints and marrow, and is able to discern the thoughts and intentions of the heart.
2 Timothy 3:16
Every Scripture is God-breathed and profitable for teaching, for reproof, for correction, and for instruction in righteousness,
Romans 10:17
So faith comes by hearing, and hearing by the word of God.
Exodus 3:2-4
The Lord's angel appeared to him in a flame of fire out of the middle of a bush. He looked, and behold, the bush burned with fire, and the bush was not consumed. Moses said, "I will turn aside now, and see this great sight, why the bush is not burnt." When Yahweh saw that he turned aside to see, God called to him out of the middle of the bush, and said, "Moses! Moses!" He said, "Here I am."

I don't know about you, but I haven't been spoken to through a burning bush lately. I haven't heard an audible voice of God teaching me, reproofing me or giving me specific instructions. I have, however, received guidance, encouragement, hope, comfort, and understanding (among other great gifts) from God through the Bible. How is it possible that a text written about 2000 years ago can speak to us so specifically, directly and accurately if it were not only God inspired but actually written By God through dozens of authors? Your Bible, His Word is waiting... What are you waiting for? Go have a conversation with Him!

- Day 333 -

Waiting Upon The Lord. That is the hardest part for the flesh... Waiting. It's not the asking through prayer that's tough. It's the middle part when we wait in silence for an answer. Often the silence is deafening.

Psalm 27:14
Wait for Yahweh. Be strong, and let your heart take courage. Yes, wait for Yahweh.
Jeremiah 14:22
Are there any among the vanities of the nations that can cause rain? or can the sky give showers? Aren't you he, the Lord our God? therefore we will wait for you; for you have made all these things.
Psalm 145:15-16
The eyes of all wait for you. You give them their food in due season. You open your hand, and satisfy the desire of every living thing.
Psalm 25:5
Guide me in your truth, and teach me, For you are the God of my salvation, I wait for you all day long.
Hosea 12:6
Therefore turn thou to thy God: keep mercy and judgment, and wait on thy God continually.
Lamentations 3:25
The LORD is good unto them that wait for him, to the soul that seeketh him.

There are several dozen other verses that I wanted to share with you about Waiting On The Lord. There are nearly a dozen uplifting verses about waiting on The Lord in Isaiah alone but I'll let you go explore those on your own! It's true that waiting is the hardest part but while you're waiting stay in faith, stay in prayer and study His Word. Start in Isaiah with 40:31 and see if you can find all 12 encouraging verses about waiting in that book alone.

- Day 334 -

Have you read the account of Joseph being visited by the angel Gabriel in his dream? I thought it was pretty clear cut that the angel told Joseph that Mary was pregnant with God's baby by the Holy Spirit, Joseph was to marry her and call the baby Jesus. I thought it was also pretty clear cut that Joseph was OBEDIENT to God's will and did what the angel told him to do.

Recently I heard another interpretation of that story told by a pastor whereby Joseph was just having a bad night's sleep knowing that Mary was pregnant. He got up after a particularly bad dream, made a cup of coffee and decided that no matter what the elders, Pharisees or Sadducees said about marrying a lying, cheating, pregnant woman, he was going to do it anyway, darn the consequences, it was just the right thing to do.

SO, what's the difference between the first and the second story?

2 Timothy 4:4
And they shall turn away their ears from the truth, and shall be turned unto fables.
Matthew 1:18-25
Now the birth of Jesus Christ was on this wise: When as his mother Mary was espoused to Joseph, before they came together, she was found with child of the Holy Ghost. Then Joseph her husband, being a just man, and not willing to make her a public example, was minded to put her away privily. But while he thought on these things, behold, the angel of the Lord appeared unto him in a dream, saying, Joseph, thou son of David, fear not to take unto thee Mary thy wife: for that which is conceived in her is of the Holy Ghost. And she shall bring forth a son, and thou shalt call his name Jesus: for he shall save his people from their sins. Now all this was done, that it might be fulfilled which was spoken of the Lord by the prophet, saying, Behold, a virgin shall be with child, and shall bring forth a son, and they shall call his name Emmanuel, which being interpreted is, God with us. Then Joseph being raised from sleep did as the angel of the Lord had bidden him, and took unto him his wife: And knew her not till she had brought forth her firstborn son: and he called his name Jesus.

How are the two versions different? Joseph had a dream, he decided to marry Mary and that's all that's important, RIGHT? WRONG! One version of the story teaches obedience to God and the other teaches it's 'OK' to be disobedient. One version teaches humility, the other teaches pridefulness. One is Godly, the other is blasphemous. One leads to heaven, the other to hell. One is the TRUTH, the other is a myth or a FABLE which God warns us against in 2 Timothy 4:4. Do you know the TRUTH well enough to discern it from the Myths and Fables? Do you know the GOOD NEWS well enough to discern it from the "Fake News"?

- Day 335 -

Ever felt so busy and scheduled that you were running around endlessly without a chance to take a breath? I see people doing this more and more...

Song of Solomon 2:1
I am the rose of Sharon, and the lily of the valleys.
Genesis 2:2-3
And on the seventh day God ended his work which he had made; and he rested on the seventh day from all his work which he had made. And God blessed the seventh day, and sanctified it: because that in it he had rested from all his work which God created and made.
Jeremiah 2:25 (MSG)
"Slow down. Take a deep breath. What's the hurry? Why wear yourself out? Just what are you after anyway? But you say, 'I can't help it. I'm addicted to alien gods. I can't quit.'

Take time to smell the roses... When was the last time you took the time to slow down, catch your breath and smell the roses?

Ever made a wrong turn by accident and saw the big red signs that say: ONE WAY... GO BACK!... DO NOT ENTER!... ? Scared the living daylight out of you, didn't it? It's not like you weren't warned by the first sign that said ONE WAY, but you either didn't see it, you were distracted or you ignored it and by doing so, you put yourself in a dangerous situation.

John 14:6
Jesus said to him, "I am the way, the truth, and the life. No one comes to the Father, except through me.
Matthew 7:13-14
"Enter in by the narrow gate; for wide is the gate and broad is the way that leads to destruction, and many are those who enter in by it. How narrow is the gate, and restricted is the way that leads to life! Few are those who find it.
Acts 4:12
There is salvation in none other, for neither is there any other name under heaven, that is given among men, by which we must be saved!"
Romans 10:13
For, "Whoever will call on the name of the Lord will be saved."

The Bible clearly says there's only ONE WAY to heaven. There are two gates. One is really attractive, wide and easy to get through but God has put signs above it saying, "WARNING- GO BACK- DO NOT ENTER". There is another gate that's really narrow and tough to find without the help of a friend or family member. The wide gate leads to eternal separation from God, the narrow gate leads to eternity with God in Heaven. The ONE and ONLY WAY to salvation is through Jesus. He is the narrow gate. Who will you help find the narrow gate today?

- Day 337 -

Isn't it interesting that people tend to be OK with saying 'GOD' or 'Lord' out loud and they feel comfortable ending a prayer in 'His name' but when it comes to the name above all names, JESUS, there appears to be some hesitation? I find that during conversations in the office centered around the Bible people will tend to whisper when they say 'JESUS'. Why is that?

Romans 1:16
For I am not ashamed of the gospel of Jesus Christ: for it is the power of God unto salvation to everyone that believeth; to the Jew first, and also to the Greek.
Luke 18:38
And he called out, saying, "Jesus, Son of David, have mercy on me!"
Philippians 2:8-10
And being found in fashion as a man, he humbled himself, and became obedient unto death, even the death of the cross. Wherefore God also hath highly exalted him, and given him a name which is above every name: That at the name of Jesus every knee should bow, of things in heaven, and things in earth, and things under the earth;

Perhaps the day has come where we should proclaim Jesus' holy name, out loud, unashamedly, so that all can hear it. We should spread the Gospel of Jesus Christ out loud, sharing his message and demonstrating the power in His name. Jesus' name is above all names let's exalt Him. How does it make you feel when you hear someone call you by your name? I've heard that the sweetest sound we can hear is our own name. How do you think Jesus feels when we use His name, out loud, praising and glorifying Him?

Tonight in church the priest that retired a few years ago came back to 'pinch hit' for our current priests. Perhaps it's the fact that Father Creedon was the priest here when I decided to return to the Catholic Church but there's something very comforting about his voice. It's kind of like listening to your earthly father or grandfather giving advice through the homily. There's one thing he does that no one else seems to do. Before he reads from the Bible, instead of just making the sign of the cross on his head, lips and heart, as he does it, he says words that are a teaching moment in and of themselves.

Philippians 4:8
Finally, brothers, whatever things are true, whatever things are honorable, whatever things are just, whatever things are pure, whatever things are lovely, whatever things are of good report; if there is any virtue, and if there is any praise, THINK ABOUT THESE THINGS.
Matthew 22:37
Jesus said to him, "'You shall love the Lord your God with all your heart, with all your soul, and with all your MIND.'
Hebrews 13:15
Through him, then, let us offer up a sacrifice of praise to God continually, that is, the fruit of LIPS which proclaim allegiance to his name.
Romans 10:9
that if you will confess with your mouth that Jesus is Lord, and believe IN YOUR HEART that God raised him from the dead, you will be saved.

As Father Creedon makes the three signs of the cross, he says, "May His Word ever be in your mind, on your lips and find a home in your heart." Simple, I know, but very profoundly biblical. Let's take a moment to contemplate how much we appreciate and love God's Word with all our MIND. May we take every opportunity to share His Word with our LIPS. May we believe His Word in full faith so that Jesus finds OUR HEART a suitable place to dwell within us. Thank you Father Creedon for reminding us of the importance of His Word in relation to our mind, lips and heart.

- Day 339 -

Tastes like chicken, but it's not. Often things are not as they appear in life or in faith. We're offered stuff in this world that's made to look and taste like heaven and the way to get to heaven… but it's not.

2 Thessalonians 2:3
Let no one deceive you in any way. For it will not be, unless the departure comes first, and the man of sin is revealed, the son of destruction,
Genesis 3:13
Yahweh God said to the woman, "What have you done?" The woman said, "The serpent deceived me, and I ate."
Leviticus 19:11
"'You shall not steal. "'You shall not lie. "'You shall not deceive one another.
2 John 1:7
For many deceivers have gone out into the world, those who don't confess that Jesus Christ came in the flesh. This is the deceiver and the Antichrist.
Galatians 2:16
yet knowing that a man is not justified by the works of the law but through faith in Jesus Christ, even we believed in Christ Jesus, that we might be justified by faith in Christ, and not by the works of the law, because no flesh will be justified by the works of the law.

There's a lie being told by deceivers. They say there are other ways to get to heaven besides through Jesus. They're saying that "if you're a 'good person' or do enough 'good stuff' that you're going to heaven". You'll be told those 'other gods' and 'other religions' are just like Jesus and can get you to heaven. Frog legs, seagulls, snakes, turtles, kangaroos, iguanas, alligators and termites all taste like chicken, but they're not. Those 'other gods and religions' seem like another way to get to heaven… but they're not. Don't be deceived.

- Day 340 -

Today, a lesson on Leadership from Fr. Creedon's homily borrowed from the book The Servant by James Hunter. Leadership is the skill of influencing people to work for the common good. Some leaders use POWER to force or coerce people into action even if their hearts are against it. Other leaders use Authority to Influence people to voluntarily do what they task them to do...

Matthew 7:29
for he taught them with authority, and not like the scribes.
Mark 1:27
They were all amazed, so that they questioned among themselves, saying, "What is this? A new teaching? For with authority he commands even the unclean spirits, and they obey him!"
Luke 5:24
But that you may know that the Son of Man has authority on earth to forgive sins" (he said to the paralyzed man), "I tell you, arise, and take up your cot, and go to your house."
Mark 9:35
He sat down, and called the twelve; and he said to them, "If any man wants to be first, he shall be last of all, and servant of all."

Jesus taught and acted with Authority, not Power. Authority is built on service and sacrifice and there can be no service or sacrifice without LOVE. Jesus lead by example with AGAPE LOVE through service to mankind and made the ultimate sacrifice to satisfy the needs of those He served. Jesus was fully God, fully human and was without a doubt the greatest servant-leader to have ever lived. Let us follow His example as we lead others to Christ by becoming better servants.

- Day 341 -

I recently heard a great quote: "For the unbeliever, earth is the closest to God they will ever get. To the believer, earth is the closest to hell as they will ever get.

James 4:8
Draw near to God, and he will draw near to you. Cleanse your hands, you sinners; and purify your hearts, you double-minded.
Psalm 73:28
But it is good for me to come close to God. I have made the Lord Yahweh my refuge, that I may tell of all your works.
Zephaniah 3:2
She didn't obey the voice. She didn't receive correction. She didn't trust in The Lord. She didn't draw near to her God.
Hebrews 7:25
Therefore he is also able to save to the uttermost those who draw near to God through him, seeing that he lives forever to make intercession for them.

We all had the same law to live by called the 10 Commandments. We have all fallen short of following those commandments and thus have committed sin in God's eyes. Those that believe in Jesus and have accepted Him as their Lord and Savior are saved by grace and will avoid an eternal separation from God (hell). Those that do not believe will pay the penalty for sin and will get even further from the source of light and life upon death. Are you as close to God as you'll ever get right now or have you been saved by grace and look forward to dwelling with God for eternity?

- Day 342 -

"I have often felt myself to be a point of light, connected to everyone I have ever loved, or mattered to, each also being a point of light, in turn connected to those they love, so that somehow we are all part of a vast web of twinkling lights." - Jean Shinoda Bolen in Crossing To Avalon. This was a reading at my friend Lori Heaps' memorial service.

John 8:12
Again, therefore, Jesus spoke to them, saying, "I am the light of the world. He who follows me will not walk in the darkness, but will have the light of life."
Genesis 1:15
and let them be for lights in the expanse of sky to give light on the earth"; and it was so.
Matthew 5:14-16
You are the light of the world. A city located on a hill can't be hidden. Neither do you light a lamp, and put it under a measuring basket, but on a stand; and it shines to all who are in the house. Even so, let your light shine before men; that they may see your good works, and glorify your Father who is in heaven.

Jesus calls us to be a BRIGHT LIGHT, just like He was. We are to let our light shine before all people so that they may see our good works and glorify God in heaven. Allow His Word to shine through us in our thoughts, actions and words so that even if those we meet never actually read God's Word, they encounter Jesus through the light we shine on them. Many of my friends have gone to be with Jesus as your friends have. Let it be a consolation to you that the very same light which shined through them, the light of Jesus, can continue to shine on through us. Be a BRIGHT LIGHT to honor them and to Glorify God today and ever after.

- Day 343 -

What do we do for those that desperately want to believe in God and the saving grace of Jesus but are just not able to believe for a multitude of reasons? We have prayed for these people who may be friends or family or just someone we didn't even know but were asked to pray for and they still are unwilling or unable to believe. What else are we to do?

Acts 26:18
to open their eyes, that they may turn from darkness to light and from the power of Satan to God, that they may receive remission of sins and an inheritance among those who are sanctified by faith in me.'

Romans 10:1
Brothers, my heart's desire and my prayer to God is for Israel, that they may be saved.

2 Peter 3:9
The Lord is not slow concerning his promise, as some count slowness; but is patient with us, not wishing that any should perish, but that all should come to repentance.

Luke 19:10
For the Son of Man came to seek and to save that which was lost."

1 Timothy 2:4
who desires all people to be saved and come to full knowledge of the truth.

Matthew 9:37-38
Then he said to his disciples, "The harvest indeed is plentiful, but the laborers are few. Pray therefore that the Lord of the harvest will send out laborers into his harvest."

Mark 16:15-16
He said to them, "Go into all the world, and preach the Good News to the whole creation. He who believes and is baptized will be saved; but he who disbelieves will be condemned.

So, what can we do for those that desperately want to be saved but can not or will not believe yet? Go out into all the world and continue to preach the Gospel to them. Continue to pray prayers of intercession for them. Continue to let your light shine so brightly that it illuminates their path to Christ. Take a moment now to pray for the salvation of someone who is, as of yet, unable or unwilling to believe.

- Day 344 -

When is enough, enough? There's horrible, inaccurate, negative news on the TV, Radio and internet. People we've 'befriended" on Facebook constantly post negative comments about God, faith and The Word. Pharmacopeia is pushed on all the sheeple through the media as the solution to the health crisis when it's more likely to be part of the cause of the problem. Basic biblical principles and morals are being openly attacked and sin is celebrated. What are we to do?

2 Corinthians 6:17
Therefore "'Come out from among them, and be separate, says the Lord. Touch no unclean thing. I will receive you.
Leviticus 20:26
You shall be holy to me; for I, The Lord, am holy, and have set you apart from the peoples, that you should be mine.
Ezra 6:21
The children of Israel who had come again out of the captivity, and all such as had separated themselves to them from the filthiness of the nations of the land, to seek Yahweh, the God of Israel, ate the Passover
Proverbs 13:20
One who walks with wise men grows wise, but a companion of fools suffers harm.

Turn off the TV until they only talk about positive, uplifting stories and stop sensationalizing the negativity in this world. Vote with your dollars and stop buying magazines and watching TV networks that advertise prescription drugs that tout the possible side effect of 'may cause death' with pride and arrogance. "Unfriend" the 'friends' who are constantly, blatantly, unabashedly and unapologetically sining against God in their posts. ...But wait, didn't Jesus 'hang out with sinners' you ask? As Kevin DeYoung wrote in his article 'Jesus, Friend of Sinners: But How?'- "Jesus was a friend of sinners not because he winked at sin, ignored sin, or enjoyed light-hearted revelry with those engaged in immorality. Jesus was a friend of sinners in that he came to save sinners and was very pleased to welcome sinners who were open to the gospel, sorry for their sins, and on their way to putting their faith in Him."

- Day 345 -

Perhaps the most devastating diseases are psychological disorders. Physical diseases can be terrible but there's something tangible about them, something you can see on x-ray or blood work or in some physical test. When you can see the problem, there's a better chance of being able to do something about it. Psychological problems like depression or anxiety or severe mood disorders are equally as devastating but since we can't actually see the problems on x-ray or in blood work, how do we help those that have these problems?

Psalm 23:3
He restores my soul. He guides me in the paths of righteousness for his name's sake.
Psalm 34:17-20
The righteous cry, and Yahweh hears, and delivers them out of all their troubles. Yahweh is near to those who have a broken heart, and saves those who have a crushed spirit. Many are the afflictions of the righteous, but Yahweh delivers him out of them all. He protects all of his bones. Not one of them is broken.
1 Peter 5:7
casting all your worries on him, because he cares for you.
Psalm 147:3
He heals the broken in heart, and binds up their wounds.
John 14:27
Peace I leave with you. My peace I give to you; not as the world gives, give I to you. Don't let your heart be troubled, neither let it be fearful.

Just because you can't see depression or anxiety or other psychological disorders on x-ray or blood work doesn't make them any less real. And likewise, just because you can't touch or see a prayer or faith doesn't make them any less real. Jesus is real and answers our prayers. Pray for those who are hurting. God will restore their soul, He will respond to your righteous cry. He will carry your worries. He will bear your burdens. He will heal your broken heart and bind up the wounds of those you pray for. And most of all He will provide that which you most desire... Peace and Rest. Whom can we pray for today? Add a name or two below for all to share in your intercessory prayer.

- Day 346 -

In ancient times a bond-servant was also considered a slave. These bond-servants often willingly and voluntarily agreed to be a servant (slave) for another person. In the New Testament, the term bondservant is also used to describe someone that devoted themselves to Jesus.

Colossians 4:7
All my affairs will be made known to you by Tychicus, the beloved brother, faithful servant, and fellow bondservant in the Lord.
Romans 1:1
Paul, a servant of Jesus Christ, called to be an apostle, set apart for the Good News of God,
James 1:1
James, a servant of God and of the Lord Jesus Christ, to the twelve tribes which are in the Dispersion: Greetings.
2 Peter 1:1
Simon Peter, a servant and apostle of Jesus Christ, to those who have obtained a like precious faith with us in the righteousness of our God and Savior, Jesus Christ:
1 Corinthians 7:22
For he who was called in the Lord being a bondservant is the Lord's free man. Likewise he who was called being free is Christ's bondservant.

Have we agreed to be bondservants (slaves, servants) of Jesus as Christians? Are there "Christians" only by name that have decided not to become bondservants of Christ? Are they really Christians then? If you say you're in but you're not ALL IN, are you OUT? Remember, God knows the heart. So, are you ALL IN?

- Day 347 -

There are lots of prophets in the Bible. Prophets in the Bible are inspired teachers or a person that proclaims the will of God and they are able to see the future. There are 4 major prophets and lots (over 100) of minor ones. How can we know a true prophet from a false prophet?

Matthew 7:15-16
"Beware of false prophets, who come to you in sheep's clothing, but inwardly are ravening wolves. By their fruits you will know them. Do you gather grapes from thorns, or figs from thistles?

2 Corinthians 11:13-15
For such men are false apostles, deceitful workers, masquerading as Christ's apostles. And no wonder, for even Satan masquerades as an angel of light. It is no great thing therefore if his servants also masquerade as servants of righteousness, whose end will be according to their works.

Deuteronomy 13:1-5
If a prophet or a dreamer of dreams arises among you, and he gives you a sign or a wonder, and the sign or the wonder comes to pass, of which he spoke to you, saying, "Let us go after other gods" (which you have not known) "and let us serve them"; you shall not listen to the words of that prophet, or to that dreamer of dreams; for Yahweh your God is testing you, to know whether you love Yahweh your God with all your heart and with all your soul. You shall walk after Yahweh your God, fear him, keep his commandments, and obey his voice, and you shall serve him, and cling to him. That prophet, or that dreamer of dreams, shall be put to death, because he has spoken rebellion against Yahweh your God, who brought you out of the land of Egypt, and redeemed you out of the house of bondage, to draw you aside out of the way which Yahweh your God commanded you to walk in. So you shall remove the evil from among you.

So, there are lots of people that will pretend to be prophets but are just frauds. In old Judaic times the test was that 100% of their prophecies had to be accurate. Another good test is to be sure prophet's teachings are consistent with the Bible. Still another good test is to inspect what the fruits of their teachings are. Good trees produce good fruit, bad trees produce rotten fruit. Either way, be careful as we are warned that false prophets will be disguised as good people and they will perform signs and wonders but their teachings will not be Biblically sound. In the end, the best way to discern the truth from a lie and a prophet from a fraud is to study the Truth. Have you studied the Truth today?

- Day 348 -

The O'Jays were a singing sensation in the 70's. Their dozens of billboard top hits include Love Train, Lovin You, I Love Music, For The Love of Money, and over 30 more. As it turns out, they're still singing their 70's hits today in their 70's. When asked what they would like the legacy of their music to convey, their reply was, "LOVE is the only thing that matters."

1 Corinthians 13:13
But now faith, hope, and love remain—these three. The greatest of these is love.
1 John 4:8, 16
8 He who doesn't love doesn't know God, for God is love. 16 We know and have believed the love which God has for us. God is love, and he who remains in love remains in God, and God remains in him.

Isn't it about time you get on The Love Train?

https://www.cbsnews.com/video/the-ojays-the-love-train-continues/

- Day 349 -

Lots of people have good intentions of starting to read the Bible but it all seems overwhelming. So, where do you start? The Bible is actually a collection of books that was written in several languages over 1500 years. Often starting at the beginning and reading to the end is not the best idea and can be a little daunting. My suggestion is to start in the Gospels (Matthew, Mark, Luke, and John) to get an understanding of Jesus, His life and ministry. To get a taste of the Old Testament, check out Genesis to get a first hand look at how God created the world and how it fell into sin.

2 Timothy 3:16
Every Scripture is God-breathed and profitable for teaching, for reproof, for correction, and for instruction in righteousness,
Psalm 119:105
Your word is a lamp to my feet, and a light for my path.
Romans 15:4
For whatever things were written before were written for our learning, that through patience and through encouragement of the Scriptures we might have hope.
John 17:17
Sanctify them in your truth. Your word is truth.

Into poetry? Check out Psalms through Song of Solomon. Into history? Read Joshua through Chronicles. Into the law? Try Exodus, Leviticus, Numbers, and Deuteronomy even though they are a little harder to digest. Want to know how to live a life that honors God? Find that out in the epistles (letters) like Romans; I and II Corinthians; Galatians; Ephesians; Philippians; Colossians; I and II Thessalonians; I and II Timothy; Titus; and Philemon. OK, so what are you waiting for? Pick a place in the Bible that interests you and get started there. Well? Don't just sit there. Get going!

Ash Wednesday is the beginning of the Lent which is the 40 day period of fasting, praying and repenting that comes before Easter. There has long been a tradition, even before the Christian church, of covering one's self in sackcloth and ashes to demonstrate humility during times of mourning and repentance. Today the ashes are placed on the forehead of the faithful as a symbol of God's seal.

Revelation 7:3
saying, "Don't harm the earth, neither the sea, nor the trees, until we have sealed the bondservants of our God on their foreheads!"
Revelation 9:4
They were told that they should not hurt the grass of the earth, neither any green thing, neither any tree, but only those people who don't have God's seal on their foreheads.
Genesis 3:19
In the sweat of thy face shalt thou eat bread, till thou return unto the ground; for out of it wast thou taken: for dust thou art, and unto dust shalt thou return.
Daniel 9:3
And I set my face unto the Lord God, to seek by prayer and supplications, with fasting, and sackcloth, and ashes:

Ever wonder where the ashes come from? They're from the previous year's palms from Palm Sunday. The ashes are to remind us of our mortality. The priest marks our forehead in the sign of the cross and says, "Remember that thou art dust and unto dust thou shalt return." How can we use this time, these 40 days of purification and enlightenment, to help us grow closer to God through Jesus? When choosing what to 'give up' for lent, let's ask ourselves what we can give from our sustenance, not from our surplus, for Jesus during these 40 days?

- Day 351 -

So many messages from God to us in His Word are misunderstood. The Gospel in the Bible is not about and has never been about making bad people good. The gospel is about making dead people alive.

Proverbs 16:25
There is a way which seems right to a man, but in the end it leads to death.
Mark 10:18
Jesus said to him, "Why do you call me good? No one is good except one—God.
Ephesians 2:4-10
But God, being rich in mercy, for his great love with which he loved us, even when we were dead through our trespasses, made us alive together with Christ (by grace you have been saved), and raised us up with him, and made us to sit with him in the heavenly places in Christ Jesus, that in the ages to come he might show the exceeding riches of his grace in kindness toward us in Christ Jesus; for by grace you have been saved through faith, and that not of yourselves; it is the gift of God, not of works, that no one would boast. For we are his workmanship, created in Christ Jesus for good works, which God prepared before that we would walk in them.

No amount of good works ("being a good person") can save us… but… We are compelled to do good works because we are saved through Jesus Christ. That might sound like semantics but it's not. Listen, it's cool to try to be a good person but there's only one way to get to heaven and be fully alive. Invite Christ into your heart and see what it feels like to be loved unconditionally, have hope restored in your life and be confident in life everlasting.

Day 352

If we depend on this world and the things in it rather than God to make us happy, we will always come up short and unsatisfied. We clutter our lives, hearts and minds with things of this world and then we try to add God to the mix. The fact is that there is NO THING, Nothing that can satisfy our desire to be happy but God.

Psalm 144:15
Happy are the people who are in such a situation. Happy are the people whose God is The Lord.
Isaiah 12:3
Therefore with joy you will draw water out of the wells of salvation.
1 Peter 4:13
But because you are partakers of Christ's sufferings, rejoice; that at the revelation of his glory you also may rejoice with exceeding joy.
2 Chronicles 9:7
Happy are your men, and happy are these your servants, who stand continually before you, and hear your wisdom.

The Author A. W. Tozer put it best when he said, "You're made in the image of God and nothing short of God will satisfy you. And even if you're one of those "nickel-in-the-slot, get saved, escape hell and take heaven" Christians, remember one thing- even you will find over the years that you are not content with "things plus God." You'll have to have God minus all things." He goes on to ask these questions: In what ways do you depend on the Things of the world for your happiness? Could your faith survive the loss of all things?

- Day 353 -

So, what's your reaction if I described you as Pulchritudinous? At first you might be a little offended. That doesn't sound like a flattering way to be described does it? Well how would you react if I said I find Jesus to be Pulchritudinous as well? Before you get all bent out of shape, consider these verses...

Psalm 27:4
One thing I have asked of The Lord, that I will seek after, that I may dwell in The Lord's house all the days of my life, to see The Lord's beauty, and to inquire in his temple.
Isaiah 33:17
Your eyes will see the king in his beauty. They will see a distant land.
1 Peter 3:4
but in the hidden person of the heart, in the incorruptible beauty of a gentle and quiet spirit, which is in the sight of God very precious.
Song of Solomon 4:7
You are all beautiful, my love. There is no flaw in you.

Though it may not sound like it, to be Pulchritudinous is to be one who has great physical beauty. Each and every one of us was created by God and we were created perfect and beautiful in His sight. In addition, our spirit was created in His image. Can you think of an image that is more Pulchritudinous? I think you are Pulchritudinous and God does too and like it or not, there's not a thing you can do about that!

- Day 354 -

Last night I visited my friend Doris at her home to give her a Chiropractic adjustment and to pray fiercely for a miracle that she desires for God to provide. She was given a very bad medical report in November of 2016. In the natural, it appeared as though she did not have much time to live having been diagnosed with two life threatening conditions but here she is in February of 2018. In the natural, her physical body may not look vibrant but in the spiritual, she is a strong brilliant light. Over and over she prayed out loud, "Trust in God and Let It Go."

Proverbs 3:5-6
Trust in The Lord with all your heart, and don't lean on your own understanding. In all your ways acknowledge him, and he will make your paths straight.
2 Kings 18:5
He trusted in The Lord, the God of Israel; so that after him was no one like him among all the kings of Judah, nor among them that were before him.
2 Corinthians 1:9
Yes, we ourselves have had the sentence of death within ourselves, that we should not trust in ourselves, but in God who raises the dead,
Hebrews 2:13
Again, "I will put my trust in him." Again, "Behold, here I am with the children whom God has given me."

I believe for a miracle for Doris. Together, last night we both prayed for a complete and total healing. But, what makes Doris so special is the fact that she acknowledged that healing comes in many forms and if her physical body is no longer supposed to be the home for her spiritual body, she will TRUST GOD AND LET IT GO. Oh that we would all have that kind of faith in God. This is my prayer for us all.

- Day 355 -

One of my friends sent me a message tonight commenting about family, siblings, and friends. He observed that we are born into our family and we are given our siblings and there's not much we can do to change that. He found it interesting however, that 'regular folks' can become 'family' while often our family and siblings end up becoming strangers. Is blood really thicker than water or is it possible that water can be made into wine (so to speak)?

Leviticus 25:35
"'If your brother has become poor, and his hand can't support himself among you; then you shall uphold him. He shall live with you like a stranger and a temporary resident.
Luke 10:25-37
Behold, a certain lawyer stood up and tested him, saying, "Teacher, what shall I do to inherit eternal life?" He said to him, "What is written in the law? How do you read it?" He answered, "You shall love the Lord your God with all your heart, with all your soul, with all your strength, and with all your mind; and your neighbor as yourself." He said to him, "You have answered correctly. Do this, and you will live." But he, desiring to justify himself, asked Jesus, "Who is my neighbor?"

Jesus answered, "A certain man was going down from Jerusalem to Jericho, and he fell among robbers, who both stripped him and beat him, and departed, leaving him half dead. By chance a certain priest was going down that way. When he saw him, he passed by on the other side. In the same way a Levite also, when he came to the place, and saw him, passed by on the other side. But a certain Samaritan, as he traveled, came where he was. When he saw him, he was moved with compassion, came to him, and bound up his wounds, pouring on oil and wine. He set him on his own animal, and brought him to an inn, and took care of him. On the next day, when he departed, he took out two denarii, and gave them to the host, and said to him, 'Take care of him. Whatever you spend beyond that, I will repay you when I return.' Now which of these three do you think seemed to be a neighbor to him who fell among the robbers?" He said, "He who showed mercy on him." Then Jesus said to him, "Go and do likewise."

To my friend, I say you're absolutely right, you can't pick your family but God admonishes us to take special care of them. My friend is also right that 'ordinary people' or 'strangers' can truly become like family. In fact, the Bible admonishes us to be like the Good Samaritan. We are to treat all people including strangers like family and show mercy on them. In essence, we should treat our family and strangers with unconditional love. In this way we emulate Jesus' first miracle and symbolically turn water (strangers) into wine (family).

So, today I would like to pay my respect to a great man that went to be with his heavenly Father yesterday, the Reverend Billy Graham. I was told that his ministry was only mediocre at best when he started until one day, while on a golf course, while his mind was distracted by a falling leaf, he had a divine revelation. He realized that he had not accepted the Bible in Full Faith. When he did, tents began to fill, then auditoriums and then stadiums began to fill to capacity to hear Rev. Graham preach a simple message from the Bible he accepted in full faith.

Hebrews 11:1-3
Now faith is the substance of things hoped for, the evidence of things not seen. For by it the elders obtained a good report. Through faith we understand that the worlds were framed by the word of God, so that things which are seen were not made of things which do appear.
Mark 16:15-16
And he said unto them, Go ye into all the world, and preach the gospel to every creature. He that believeth and is baptized shall be saved; but he that believeth not shall be damned.
Matthew 25:23
His lord said unto him, Well done, good and faithful servant; thou hast been faithful over a few things, I will make thee ruler over many things: enter thou into the joy of thy lord.

His was a life well lived. He accepted the Word in full faith and Jesus Christ as his Savior. He went out into all the world and preached the gospel and saved literally millions of souls. And, I am confident, based on God's promise in the Word, Reverend Billy Graham has entered into the joy of The Lord. "Some day you will read or hear that Billy Graham is dead. Don't you believe a word of it. I shall be more alive than I am now. I will just have changed my address. I will have gone into the presence of God."- Billy Graham

- Day 357 -

At Bible study this week, my friend Gary posed a question. Are we being sensitive to the opportunities that God gives us to spread the Gospel? On days when we pray that God will put someone in our path for us to share the Good News with, inevitably we bump into someone and the topic of faith seems to present itself. What about the days that we don't pray for that opportunity, we are not sensitive and we pass up the chance to share our life-saving message?

Isaiah 6:8
Also I heard the voice of the Lord, saying, Whom shall I send, and who will go for us? Then said I, Here am I; send me.
Proverbs 11:30
The fruit of the righteous is a tree of life; and he that winneth souls is wise.
Acts 22:15
For thou shalt be his witness unto all men of what thou hast seen and heard.
Luke 15:4
What man of you, having an hundred sheep, if he lose one of them, doth not leave the ninety and nine in the wilderness, and go after that which is lost, until he find it?
Matthew 11:15
He that hath ears to hear, let him hear.
John 14:6
Jesus saith unto him, I am the way, the truth, and the life: no man cometh unto the Father, but by me.

Here's why we need to stay sensitive to the opportunities for evangelism each day: What's at stake is Life or eternal death, Heaven or hell. Will we be sensitive enough to recognize when we should share the Good News? Will we be bold enough to speak up and save a soul destined to an eternity separated from God? Jesus wants to have a relationship with ALL of His children. Will we take the time to introduce a friend, family member or a complete stranger to Jesus today to begin that relationship? Stay Sensitive To The Opportunities God Puts In Our Path My Friends.

- Day 358 -

Martin Luther is quoted as having said, "I have so much to do that I shall spend the first three hours in prayer." In effect he was saying that there's no way I'll get everything done in the time I have, BUT with God's help, I can do all the things I need to.

Genesis 2:2-3
And on the seventh day God ended his work which he had made; and he rested on the seventh day from all his work which he had made. And God blessed the seventh day, and sanctified it: because that in it he had rested from all his work which God created and made.
2 Peter 3:8
But, beloved, be not ignorant of this one thing, that one day is with the Lord as a thousand years, and a thousand years as one day.
Ecclesiastes 3:11
He has made everything beautiful in its time. He has also set eternity in their hearts, yet so that man can't find out the work that God has done from the beginning even to the end.
Psalm 90:12
So teach us to number our days, that we may gain a heart of wisdom.
James 4:13-15
Come now, you who say, "Today or tomorrow let's go into this city, and spend a year there, trade, and make a profit." Whereas you don't know what your life will be like tomorrow. For what is your life? For you are a vapor, that appears for a little time, and then vanishes away. For you ought to say, "If the Lord wills, we will both live, and do this or that."

Do you get that? If you only have 4 hours to get 6 hours of stuff done, spend the first 3 of the 4 hours in prayer. God can get more done in 20 minutes than we can get done in 20 years. Give Him 7 days and he can create EVERYTHING from nothing.

- Day 359 -

A little boy was flying his kite on a particularly windy day when there was a thick low cloud cover. He let out so much string that the kite disappeared above the clouds. A passer-by looked at him holding the ball of string and asked what he was doing. He replied, "I'm flying a kite." The passer-by said, "I don't see any kite in the sky. How do you know it's still there?" The boy replied, "I can feel the tug."

Romans 8:14
For as many as are led by the Spirit of God, these are children of God.
Deuteronomy 8:2
You shall remember all the way which Yahweh your God has led you these forty years in the wilderness, that he might humble you, to prove you, to know what was in your heart, whether you would keep his commandments, or not.
Proverbs 16:9
A man's heart plans his course, but the Lord directs his steps.
2 Thessalonians 3:5
May the Lord direct your hearts into the love of God, and into the patience of Christ.

If Jesus truly lives in our heart but we can not physically see Him, how do we know that He's really there? I'll tell you how. Every once in a while you will feel the tug. Perhaps your fleshy body wants to do something that's immoral... you will feel the tug to remind you not to do it. You pass a beggar on the street... you will feel the tug to go back to offer food and pray with him or her. Perhaps something terrible happens that causes you to be sad or depressed... you will feel the tug to remind you that He loves you, will never leave you nor will He forsake you. Have you felt the tug lately?

- Day 360 -

Have you ever been asked, "When were you saved?" For some it's a really easy answer and they have the year, month, day and time readily available to recite. For others it's not that cut and dry. For some it was a gradual thing starting as acquaintances, moved into friendship and now you're "just like family". And yet wasn't the day we were all saved, the same exact day when you think about it?

Romans 5:8
But God commends his own love toward us, in that while we were yet sinners, Christ died for us.
Romans 6:3
Or don't you know that all we who were baptized into Christ Jesus were baptized into his death?
Hebrews 2:9
But we see him who has been made a little lower than the angels, Jesus, because of the suffering of death crowned with glory and honor, that by the grace of God he should taste of death for everyone.
John 11:25
Jesus said to her, "I am the resurrection and the life. He who believes in me will still live, even if he dies.

Weren't we all saved the day that Jesus died on the cross for us? And, isn't it through His resurrection that we were all saved at the same moment in time when He defeated death? Though our decision to accept Jesus into our hearts and make Him our Lord and Savior may have happened at different times and places, it would be of little consequence without the events that took place that led to that moment of self-sacrifice at Calvary. So, we know when we were saved. When did you accept Him as your Lord and Savior?

- Day 361 -

What exactly is the relationship between sin and grace? We as Christians are not 'sinless', we just strive to 'sin less'.

John 8:3-11
The scribes and the Pharisees brought a woman taken in adultery. Having set her in the middle, they told him, "Teacher, we found this woman in adultery, in the very act. Now in our law, Moses commanded us to stone such women. What then do you say about her?" They said this testing him, that they might have something to accuse him of. But Jesus stooped down, and wrote on the ground with his finger. But when they continued asking him, he looked up and said to them, "He who is without sin among you, let him throw the first stone at her." Again he stooped down, and with his finger wrote on the ground. They, when they heard it, being convicted by their conscience, went out one by one, beginning from the oldest, even to the last. Jesus was left alone with the woman where she was, in the middle.

Jesus, standing up, saw her and said, "Woman, where are your accusers? Did no one condemn you?" She said, "No one, Lord."

Jesus said, "Neither do I condemn you. Go your way. From now on, sin no more."

Grace means that God grants love where apathy is merited. Grace means God gives forgiveness where there should be judgement. Grace means that God sent his only Son to descend into hell on a cross so that we, the guilty, could be reconciled, made righteous, and be received into heaven even though we did not deserve it. Grace means that you can sin MORE than you want to, NOT as much as you want to. With Jesus in your heart, you are forgiven for this and all your other sins. Go your way and sin no more.

What is the importance of the soil to the seed? We all have the seed inside us which is the Holy Spirit. The seed has unlimited potential but where the seed is planted makes all the difference. Some soil is too hard, some soil has too many stones, some soil is contaminated with weeds and thorns and some soil is good and dark and rich and full of nutrients...

Matthew 13:3-8, 18-23
3-8 He spoke to them many things in parables, saying, "Behold, a farmer went out to sow. As he sowed, some seeds fell by the roadside, and the birds came and devoured them. Others fell on rocky ground, where they didn't have much soil, and immediately they sprang up, because they had no depth of earth. When the sun had risen, they were scorched. Because they had no root, they withered away. Others fell among thorns. The thorns grew up and choked them. Others fell on good soil, and yielded fruit: some one hundred times as much, some sixty, and some thirty.
18-23 "Hear, then, the parable of the farmer. When anyone hears the word of the Kingdom, and doesn't understand it, the evil one comes, and snatches away that which has been sown in his heart. This is what was sown by the roadside. What was sown on the rocky places, this is he who hears the word, and immediately with joy receives it; yet he has no root in himself, but endures for a while. When oppression or persecution arises because of the word, immediately he stumbles. What was sown among the thorns, this is he who hears the word, but the cares of this age and the deceitfulness of riches choke the word, and he becomes unfruitful. What was sown on the good ground, this is he who hears the word, and understands it, who most certainly bears fruit, and produces, some one hundred times as much, some sixty, and some thirty."

Lord God, grant us ears to hear your Word. Lord God allow us to receive and rejoice in your Word. May your Word take root within us so that we do not stumble when we are oppressed or persecuted. Lord God protect us from the deceit of riches so that the seed of your Word becomes fruitful within us. Jesus, grant that we will understand the Word which we have heard so that it grows inside us and bears fruit. Lord God, it is our prayer that we become fertile ground for the Holy Spirit to not just dwell within us but to grow and release it's unlimited potential.

- Day 363 -

Eternal Security. Doesn't that sound great? To be eternally secure. Wow. When we are brought into a relationship with Jesus as our Lord and Savior, we are also guaranteed the security of an eternity with God. Once we accept Jesus into our hearts, eternal life is ours and no one can snatch us out of God's hand.

John 3:15
That whosoever believeth in him should not perish, but have eternal life.
John 10:28-29
And I give unto them eternal life; and they shall never perish, neither shall any man pluck them out of my hand. My Father, which gave them me, is greater than all; and no man is able to pluck them out of my Father's hand.
Ephesians 4:30
And grieve not the holy Spirit of God, whereby ye are sealed unto the day of redemption.
Romans 8:38-39
For I am persuaded, that neither death, nor life, nor angels, nor principalities, nor powers, nor things present, nor things to come, Nor height, nor depth, nor any other creature, shall be able to separate us from the love of God, which is in Christ Jesus our Lord.

How does this sound?... The state of feeling safe, stable, and free from fear or anxiety or danger lasting and existing forever without end. That's Eternal Security and you have exactly that when you are in Christ and Christ is in you. Our Eternal Security was bought for us by Jesus, promised to us by God and secured by The Holy Spirit. Are you feeling Eternally Secure yet?

- Day 364 -

IT'S ALL FREE!! You can't buy it. You can't earn it. You can't be nice enough to merit it. You can't be good enough to deserve it. Once you've got it, it can never be taken away. It's FREE for the asking but costly not to accept.

Ephesians 2:8-9
for by grace you have been saved through faith, and that not of yourselves; it is the gift of God, not of works, that no one would boast.
Romans 5:15
But the free gift isn't like the trespass. For if by the trespass of the one the many died, much more did the grace of God, and the gift by the grace of the one man, Jesus Christ, abound to the many.
Romans 6:23
For the wages of sin is death, but the free gift of God is eternal life in Christ Jesus our Lord.
1 Corinthians 1:18
For the word of the cross is foolishness to those who are dying, but to us who are saved it is the power of God.
John 8:32
You will know the truth, and the truth will make you free."

Jesus is offering us eternal life through the grace He and only He can provide because of His sacrifice for us. You can not beg, borrow, buy, steal or earn this grace. It is offered for free just by responding to the call to believe in Jesus as your Lord and Savior. So, I guess it's true... The best things in life (and life everlasting) are FREE. It's also true that Freedom isn't free. It is paid for by sacrifice. Jesus's sacrifice at Calvary was the ultimate sacrifice for sure! Thank you Jesus!

- Day 365 -

Father Matthew Glover gave an insightful homily at morning mass about the rich man and Lazarus. One of those insights included a remembrance of a scene from the 1973 movie The Exorcist. In the movie, Father Damien Karras was rushing through a train station to get to his mother when he hears the plea of a beggar: "Can you help an old altar boy Father?" Father Damien looks over at the beggar but doesn't take the time to stop and help him.

Luke 16:19-26
"Now there was a certain rich man, and he was clothed in purple and fine linen, living in luxury every day. A certain beggar, named Lazarus, was laid at his gate, full of sores, and desiring to be fed with the crumbs that fell from the rich man's table. Yes, even the dogs came and licked his sores. The beggar died, and he was carried away by the angels to Abraham's bosom. The rich man also died, and was buried. In Hades, he lifted up his eyes, being in torment, and saw Abraham far off, and Lazarus at his bosom. He cried and said, 'Father Abraham, have mercy on me, and send Lazarus, that he may dip the tip of his finger in water, and cool my tongue! For I am in anguish in this flame.'

"But Abraham said, 'Son, remember that you, in your lifetime, received your good things, and Lazarus, in the same way, bad things. But now here he is comforted and you are in anguish. Besides all this, between us and you there is a great gulf fixed, that those who want to pass from here to you are not able, and that no one may cross over from there to us.'

The Devil torments Father Damien by reminding him over and over of how he passed the beggar and didn't stop to help him. Symbolically, Father Damien did not stop to give Lazarus the crumbs off his table by offering a dollar or two to go get something to eat. The devil reminds Father Damien that he didn't just pass a beggar in that train station, he symbolically passed Jesus and did not take the time to feed or clothe Him. How many beggars have we passed? Could they have been Lazarus begging for our crumbs? Could they have been Jesus hoping we would pass the test by stopping to pray with Him and offer something for Him to eat?

Made in the USA
Middletown, DE
17 January 2021